Selçuk İpek / Adnan Gerçek (eds.)

Current Perspectives in Public Finance

PETER LANG

Bibliographic Information published by the Deutsche Nationalbibliothek
The Deutsche Nationalbibliothek lists this publication in the Deutsche Nationalbibliografie; detailed bibliographic data is available online at http://dnb.d-nb.de.

Library of Congress Cataloging-in-Publication Data
A CIP catalog record for this book has been applied for at the Library of Congress.

Printed by CPI books GmbH, Leck

ISBN 978-3-631-77446-5 (Print)
E-ISBN 978-3-631-77584-4 (E-PDF)
E-ISBN 978-3-631-77585-1 (EPUB)
E-ISBN 978-3-631-77586-8 (MOBI)
DOI 10.3726/b15236

Peter Lang – Berlin · Bern · Bruxelles · New York · Oxford · Warszawa · Wien

This publication has been peer reviewed.

www.peterlang.com

Current Perspectives in Public Finance

Preface

This book investigates the different issues of taxation, public expenditures and intervention. It covers the current perspectives in public finance such as taxation of digital economy, delegating the power of taxation, the desperation of tax administration, human rights budgeting, economic growth and tax revenues, minimal state and government expenditures, consumer behaviours, incentives of green energy, and trade wars alike. The book consists of eleven chapters related to the "new public finance" issues mentioned above. The large part of chapters published in this volume was selected among the presented papers in the 33th International Public Finance Conference/Turkey in May, 2018. They also went through a review process before publication.

Biyan and Yılmaz examine the virtual establishment concept by literature review using international developments and comparative law. Also they give proposal for the concretisation of the virtual establishment concept.

Bozdoğanoğlu studies the main features of cryptocurrencies and virtual money, especially the ones that have emerged recently, and explains the differences. In addition, the study examines the difficulties concerning cryptocurrencies, such as anonymity feature of cryptocurrencies, and taxation and regulation discrepancies according to countries.

Çomaklı and Uzun discuss the issue of delegating "the power of taxation", which is possessed to "be able to be a state" in relation with the United States of Europe goal. In this context, the political mechanisms and priorities necessary "to become a united states" are briefly examined.

Erdoğdu and Siverekli investigate the relationship between gross domestic product, a general measure of the growth of the country's economy, and tax revenues, the output of taxation which is the main action of governments' fiscal policies, in the period 2006–2017 in Turkey, using monthly data. The empirical results of the study help the policymakers to make a better assessing of the relationship between tax revenues and gross domestic product to formulate tax policies.

Güngör Göksu analyses the relationship between human rights and state budget and finds out what changes human rights budgeting practices cause on state budgets. Also the study determines the points regarding with analysing human rights budgeting.

Özel Özer, Özer and Mastar Özcan attempt to shed light on how the primary institutions of the public sector keep up with the minimal state objective in Turkey.

In addition, the effort strives to measure and evaluate whether this tendency has been in effect for public expenditures and government budget expenditures for the Turkish case in her historical, political economy development.

Selen evaluates the reflection of the free trade system on public finance understanding. In today's world trade system, the state, especially for conservation purposes, taxation and expenditure initiatives are significantly limited.

Şener makes some psychological analyses about explaining the irrationality problem. Also he evaluates the behaviours of Turkish consumers whose economic choices are dominated by conspicuous consumption motivation.

Tirgil and Yorulmaz investigate the monthly aggregate cigarette sales data before and after the tobacco control policies to declining cigarette consumption in Turkey. They find that cigarette consumption increased until the 2000s, but the cigarette consumption immediately declined after the public smoking regulations in 2008.

Yiğit Şakar studies the financial incentives used to finance energy efficiency in buildings in terms of Turkey and European Union and to make inferences for Turkey. As a result the study determined that the same financing methods have been adopted both in Turkey and European Union, however, Turkey, compared to European Union, has newly begun to implement the tax incentives.

It is our hope that the current volume would be very useful for both academics and policy makers not only in Turkey, but also in many developing and developed countries alike.

Selçuk İpek
Adnan Gerçek

Contents

List of Contributors

Özgür Biyan
Assoc. Prof. Dr., Bandırma Onyedi Eylül University, Faculty of Economics and Administrative Sciences, Department of Public Finance, obiyan@bandirma.edu.tr

Burçin Bozdoğanoğlu
Assoc. Prof, Bandırma Onyedi Eylül University, Faculty of Economics and Administrative Sciences, Department of Public Finance, burcindogan@gmail.com

Şafak Ertan Çomaklı
Prof. Dr., Turkish Police Academy, e-mail address: safakcomakli@gmail.com

Hamza Erdoğdu
Assist. Prof. Dr., University of Harran, Faculty of Economics and Administrative Sciences, Department of Econometrics, hamzaerdogdu@harran.edu.tr

Gonca Güngör Göksu
Res. Assist. Dr. Sakarya University, Faculty of Economics and Administrative Sciences, Department of Public Finance, ggungor@sakarya.edu.tr.

Pelin Mastar Özcan
Lecturer Dr., Manisa Celal Bayar University, Faculty of Economics and Administrative Sciences, Department of Public Finance, pelin.mastar@cbu.edu.tr

Aslıhan Özel Özer
Lecturer Dr., Manisa Celal Bayar University, Ahmetli Vocational School, Program of Accounting and Tax Applications, aslihanozel@yahoo.com

Buğra Özer
Assoc. Prof., Manisa Celal Bayar University, Faculty of Economics and Administrative Sciences, Department of Political Science and International Relations, bugraozer@gmail.com

Ufuk Selen
Assoc. Prof., Bursa Uludağ University, Faculty of Economics and Administrative Sciences, Department of Public Finance, uselen@uludag.edu.tr

Orhan Şener
Prof, Dr., Emeritus, orhansener2006@hotmail.com

Esra Siverekli
Prof. Dr., University of Harran, Faculty of Economics and Administrative Sciences, Department of Public Finance, esrasiverekli@harran.edu.tr

Abdullah Tirgil
Assist. Prof. Dr., Ankara Yıldırım Beyazit University, Department of Public Finance, atirgil@ybu.edu.tr

Murat Uzun
Res. Assist., Turkish Police Academy, e-mail address: muratuzun89@gmail.com

Ayşe Yiğit Şakar
Prof. Dr., Istanbul Arel University, Faculty of Economics and Administrative Sciences, Department of Business Administration, aysesakar@arel.edu.tr, ayseyigitsakar@gmail.com

Güneş Yılmaz
Assoc. Prof. Dr., Alanya Alaaddin Keykubat University, Department of International Trade, gunes.yilmaz@alanya.edu.tr

Recep Yorulmaz
Assist. Prof. Dr., Ankara Yıldırım Beyazit University, Department of Public Finance, ryorulmaz@ybu.edu.tr

Mesut Yücesan
Assist. Prof. Dr. Çanakkale Onsekiz Mart University, Lapseki Vocational School, mesutyucesan@comu.edu.tr

Özgür Biyan[1] and Güneş Yılmaz

A Taxation Problem Caused by Digital Economy: Definition of Virtual Establishment

Abstract: The permanent establishment has been one of the critical issues in international taxation for years. The concept of the permanent establishment has gained a new dimension with the widespread use of the internet. Economic activities in the digital environment have begun to create problems in the tax systems and have caused tax-free areas to appear. In this study, how the virtual establishment concept should be handled is examined by literature review using international developments and comparative law. The proposal for the concretisation of the virtual establishment concept has been given.

Keywords: Digital Economy, Virtual Establishment, Taxation, Tax Law

JEL Codes: K34, H20, F62

1 Introduction

While the extent of the trade carried out through the internet, amongst other economic activities, has reached dramatic levels every year, the disruptions encountered in taxation, insufficient regulations in the face of the transformations and problems manifest themselves intensively both nationally and internationally. The term "workplace/establishment", particularly in the economic activities carried out in the electronic environment, contains some uncertainties as to which country shall be entitled to use the power of taxation, for the reason that traditional definitions remain incapable in terms of scope and comprehension, which in turn undermines the foundations of the principle of fairness in taxation and leads to some non-taxable areas. International aspect and impact of the subject have increased so much so that even the international organisations had to carry out some activities as to how the concept of "workplace" had to be dealt with in the digital activities. Especially, the works that began towards the 2000s continue nonstop. In this context, the European Union took some actions to resolve such problems by itself. On the other hand, although Organisation for Economic Co-operation and Development (OECD) offered some proposals by issuing reports for the member countries, it turns out that the problem persists. Aware of the significance of the subject in question, our study underlines that the

1 Corresponding author.

concept of "workplace" should be redefined in terms of the economic activities carried out in electronic environment, in accordance with the developments in the international arena; it discusses the assessments in line with the approaches of the international organizations as well as the opinions in the doctrine and proposes some solutions. It also addresses the existing situation in the Turkish Tax System and future works.

2 Digital Economy and Its Effect on Tax Law in General

2.1 Digital Economy and General Characteristics

The term "Digital" means "the display" or "displaying the data electronically on a monitor" (www.tdk.gov.tr). In this sense, all of the electronic activities that are performed in the electronic environment through a computer today can be accepted as the digital economy. Therefore, all types of goods and services, offered via the internet as part of economic activity through mobile devices (mobile phone, tablet, etc.), particularly the computers, are included in the scope the digital economy. The digital economy, for which the legal regulations established according to traditional economic activities remain incapable, and which require particular arrangements, are closely related to the taxation that is an important area.

Particularly the development of information and communication reshaped the organisational structures, production techniques, decision-making processes and marketing strategies of the businesses. Further to that, the most significant change is that the virtual businesses have become a part of our daily lives. So, the concepts of virtual businesses, virtual traders, virtual workplace/establishment or in other words, the concepts such as e-business, e-trade, e-workplace have to be redefined, and all applications and legislative works have to be carried out accordingly (Gencer, 2013:21).

Therefore, the first assessment that can be made should be on the concept of "digital activity" and activity must satisfy the following elements to be regarded as a digital activity, according to the OECD (Hongler & Pistone, 2015: 30–31):

(1) Whole enterprise or a vast majority thereof should rely on the trading of digital goods and services.
(2) The goods and services delivered differently from the existing ones, such as the commercialisation, processing and collection of the location-related data, other IT tools, websites, server maintenance or operation should be the physical elements and activities that do not include real/material creation.
(3) Agreements should generally be finalised via the internet or phone remotely.

(4) Payments should primarily be made on credit cards, with online forms or through the electronic payment methods integrated with the connected links.
(5) Websites are assumed to be used only to enter the headquarters of a company; not to be associated with the activities of the physical stores or branches in the countries where the principal company or operating company are located.
(6) A vast majority or all of the profit should correspond to digital goods or services.
(7) The consumer should not consider the physical location and legal/taxation domicile of the vendor nor should it influence the preferences of the consumer.
(8) Performance of digital service or actual usage of digital goods should not require a physical workplace nor should it require the inclusion of physical product, other than the use of a computer, mobile device or other IT tools.

This approach of OECD was criticised in some aspects and claimed to conflict with the principle of impartiality, in particular. As an example, it is not a big deal whether all or the vast majority of an enterprise relies on the trading of digital goods and services. It may rely on digital activity partially or to a certain extent. Its volume, more or less, does not affect the essence of the matter. The same applies primarily to the payment made using a credit card and electronic payment methods. Considering the principles of fairness and impartiality, it was stated that there was no significant justification for a new workplace definition and it also did not contribute to the establishment of a relationship between digital activities and non-digital activities and formation of a new connection. A new definition should cover not only the suppliers of online advertising, e-commerce but also undoubtedly other enterprises. *A threshold must be set* to work out an outcome which is compatible with the principle of impartiality (e.g. giving/offering access to an electronic application, database, online market, storage room or providing advertising services on a website or in an electronic application) and this threshold, regardless of whether the vast majority of the activity is digital or not, should be an assurance and be used equally for everybody (Hongler & Pistone, 2015: 31). It would be fair to say that "setting a threshold", which is outlined in the literature as the most concrete proposal, is highly essential and acceptable. However, it is quite evident that the points, such as the content and level of thresholds need to be addressed and discussed.

It should be noted that the common characteristic of the transactions in the digital economy is the availability of one or more mediators. For example, cloud services consumer may outsource the services that it needs, directly from a cloud service provider or a cloud service broker. Cloud service mediator serves as a station between the consumer and service provider. While the mediators can combine more than one service request to create a new service, they may also choose to improve the available services and deliver them to their clients (Budak, 2018: 76).

Nevertheless, the transactions performed in digital economy fall into three categories when considered for the parties: Business to Consumer (B2C), Business to Business (B2B), and Consumer to Consumer (C2C). In the digital environment, almost all of the transactions are performed as B2C and B2B.

2.2 The Effect of Digital Economy on Tax Law

There are some essential points where the digital economy disables the generally accepted principles of international tax law. These can be summarised as "elimination of the need for a physical presence", "the date being the principal element of the production" and "the problem of identifying the character of income" (Uslu, 2017a: 151).

Digital economic activities that violate the taxation powers of the countries and even make it impossible for them to use these powers are at the top of the tax world agenda. The solution for some issues, such as the fact that the digital activities can hardly be controlled, the uncertainties in the delivery point for the goods and services, assessment difficulties caused by mobile applications, the difficulties in identifying the taxpayer and responsible person, etc., is still pending both in national and international context.

Furthermore, based on the developments in the digital economy, there is uncertainty in the current legal regulations in determining the subject to be taxed. Such that, since the products considered as tangible assets, such as newspaper, book, magazine, music CD, computer software, film videos, can be sold/purchased or downloaded free of charge into the hard discs in virtual environment, such digital products are now widely assessed as services, particularly in terms of taxation. In other words, the goods do not necessarily have to be delivered physically because the digital products are relocated as virtual and digital data (Kara & Öz, 2016: 35). Moreover, the business models permitted by the digital economy enable the operations to be spilt on a global scale, and business infrastructure can be set outside a particular market country. Multinational companies acquire the capability to do business in a way to reduce both direct and indirect tax burden (Turunç, 2017: 54).

Nevertheless, multinational companies may avoid being taxed in the Market country one way or another, using the infrastructure offered by the digital economy or they may erode their taxable profits in those countries. Thus, such companies avoid taxable entities. They can do that by making use of the exceptions in the definition of the workplace or through the execution of the agreement outside the market where the agreement was made and only if the local workforce is employed. They minimise the revenue that can be allocated to the assets and risks. Multinational companies may distribute their risks and assets by making intra-group agreements which do not reflect the functions of the operational units. Therefore, the profits of the assets are shared out, based on legal freehold and intra-group deals. Besides, they enjoy the tax discounts excessively. Multinational companies employ hybrid instruments and assets, to that end. Similarly, they can design the interest, copyright/royalty and service fee flow within the group, as a way to enjoy the discounts. They either pay very low or never pay a withholding tax in the source country. For that, they utilise the network of agreements (Turunç, 2017: 55).

In conclusion, based on all of the explanations herein, fundamental issues caused by a digital economy in the tax legislation can be listed as follows and these assessments involve the subjects that will change and lead the future and reality of the tax and taxation:

- Taxation of internet gaming and gambling (Van der Paardt, 2009: 525–531),
- Taxation of real-time online teaching, online advertisement, online remote equipment-controlling, and online database services (Zhu, 2014: 4),
- Whether a Web site or server can be considered a workplace (Pahlsson, 2002: 198–202; Lexner, 2010: 21–36; Gianni, 2014: 1–38),
- Which country/countries to use the power of taxation (Pahlsson, 2002: 203–206),
- Difficulties regarding the identification of the delivery of digital products and VAT (Pahlsson, 2002: 207–209; Bird & Gendron, 1998: 429–442),
- Taxation of cloud information services (Budak, 2017: 301).
- Use of digital assets, the establishment of front companies, abuse of tax agreements, in an attempt to avoid the withholding tax obtained from non-domiciled businesses, due to the payments, such as the interest or copyright/royalty, etc. (Budak, 2018: 63).
- Use of hybrid mismatch arrangements or extensive use of excess deduction mechanisms (Budak, 2018: 65).
- Taxation of the transactions and earned income, concerning the payment services (Gülhan & Turunç, 2015: 167).
- Taxation of the income obtained from the application programs and transactions (Gülhan & Turunç, 2015: 167).

- Taxation of participating network platforms (Facebook, Instagram, Tweeter, etc.) (Gülhan & Turunç, 2015: 167).
- Taxation of Online Domain and Online Domain Name Hosting Services (Ertaş, 2017: 133).
- Taxation of Freelance services (software, search engine optimisation (SEO), graphic design and translation) (Ertaş, 2017: 134).

Although these are the issues identified, which need a comprehensive solution, the top title points out that the doctrine focuses primarily on three regimes concerning the taxation of digital economy (Gülhan & Turunç, 2015: 168):

a) *Residence-based regime*: Although it means as close as generally accepted workplace definition, it does not require a physical presence and is based on an accepted system which is remotely manageable. An international consensus seems to be imperative.
b) *Source-based regime*: If any income is earned through the digital activities from a country market, it is accepted that the said country should be paid tax because such income is earned, thanks to the structure, sources and opportunities/facilities of the said country.
c) *Mixed regime*: It is based on the collective use of residence-basis and source basis.

As a result, to make a definition in a more general sense, digital economic activities result in uncertainty in the following matters regarding taxation:

- Identification of taxpayer (who will declare and pay tax)
- Identification of the type of the income (commercial, self-employment, intangible right, etc.)
- Identification of the location where the income is earned (the place of the event generating the tax, workplace)
- Identification of the amount of the earned income and taxable income (tax assessment)
- Which tax regime is to be implemented (direct taxation, withholding at source, etc.)
- How to use the tax collected on the expenses.

3 Impediment in the Use of Power of Taxation: Workplace Concept

The workplace, which constitutes a basis for taxation as a place (location), is defined as nexus which enables the commercial income to be connected to the power of taxation of the source country in which such income is earned (Yaltı Soydan, 1995: 131). One of the nexus rules in the use of the power of taxation, the subject of "workplace" is essential ground on which the tax office can raise the tax from corporate taxpayers and commercial taxpayers. Those who have a business within the political boundaries of a country shall be subject to the taxation regime of that country. The first point to be considered in applying the principle of residence, which is a fundamental principle in taxation, is whether the person/organisation has a workplace.

One of the critical issues created by the digital economy is that it causes the definition of traditional "workplace" concept to lose its meaning today, regarding tax legislation. Such that, traditional workplace forms a basis, within the context of domestic law, so that the bond between the government which is entitled to the power of taxation and the taxable activity is materialised and embodied. Above all, the concept of "workplace" had to be redefined because the cloud information systems began to be used widely as the number of the applications, which deliver services through the mobile applications or websites but the activities of which affect all countries has increased. Such that, the workplace concept at international level is defined traditionally and linked to the tax legislation mainly based on "permanent establishment". In this context, according to the explicit rule of OECD Model Convention, unless a company in a country carries out activity in another country through the means of a permanent establishment in another country, no direct tax is applied on its commercial profit based on net income in the other country (Hoffart, 2007: 106). Such a definition is indeed not suitable to understand today's digital economic activities and to implement the rules of traditional tax legislation. That is, the rules in the current traditional tax legislation lead to some problems in applying both the tax collected on Income and the consumption taxes like a VAT.

On the other hand, DTT (Double-Tax Treaty) regulations with respect to the workplace concept still underline a permanent and physical location to create a "workplace" and to accept the existence of such an establishment and therefore the countries failed to come up with a structure upon which they agree (For further information, see Kara & Öz, 2016:32). For this very reason, discussions and works continue concerning the content of the workplace concept, especially in OECD reports and in double taxation treaties and the related domestic law regulations began to address comprehensively the idea what should be understood in the workplace concept.

The discussion, experienced in practice on the concepts of "workplace" which are thought traditionally and has taken its place in the regulations as well as "e-business" that we face at the level of e-commerce, continues on these two topics over the past few years. The basic immediate question here is the point whether we can match up the scope of "e-business" with the content of "workplace" in the traditional sense, by using the basis of "web pages" and/or "web servers". Put it differently, can the "web pages" and/or "web servers" be deemed as a "permanent establishment" or "permanent agent"? (Gencer, 2013: 22).

3.1 OECD's Approach to the Concept of Workplace

3.1.1 OECD's Overall Approach since the 1990s to Present

Carrying out some works to tax the electronic commerce since the second half of the 1990s, OECD began to work on the "taxation of the digital economy", with the development of business models performed through the internet. In 1998, initial steps taken in the Ottawa Meeting began to concrete as OECD BEPS (Base Erosion and Profit Shifting) Project was put into practice in 2013. In the end, more than 70 ministers and high-level delegates representing 70 countries, including Turkey, signed the Multilateral Convention to Implement Tax Treaty-Related Measures to Prevent Base Erosion and Profit Shifting – "Multilateral Instrument" or "MLI" on June 07, 2017. Thanks to MLI (Multi-Level Instrument), the countries will be able to transfer the outcomes and measures outlined in OECD/G20 BEPS project into international tax treaties, international tax conventions and close up the gaps (Yıldırım, 2017: 54). It will prove beneficial to scrutinise the steps taken by OECD in the taxation of the digital economy from 1990 to present, for the essence of the subject.

In the meeting held by OECD between 7 – 9 October 1998 in Ottawa, Canada, it was agreed that policies had to be produced based on the principles of "*impartiality, productivity, precision and simplicity, effectivity and fairness and flexibility*" (Gülhan & Turunç, 2015: 169) and the following outcomes came forward with respect to the electronic commerce (Cangir, 2002: 24).

- New technologies, underpinning the electronic commerce as well, offer the tax offices new significant opportunities to improve and develop the services they offer the taxpayers. OECD member countries are determined to utilise these opportunities to the full extent.
- Taxation principles taken as a basis by the governments in the taxation of traditional commerce must also be referred to in the taxation of electronic commerce. Existing tax legislation is sufficient, in order to put these principles into practice, considering the development stage of technology and commerce. The new regulations to be set forth should be introduced in an attempt

to help implement the current taxational principles and not to aim at different taxation for electronic commerce transactions.

- The following three aspects should be noted in implementing the tax regulations made in the national level in order for the current tax principles to be implemented in the electronic commerce as well as the international tax principles, in the electronic commerce: "*Maintaining the financial autonomy of the countries; ensuring that the tax income collected on electronic commerce is shared out equally amongst the related countries; preventing unnecessary taxation (abuse) by means of double taxation*".

Also, it was suggested in the mentioned meeting that VAT shall be accrued in "the place of consumption" and digital products cannot be regarded as physical goods regarding customs duties and VAT. Therefore, the transactions carried out as part of electronic commerce contradicted the place of consumption. Besides, the rules and principles of assessment and realisation for the value-added tax on electronic trade have not yet been set forth thoroughly (Ertaş, 2017:136). Hence, four different solution approaches came into existence concerning the taxation of electronic commerce before the efforts were initiated towards the action plans (Alptürk, 2005: 313):

- to take the electronic environment sort of "free trade zone" and not to impose any tax,
- to impose a tax using "byte" taxation which is "an electronic sales tax", based on the taxation of the volume of the transferred data used during the sale, which is measured in "byte", regardless of the nature of the electronic transactions.
- to impose the tax under the rules available in the current legislation,
- to impose the tax according to the instructions to be outlined in the local tax legislation and double-tax treaties.

Although the first decade of the millennium went by within the frame of these opinions, OECD began to take some firm steps in 2013 using Base Erosion and Profit Shifting (BEPS) Action Plan, to clarify the concept of the electronic workplace. The leaders of G20 countries came together and agreed upon BEPS Action Plan consisting of 15 actions in order to prevent foreign tax losses, and they reached a consensus to review their legislation by this action plan (Payne & Raiborn, 2018: 472). Moreover, the first action of the mentioned action plan was determined as the "Taxation of Digital Economy" No. 1 (Gülhan & Turunç, 2015: 171). In this context, BEPS Action plan mainly included the proposals regarding the direct taxes, in the taxation of digital economy (Uslu, 2017b: 151–152). OECD favoured the idea that tax should be imposed in the place of consumption, concerning the transactions carried out "business to business" and "business to consumer" (Ertaş, 2017: 137). These proposals are listed as follows: "*Withholding at source*", "*digital equalisation levy*", "*digital presence-based establishment*".

The first action clause of BEPS Action Plan suggests that it is required to determine whether the digital economy poses a threat for the existing international tax rules, by taking both indirect and direct taxation practices into account, with an integrated approach and the alternatives dealing with these problems should be developed. Some of the points to be discussed within the scope of article #1 of the Action Plan are as follows (Turunç, 2017: 51):

a) the capacity of the companies to possess a digital existence in another country's economy, without having to pay any tax, for the reason that a sufficient connection cannot be established between the existing international rules,
b) determining the characteristics of the income earned through the new business models,
c) how to determine the VAT or goods and services tax that are caused by the use of the relevant source rule and cross-border circulation of digital goods and services.

Moreover, while determining the exceptions concerning the workplace definition set out in article #5 of the OECD Model Tax Convention, the activities covered by such exceptions were assessed as "***preparatory or auxiliary***". However, some dramatic changes happened in the operational applications of multinational companies since the beginning of these exceptions. In line with the changing conditions, the activities which were previously thought to be preparatory or auxiliary, correspond to the basic activity areas today. Intending to tax the profits which are acquired through the activities carried out in a country, it is recommended that each of the exceptions contained in the article #5 of the Model Convention is changed in order to limit those exceptions with "preparatory or auxiliary" activities (Turunç, 2017: 56).

3.1.2 OECD's Approach to the Workplace (Establishment) Concept and Changes

3.1.2.1 General Description

It is seen that the OECD Model Convention mentions the definition of "permanent establishment" in article #5/1. So, a permanent establishment means "*a permanent location in which a business is carried out wholly or partially*" (OECD,

2017:12). Likewise, the OECD Model Convention stipulates that a permanent establishment is required to include the following features (art. 5/2) notably:

a) place of management;
b) a branch;
c) an office;
d) a factory;
e) a workshop/plant and
f) using different methods for mining, drilling oil, gas well, extracting stones, natural resources from the quarry, etc.

Also, the 2017 draft of the Convention underlines ***what a permanent establishment cannot contain***, as well. Hence (OECD, 2017: art. 5/4):

a) the facilities must be used to store, display or deliver the goods and items of the establishment, only;
b) the goods and items of the establishment should be stocked only for storage, display or delivery;
c) to maintain the goods or item stocks of the establishment so that they can be processed by another organisation, only;
d) to maintain a fixed/permanent location of the establishment in order to sell goods and commodities or collect data, only;
e) to maintain permanent location regarding the business, to keep any other activity of a preparatory or auxiliary character, only for the establishment;
f) to maintain a permanent location only, for any combination of the business.

The element of "Permanent location" includes the elements of permanency and continuity, in a geographical sense. Concerning a business, a location, which constitutes a whole commercially and geographically, can be regarded as an establishment. A major element concerning "permanent establishment" is the element of continuity. Therefore, a permanent location regarding the business can only be considered an establishment if it is used on a continuous basis, rather than temporary. It is open to comment under what circumstances a business can be considered to be used on a continuous basis. Nevertheless, it is still possible to recognise the existence of an establishment if the business is carried on at the same location for a specified period (six months) or at shorter intervals but in more than one occasions. Also, in case a permanent location, which was initially secured for long-term commercial activity, abandoned for a short time due to an unpredictable reason, it should be accepted that the establishment has been formed. The main point here is the purpose (Cangir, 2000a: 57) and intention.

Pursuant to the article #5/5 of the Model Convention, if a person other than an agent operating independently is entitled to act on behalf of the enterprise in another contracting country and to execute a contract on behalf of the enterprise and also if such person regularly uses the power of executing a contract, then such enterprise will be accepted to own a permanent establishment in such other contracting country unless he/she carries out any activity which will not necessitate the formation of a permanent establishment, as specified in article # 5/4. Furthermore, if an enterprise carries on its commercial activities in another contracting country, through the means of an independent broker that performs as part of its own business, general commission agent or similar agent, a permanent establishment will not necessarily be formed in such another contracting country (Organ & Kara, 2017: 5). It is important whether or not the contracts supplemented by the dependent agency are executed on behalf of the enterprise. However, if the supplemented contract is binding the enterprise – even though it is not made on behalf of the enterprises, the agency executing the contract will be accepted as having an establishment (Işık, 2014: 117). At this critical point, one of the proposal that could be introduced into the definition of establishment (workplace) in the context of BEPS Action Plan No #7 is the point by which the locations used for purposes such as, "storage, exhibition, goods transfer centre, data collection centre, etc.", that are considered to be auxiliary and preparatory activities yet do not constitute an establishment, in the context of the Model Convention, can, from now on, be accepted as establishments by looking at the characteristic of the commercial activity (Uslu, 2017b: 160).

In general terms, it should be checked whether the activity being carried out at a permanent establishment constitute a ***substantial and significant part*** of the activity concerning the entire business. If the activity of an establishment is a separate, distinctive activity which is destined for a single purpose within the general line of business of the establishment, the preparatory and auxiliary feature cannot be mentioned (Yaltı Soydan, 1995: 134). Based on the works carried out so far within the scope of BEPS Action Plan No #1, while a permanent location cannot be regarded as a "permanent establishment" only if it is not preparatory and auxiliary, other permanent locations, which have a significant number of employees and attach great importance to quick delivery to their customers on time and on-site, will be accepted as a permanent establishment and subject to taxation for the seller (for more information, see Kara & Öz, 2016: 33).

In the guidelines published for the Action No #1 of BEPS Action Plan, the following proposals were suggested to the member countries concerning the digital workplace/business applications (OECD, 2014a: 43):

- to impose a minimum tax in the country of origin by regulating the deductions on the paying side,
- to impose no or low tax on the source,
- to impose less tax or impose no tax on the income, which is not continuous, using intra-group regulations (to cover the income that can be earned through law tax legislation, preferential regimes or hybrid mismatch),
- not to impose any tax for low income at the level of parent/principal company.

3.1.2.2. Website and Server Arguments

Considering the comments on OECD Model Convention, it was stated that the websites with respect to electronic commerce cannot always be accepted as an establishment unless they are also equipped with machinery, equipment and items regarding the fixtures and therefore the websites, which consist of electronic data or software only, cannot be accepted as an establishment, on their own (OECD, 2017: 117 § 123). This comment does not make it possible to accept the websites as an establishment unconditionally (Hongler & Pistone, 2015: 12). On the contrary, since the server, on which the website is installed and which allows access to the site, is an equipment with physical presence, the location where the server in relation with the website on which electronic trade is performed, raises the issue whether or not the server can be considered as an establishment provided that the server has remained in such location for a specified period (long enough to cause this existence to be considered permanent/continuous) (Batun, 2014: 70).

According to the interpretation on the article #5 of OECD Model Convention, concerning the concept of a permanent establishment in the digital economy, there were some arguments on whether or not the mere use of computer equipment in the electronic commerce transactions taking place in a country could constitute an establishment. There must be a distinction between the computer equipment that can be installed in a way to constitute an establishment in a location under certain circumstances even though such equipment can constitute an establishment in a country in a territory where automatic equipment is operated by an enterprise and the data/software used or stored by such equipment. As an example, a website, which is the combination of software and digital data, does not constitute a presence, on its own. Therefore, it does not have a location to constitute "a place for the business"; because, in the context of the software and data which make up of such website, there is not "a plant like the buildings or machinery or equipment in certain conditions" (Budak, 2018: 113–114).

The summary of the final report as regards the Action 7 following the update in 2017 set out two amendments in general (Yıldırım, 2017: 54):

1) If now an affiliated company/person plays a key/principal role in the process in a way to lead to the outcome that the contracts are made and finalised in the country where they operate and such contracts are approved by the company (the company for which the contracts primarily are made) without being modified, such company/person playing a vital role in the contracting process shall be considered to have formed an "establishment" in the country they are based. (Except for the businesses regarding the preparatory/auxiliary operations of such companies/persons as specified in paragraph #4 of article #5 in the model convention and the operations of such companies/persons as independent agents).

2) The second basic amendment is about the preparatory/auxiliary operations as specified in paragraph #4 of article #5 in the model convention and the cases that exclude such operations to constitute an establishment. This amendment was intended to split the operations and businesses, which are a meaningful whole, into smaller operations by dividing them into segments in various shapes, in an attempt to prevent the inhibition of workplace formation by ensuring that each operation is rendered preparatory/auxiliary. If the persons/companies that are closely associated with each other carry out operations in different locations, which supplement each other and constitute a significant whole in total and the total of such operations are no longer preparatory/auxiliary, then it will be possible to say that an "establishment" was formed in the locations where such operations are carried out.

However, the enterprise that carries out commercial activity by operating a website can vary from the enterprise that operates the server on which such website is installed and through which it delivers services. Therefore, the distinction between "website" and "server" is important in that respect, as well. What is mostly encountered in practice is that the website on which an enterprise carries out commercial operations is installed on the server of "an internet service provider". Even though in this example, a fee is paid to the internet service provider by the enterprise operating the website, based on the disc space required to store the software and data on the server, it is not possible to agree that the server will be at the disposal of the enterprise operating the website. Here, the services are offered for a fee by an internet service provider. Therefore, in this case, we cannot say that the enterprise operating the website owns the establishment (Batun, 2014: 71).

Another point being discussed in the context of the fact that a server is required to be considered an establishment is an issue of how the revenue to be attributed to the establishment (server) will be determined. Some commentators claim that even though a server can be accepted as an establishment, they argue that a server should not be deemed as an establishment for that reason alone, by underlining the problems to be encountered in distributing the revenue. This approach emphasises the diversity of the business functions as part of the commercial activity in the electronic commerce environment and the difficulties in the implementation of the article #7 of the Model Convention. Nevertheless, it seems quite difficult to associate this approach with the underlying rationale of the Model Convention. Because under the provision of the first clause of the article #7 in the Model Convention, if an establishment exists, some income should be allocated to that establishment. The rationale here is to determine the "existence of an establishment" first and then "the income" to be allocated here too. However, this rationale works the other way around in the approach arguing the idea that a server should not be considered an establishment due to practical difficulties (Cangir, 2000a: 59).

Both this situation and the fact that the website publishers that rent the servers have no control and right over the technical equipment and assets on which their websites are installed, other than receiving a rental service, make it impossible to determine an establishment and/or a representative by using the concept of "web pages" and/or "web servers" (Gençer, 2013: 22).

Based on what's concluded here, it will not be a fair approach to accept each web page or web server as an "establishment". The decisions taken in Ottawa Meetings favours the idea that a separate taxation regime would not be required concerning the taxation of electronic commerce. However, the idea that this approach should be abandoned is more prevalent today, based on both the current situation today and the approach of OECD in the last few years. Such that, traditional taxation principles and definitions are open to abuse and can create an unfair competition environment, as they remain incapable of comprehending the electronic trade. On the other hand, the fact that a website or web server should be accepted as an establishment in any case and condition will lead us to a unifactorial and accordingly to uniform taxation. For instance, a matter to be taxed as an element of "agricultural income", without taking the existing taxation rules into account, needs to be taken into account and taxed as a "commercial income", with the establishment approach that is attributed to the websites. With regards to the element to be taxed, the distinctions set out in the current legal regulations will eventually be taxed as a "commercial income", by rendering them down to a single revenue item. Hence, despite what's been achieved so far since 1998, it is evident that more accurate assessments should be made in defining the digital workplace and previous assessments are still insufficient.

3.1.2.2. Threshold Proposals

In the report regarding the Action No #1, an international agreement was reached on the proposals in the collection of VAT and Sales Tax, which entitle the country where the end user or the customer is located, to power of taxation, in the collection of VAT of the products submitted from the cross-border "business to consumer" (B2C). Concerning other taxation challenges, the uncertainty in the fact of the "location of the economic activities" and "the location where the value is created" continues to cause a disagreement on the subject of taxation (Kahraman, 2017: 1).

The Final Report #7 of BEPS on "Preventing the Artificial Avoidance of Permanent Establishment Status" was intended to offer some changes in the text of OECD Model Convention, with regards to the formation of the establishment, which are listed as follows (Kahraman, 2017: 2):

- Expanding the dependent agent test,
- Limiting the independent agent exemption,
- Limiting the business exemptions concerning the use of enterprise facilities for storage, display or delivery of the goods (including an anti-fragmentation test to prevent the activities from being split into separate enterprises),
- Preventing the abuse of the business rule dependent on 12-month construction site.

"Action 15 – Multilateral Convention" was established to put the changes regarding the Action #7 of BEPS into practice in the short term. So, "Multilateral Convention to Implement BEPS Actions Regarding the Tax Treaty Related Measures to Prevent Base Erosion and Profit Shifting" which is the Action #15 was executed on 7 June 2017 at a signing ceremony joined by the representatives of more than 70 countries. Moreover, Turkey was one of the countries to sign the Convention.

It was emphasised that the term "workplace" mentioned in the Action Plan #7 of BEPS had to be redefined and mainly it was suggested that e-commerce income should be shared uniformly between the country of residence and the country of origin and also it was expressed that it would be appropriate to make a distinction between the delivery of the physical goods and the digital activities (Hongler & Pistone, 2015: 24). In this sense, it can be appropriate to make a definition by considering the concrete proposals and elements, regarding taxation (Hongler & Pistone, 2015: 25):

- Electronic application, database, online selling domains, storages of the residents of the other contracting country, the areas reserved for advertising on a website or application,
- User threshold, the quantity of the people using the electronic application or website (e.g. more than 1.000 users, data usage in a month),
- Certain time threshold (e.g. observation regarding the violation of the user threshold in 12 month period),

- The amount of the income earned (EUR, USD, GBP, CNY, CHF, etc.) (mainly, small business to avoid facing a heavy tax burden),
- The terms such as electronic application, access, database, online activity area, storage, advertising services, website, monthly user period, resident, total income and service must be redefined.

Even though the OECD Report (Addressing the Tax Challenges of the Digital Economy) did not address a particular figure (threshold) (article 5), it mentioned that "digital sales, number of contracts, number of users and consumption level" should be emphasised. Moreover, the report put forth some solutions while it underlined that double taxation should be avoided, as the primary objective. Also, it was emphasised that the companies sustaining any loss during the use of the power of taxation have to be taken into account, as well and mainly it would be appropriate to take this situation into account when taxing the country of origin. (Hongler & Pistone, 2015: 26–27).

Accordingly, it was suggested that if a certain percentage of the total sales of a company based in the country A is made up of the sales carried out in the country B, the country B should assume that such country is doing business in the country B, as well (as if it has a workplace) (OECD, 2014b: 7). Furthermore, if a company, which carries out business in a country but does not have a physical workplace (nexus) and yet does business entirely through the internet, offers its services via a website in the local language of that country, uses the banking and finance system of that country or carries on its business by making use of the suppliers in that country, then it must be considered to carry out business in that country even if it does not have any physical establishment and therefore should be taxed by the country of origin (OECD, 2014b: 41).

It was not deemed appropriate to implement a separate tax system or a differential taxation regime for the digital economy. Instead, it was recommended that some arrangements be made to promote the digital economy. OECD report also includes some possibilities, such as "partial sharing, profit methods, withholding tax in digital transactions and equalisation tax" (Budak, 2018: 134).

Moreover, lastly, in the meeting held by the Ministers of Finance of G20 in Buenos Aires between 19 and 20 March 2018, Tax Challenges Arising from Digitalization – Interim Report regarding the BEPS Action Plan #1 was issued, and it was announced that they would work towards a consensus-based solution by 2020. The report sets out the applications of the countries in the short term. However, it is emphasised that the primary objective in OECD is to pave the way to proceed towards "a long-term multilateral solution" in the next stage (Kahraman, 2017: 2).

3.2 European Union's Approach to Workplace/Establishment

A proposal called "**target country-based cash flow tax**" was made in the studies conducted by a Group of Specialist on Taxation of Digital Economy in European Commission, within the scope of EU. As part of the mentioned proposal, VAT is supposed to be calculated based on the cash flow, as a principle. Likewise, "Common Consolidated Corporate Tax Basis" was suggested concerning the Corporate Tax. In this way, the companies earning income from several countries within the union will be taxed based on a single regime (Budak, 2018: 136–137).

European Union Commission for Taxation of Digital Economy is in the opinion that it will not be possible to impose a tax on a seller (vendor) who does not mainly reside in a country, does not have a permanent establishment, but markets physical or digital product via online selling only, by relying on the rules of a permanent establishment (Hongler & Pistone, 2015: 13–14).

As in the example of Rubik Agreements signed between Switzerland, United Kingdom and Austria, the power of collection can be shared among the countries as a significant step towards the distribution of the tax revenue. One or more countries can collect on behalf of others and share the tax revenue. Alternatively, they can let a single country to impose the tax, using a system called "one-stop shop" as in the European Union and agree on the sharing of the tax collected, as a solution (Hongler & Pistone, 2015: 37).

In EU's universal VAT system, it was agreed that indirect tax, just like the VAT in cross-border trade, is supposed to be collected in the place where the service is consumed. The international acknowledgements regarding the country from which the VAT arises are seen as similar with the article #6 of the VAT Law No. 3065. Even though the European Union points out the place of consumption for VAT assessment, it introduced a system called MOSS (Mini-One-Stop-Shop), by taking advantage of being a union. MOSS is a VAT system designed by the European Union. Based on this system, the sellers can register to MOSS in any one of the EU member countries and submit VAT returns electronically in three-month periods. So, the collected VAT is transferred to MOSS, which transfers such amounts electronically to the related countries.

On the other hand, the sellers who are not a member of MOSS submit their VAT returns and pay directly to the related country in three-month periods. However, as it is seen, the system in question runs on voluntary registration. Therefore, it may not be seen as an efficient solution in preventing the assessment losses (Ertaş, 2017: 137).

The regulation of EU, called "digital taxation package" which allows imposing a tax without having "a physical presence/nexus", is one of the significant and final steps regarding the taxation of digital activities (Kahraman, 2017:4). The arrangement, which aims at ensuring that online businesses contribute to the same taxation regime as the companies associated with a traditional physical establishment, contains a recommendation to change Double Tax Treaties with the third countries. The practice, called "Digital services tax", allows the member countries to impose a tax on the income earned in their soils, without having "a physical connection/nexus".

Specific digital services, including the provision of advertising area, availability of market areas and transmission of collected user data, while offering digital content or payment services, were introduced into the subject of Digital Services Tax. Taxpayers are the organisations with an annual global revenue above €750 million and annual revenue above €50 million stemming from the digital services in EU (Kahraman, 2018: 3).

In this context, as the criteria to be considered in recognising a business operating in a country as a digital establishment even though it does not have a physical presence in that country, it was proposed that such business is to be associated with the income which will require the "significant digital presence" to be acknowledged, user and agreement thresholds. Therefore, a company, if it possesses any of the following criteria, will be considered to have a "significant economic digital presence" in a Member Country:

- if it exceeds the threshold of €7 million revenue in a fiscal year, from the digital services in a Member Country (e.g. earning income from ad placement according to user data),
- if more than 100.000 users had access to the digital services in a fiscal year in a Member Country (e.g. earning income from the services giving the users access in the shared economy and online markets),
- if over 3000 labour contracts are executed in a fiscal year for the digital services between the company and the business users (e.g. income earned from broadcast streaming services delivered to its subscribers).

"Digital Services Tax", defined temporarily by EU Commission, is projected to be implemented as from January 1st, 2020 and collected by 3% based on gross income. However, it has to be remembered that they will also need the approval of 28 member parliaments in order for them to be implemented. In case a tax is imposed by 3% under the proposal of the Commission, this will mean an opportunity for the member countries to earn approximately €5 billion annually. When applied to the EU, this single-rate tax could promote "tax exchange" and "avoidance in tax distortion" in a single market. If the bill becomes a law, the technology giants such as Google, Amazon, etc. will have to pay 3% of their revenue as a tax in the country where the activity is carried on. The fact that the tax will be paid in the country where the activity is executed could undoubtedly affect negatively the tax revenue of the countries like Ireland in which such companies are based (Kahraman, 2018, s.4).

3.3 The Situation in Turkish Tax Law

Based on TSI data, the percentage of internet users shopping online in Turkey appears to be 24.9 % as of April/2017. According to the same study, those who purchase goods/services via the net purchase services apart from physical products are: 2.7 % e-learning, 24.1 % travelling services, 13.6 % sportive and cultural activities, 14.5 % holiday and accommodation. The data in question indicate that a considerable amount of internet users in Turkey tend to buy online. The data obtained in the recent study is estimated to cover both domestic and overseas online service purchases (Ertaş, 2017: 133).

Before we move on to define the concept of "workplace/establishment" in Turkish Law, it will be appropriate to make a quick mention of the legal arrangements made concerning the digital economy. The initial step taken to control the activities of the digital economy began with the Electronic Signature Law No. 5070 (Official Gazette, 23.01.2004/25355). Then, the Law on Regulation of Publications on the Internet and Combating Crimes Committed Using Such Publications No. 5661 (Official Gazette, 23.05.2007/26530), Consumer Protection Law no. 6502 (Official Gazette, 28.11.2013/28835), Law on Regulation of Electronic Commerce no. 6563 (Official Gazette, 05.11.2014/29166), Privacy Act no. 6698 (Official Gazette, 07.04.2016/29677) entered into force, and some arrangements were introduced towards the activities carried out in the digital environment. Besides, the Electronic Notification application was launched.

3.3.1 Today: Current Regulations

Natural persons who are under a full obligation (as taxpayers) under the Income Tax Law are subjected to taxation based on the profits and income they earn both at home and abroad (ITL art. 3). On the other hand, those with limited liability (as taxpayers) are bound up with special arrangements. Especially, regarding commercial income, the income earner is required to have an establishment or keep a permanent representative in Turkey and earn its income at such locations or through such representatives.

Under the Corporate Tax Law, of the taxpayers listed in the law, only those whose registered or head offices are based in Turkey are required to pay tax as fully obligated taxpayers based on the total income they earn both in and outside

Turkey. Those who have neither a registered nor a head office in Turkey are taxed based only on their income in Turkey. Furthermore, the commercial income earned by foreign organisations which have an establishment or keep a permanent representative in Turkey, from the transactions carried out at such locations or through such representatives.

Moreover, yet, it is seen that the concept "establishment" is discussed as a nexus, as a headline in taxation regarding the national law.

It is observed that the workplace in our legislation is defined and regulated directly in Tax Procedure Law. Pursuant thereto, a workplace is defined as follows "*a workplace in a commercial, industrial or professional activity is a location allocated for the execution of any commercial, industrial or professional activity or used in such activities, such a store/shop, office, bureau, surgery, workshop/plant, branch, warehouse, hotel, café, leisure and sports centres, farm fields, orchards, garden, farm, livestock plants, fisheries and dive-in fishing spots, mines, quarries, construction sites, ferry buffets/snack bars, etc.*". As can be seen, a suitable arrangement dealing with the digital workplace is in place in the domestic law.

The Cabinet was authorised in Turkey by adding a clause into the article #9 of the Law No. 6745, dated 20 August 2016 as well as into the article #11 of Tax Procedure Law. Upon this regulation, the Cabinet was authorised to impose tax withholding on those who are a party to or mediator in the taxable transactions and to set different rates of withholding/deduction, – but only between the lower and upper limits set out in the tax legislations – as regards the taxable transactions, in respect of business groups, business types, sectors and commodity groups, regardless of whether or not the payees are taxpayers, whether the payer or the mediator in the payment is obliged to withhold tax as per the tax law, whether the payment is destined to cover the purchase of goods or services, whether it is carried out in electronic environment and whether the payee used such amount to get a discount, in determining the basis of tax assessment.

Upon the authorisation in question, those who are "party to" or "mediator in" the transactions, "business to business", "business to end consumer", "consumer to consumer", "thing to thing" and "server to server" as part of internet of things, can be burdened with "tax obligation", but only within the lower and upper limits set out in income tax or corporate tax laws (Kahraman, 2017: 4).

3.3.2 The Situation in Draft Tax Procedure Law

The use of the concept, "establishment in the electronic environment", in TPL draft, which is likely to become law soon, appears as an outcome of the studies carried out in the international arena, in order to tax the digital economy more effectively. The article #130 of the draft law states that in case the internet, extranet, intranet or a similar telecommunication media or tool is allocated to a commercial, industrial or professional activity or used in such activities, a workplace will be formed in an electronic environment. Nevertheless, the electronic environment was also added to the extent of "workplace", as mentioned in the article #129 of the Draft. However, electronic environments like a website are merely tools (Ertaş 2017: 137).

According to the article #129 of the TPL Draft, "a workplace/establishment" is "*a location allocated for the execution of any commercial, industrial or professional activity or used in such activities, such a store/shop, office, bureau, surgery, manufacturing plant, branch, sales point, workshop, warehouse, laboratory, showroom and exhibition hall, education/training and course locations, home office, auction hall/room, hotel, café, leisure and sports centres, farm fields, orchards, garden, farm, livestock plants, fisheries and dive-in fishing spots, salt works, mines, quarries, construction sites, cargo and passenger transport vehicles, ferry buffets/snack bars,* ***mobile devices, electronic media or fields,*** *etc.*"

According to the article #139 of the TPL Draft, "a workplace/establishment in electronic environment" is "(1) *In case of internet, extranet, intranet or a similar telecommunication media or tool is allocated to a commercial, industrial or professional activity or used in such activities; a workplace will be formed in the electronic environment. (2) Ministry of Finance is authorised to determine the matters regarding the scope of the workplaces formed in an electronic environment and the fulfilment of the duties concerning the tax obligation; hold the mediators in supplying the goods and services by means of the workplaces formed in electronic environment or in paying the price of such goods and services as well as the buyers of the goods and services, severally responsible for the payment of the related taxes and to determine the rules and principles regarding the application.*"

The regulations for the current establishment (TPL 156) do not cover or embrace the "digital activities." TPL Draft Law acknowledges "a location allocated for the execution of any commercial, industrial or professional activity or used in such activities, such as mobile device, electronic media or fields" as the workplace/establishment. The terms "allocation" and "usage", which are included in the regulations, need clarification. Moreover, the authority granted to the Ministry of Finance is controversial regarding the Constitution.

3.4 Consequences of the Lack of Definition of Establishment

Three significant questions emphasised by OECD BEPS Action Plans need to be answered correctly:

1. Where is the economic-commercial activity carried out?
2. Where is the economic value created?
3. Where (or what) do the taxable income stem from, arising from the created value?

When the permanent establishment was defined and theoretically developed, there was no such term as the digital economy, and neither the computers nor the digital world was a part of the economy (Hongler & Pistone, 2015: 21). The traditional concept of "establishment" has become more restrictive for the source countries over time and almost formed a "cage" for them, which in turn paved the way for adopting an international tax planning (Hongler & Pistone, 2015: 10).

Since the digitalised activities allow the companies to perform a commercial activity without them showing a physical presence, they rule out the requirement of physical presence – which is available in the local regulations of that countries – to tax the company profits.

The person or organisation trading via the net can get in touch with the customers anytime and anywhere in the world. In traditional taxation systems, the domicile of the vendor is highly relevant in that a connection can be established with the taxable event and the tax can be assessed. Whereas, the digital activities do not require a nexus (a permanent workplace) or a head office to manage the business. This is because, what is meant by the domicile, is, in fact, the entire world (Alptürk, 2005: 317). Therefore, the fact that the definition of traditional establishment is associated with a permanent and physical location results in the failure to tax the digital economic activities.

The first step to collect tax on internet sales is to establish a collection and payment mechanism, to that end. It is still unclear whether it is required to simplify the sales tax during this formation or to provide the suppliers or credit card companies with sophisticated software. It can also obstruct the development of the sector unless it is easy and sustainable (Alptürk, 2005: 315).

Since the arrangements within the scope of OECD Model Convention seek to produce a solution based on the fact that a place has to be permanent, it fails to find a practical solution for the digital establishments introduced by the digital economy. For instance, it is still unclear whether or not a website will be considered an establishment or what type of taxation will be adopted towards the income earned through the applications operated via mobile devices (Hongler & Pistone, 2015: 2).

Direct taxes have some problems, too. The consequence caused by the lack of the definition of the workplace, what the information transmitted in a virtual environment is used for (trade-in, paid, free, etc.), failing to identify the nature of the income are some of the major problems (Budak, 2018: 80–81).

- Server and website owned by separate persons,
- Can a server alone make an establishment on its own?
- Can we say that the business of an establishment is operated entirely or partially via the server?

3.5 Opinions to Redefine the Establishment

The fact that multinational companies can get around the concept of "establishment" included in the international regulations and the local codes of law in the countries they do business, due to the complicated company structures and business models (Uslu, 2017b: 160), requires the definition of "establishment" be restructured. The fact that the definition of establishment is made accurately causes the country, where the establishment is based, to be subjected to taxation, due to the income to be attributed to such an establishment. Therefore, the broader the definition of establishment, the higher the possibility of taxing the country where it is located (Yaltı Soydan, 1995: 131). While the OECD Model has a narrow-scoped definition for Establishment, UN Model has a broader perspective (Işık, 2014: 109). In UN Model, expansionary arrangements made about construction sites, acknowledging the places and stocks – which are kept in order to "deliver" the goods and commodities left outside the establishment – as an establishment (e.g. warehouse), regulations related to insurance operations, distinctions related to the subsidiary companies which do stocking for continuous delivery on behalf of parent companies, draw attention as some of the points that expand the power of taxation of the source country (Yaltı Soydan, 1995: 138). The necessity to bring a new definition about the term "establishment" enables the country of origin to exercise its right of taxation on the commercial revenue, regionally and legally, rather than resolving the problem by performing a transaction based on withholding tax (Hongler & Pistone, 2015: 2).

Hardware law, software law as well as the rules of tax law compatible with the principles of impartiality, efficiency, certainty and simplicity, effectivity and fairness and flexibility are the subjects that need to be taken into consideration collectively when establishing a new nexus (Hongler & Pistone, 2015: 40–43).

Virtual workplace concept is invented in an attempt to make it easier to call a commercial activity an establishment, in other words, to stretch the definition of establishment. This was intended to pave the way to call it an establishment by way of a tax nexus and to impose a tax, even if an activity, which is carried out in a country, cannot be executed using a permanent establishment. This nexus works "as if it is a permanent establishment" in a sense and allows the country of origin to impose a tax on the income attributed to this establishment (Kara & Öz, 2016: 33). So, the nature of "tax nexus" becomes more of an issue.

The activities carried out without a physical connection, such as a website or mobile phone application, result in significant problems for the source countries, as well. Failing to establish a nexus with the country of income results in the formation of a tax-free (non-taxable) domain. This result has led to the idea that a remarkable digital presence can be referred alternatively in different situations. For instance, it was suggested that an alternative establishment can exist in the event that a number of agreements are made between a business carrying out digital activity and the customer(s) in the country of origin; the goods or services offered digitally are used widely in the country of origin; payments of large amounts are made from the country of origin to the business carrying out digital activity. However, in that case, some liabilities could be imposed on such business carrying out digital activity, nearly worldwide, which is not applicable (Budak, 2018: 85).

Although the digital economy appears to be an abstract cycle, it will be fair to say that it is recorded since the payments are made through the agency of financial intermediaries. Financial institutions keep a record of payers and payees of the payments. Therefore, it seems possible to identify at least the major global companies supplying digital services and get the financial institutions to withhold VAT based on the payments to be made for them from Turkey. It is for sure that a new legal arrangement will be required to get the financial institutions to withhold such tax. Finance Administration took a step similar to this approach, in the General Communique on Tax Procedure Law, Item No. 464, which was published in December 2015. The Communique stipulates that data, concerning the payments towards the selling and renting transactions performed online, will be transferred periodically in the electronic environment from the banks operating within the scope of the Banking Law No #5411 to RA (Revenue Administration) system. As can be seen from the provision of the communique, Finance Administration indicated that it would resort to using of the records of the banks, for some ongoing transactions in the digital economy. Concerning the services received electronically from overseas, the same method can be adopted and further to that, a legal infrastructure should be prepared, to withhold VAT (Ertaş, 2017: 139).

Theoretically, splitting a commercial income would also result in the distribution of the power of taxation. Therefore, a nexus (association with a permanent establishment) will always exist, physically or digitally or whatever, in a country where the value is created (Hongler & Pistone, 2015: 23). On the other hand, distribution of the power of taxation ought to be evaluated regarding the utility theory. Since the primary utility of digital economy leads to proper functioning of a country's infrastructure (electricity, internet, communication, etc.), this situation will require that the power of taxation of the country, the infrastructure of which is used, should also be taken into account (Hongler & Pistone, 2015: 24).

In case a threshold is set depending on the number of users, the resulting outcome is to be assessed regarding the VAT, as well. If a threshold is set based on a certain number of users and the presence of a digital establishment is recognised when such threshold is exceeded, it is still unclear whether VAT is to be collected by the country to which the user is associated or the country where the enterprise is located.

An enterprise based in a contracting country will be deemed to have a permanent establishment in another contracting country if the enterprise earns more than …. (TL, EUR, USD, GBP, CHF, etc.) annually in such contracting country, through an electronic application, database, online, market area or storage, website advertising service or through an electronic application which has over 1000 individual users every month, residing in such contracting country (Hongler & Pistone, 2015: 3). The proposal in question was brought to adding it as clause #8 into the article #5 of the OECD Model Convention. The authors underlined that the term "user" here should be defined clearly and emphasised whether the persons who are subscribers or the persons who receive the service directly are supposed to be considered. Also, it was also expressed that the terms "database", "advertising services", "website", "each month" and "resident" need to be clarified, as well.

One of the views outlined in the literature is to adopt the principle of economic presence, instead of physical presence, for an establishment. Within this framework, as an example, when the number of commercial activities carried out in a country by a resident of another contracting country exceeds a certain threshold (e.g. $1 million US), it will acknowledge that an establishment is formed, so such income should be taxed in the source country. A concept of "virtual establishment" (virtual PE) was suggested, based on the idea that an establishment will be considered to have formed in case of the presence of a continuous and significant commercial activity in a country (Batun, 2014: 74).

3.6 Practices in Some Countries to Tax Digital Activities

Spanish Tax Court ordered that a company, which makes sales in Spain over an internet site based outside Spain (web-hosted outside Spain) although it is not a resident of Spain, could be subjected to direct tax liability in Spain, based on its revenue earned from such sales, as a commercial income, within the framework of the approach "virtual establishment" (virtual PE) (Erdem, 2016:23).

"Diverted Profit Tax" that became law in 2015 in the UK is regarded as one of the leading steps taken by taxing the largest technology companies. "Diverted Profit Tax" targets the tax structures of large-scale taxpayers only. It advocates that the income earned as a result of the activities in the UK should be above a certain amount and also considers the overseas structuring and tax burden of UK group companies.

Australian Government launched "Australia Goods and Services Tax" act in February 2017 for the international service sales as well as digital products, to be implemented on the Australian consumers. This act introduced two major taxes. A brand new tax, called "Netflix Tax", was introduced into the consumption taxes act, to tax the foreign taxpayers offering entertainment services using the online subscription model. Moreover, a new tax liability, called "Amazon Tax", was launched in order to tax the foreign companies selling products in Australia by way of e-commerce (Uslu, 2017a: 152).

While the businesses can be monitored more strictly in e-commerce, within the scope of the Action Plan #7 of BEPS, with respect to the taxes collected on the revenue in the People's Republic of China, the Government of Vietnam announced its arrangement plans with regards to the establishment of tax liability, declaration, tax returns and tax payment obligations of foreign digital companies. On the other hand, India put a practice, called "equalisation tax", into operation, aiming at taxing the e-commerce-based transactions, to be effective from June 1, 2016. Upon this arrangement in Law, India imposed tax by 6 % on the payments made in cash or on account, to the limited taxpayers who do not have an establishment in India, with respect to the "specific services, such as the provision of online advertising, digital advertising space" (Kahraman, 2017: 3).

In 2016, South Dakota State of USA introduced its principle of nexus in its legislation. The law will enable the vendors, who do not have a physical presence for the sales tax based on the principle of an economic nexus, to be taxpayers. Tax liability threshold was determined as "the vendor has to make 200 separate sales or make a total of $100.000 US sales".

Belgian Government annulled the VAT exemption offered to the companies delivering online gaming service, upon the amendment to the law in 2016. However, an online game company escalated the case to the Constitutional Court on the ground that the amendment in question is against both the Belgian VAT law and straight games legislation. The Court cancelled the execution of the law, upon its recent decision, as it acknowledged the company to be right (SBC News, 2018).

4 Conclusion

Development of digital economy requires that the rules in every field affected by the economic activity be readdressed and rediscussed. In that sense, the tax legislation is one of the closely affected fields. The fact that the number of economic activities via internet in an electronic environment, as well as the users who enjoy such activities, keep increasing every year began to influence the tax revenue of the countries, as well and caused the formation of non-taxable areas by creating the unfair competitive environment. Although OECD and EU agree upon the fact that existing applicable international taxation rules remain incapable in taxing the digitalised economy, OECD members have not yet introduced a new and stable taxation rule in this respect at international level. As a short-term solution, OECD member countries adopted the taxation method, which is mostly collected based on the sales and it is mentioned that a long-term solution will be achieved in 2020. On the other hand, EU strives to introduce new rules and settle the problem on its own merits. However, there are still specific rules that have to be approved by the parliaments of 28 countries and also some lingering uncertainties and challenges encountered in the implementation by non-member countries

Primarily, the economic activities offered via the websites, cloud systems, the applications on mobile devices which are deemed as virtual workplace have long exceeded the limits of the tax-raising powers of the countries, thanks to their extensive features. Therefore, the outcome, likely to come out of either international or national works, favours the idea that the virtual workplace has to be redefined and taxation arrangements will be required, accordingly.

In this sense, the following considerations have to be resolved immediately:

- clarifying and defining the nature of digital products and services, comprehensively,
- defining and clarifying the considerations to be recognised as "establishment" in a virtual environment,
- how to assess the status of the limited taxpayers regarding the taxes collected on income,
- how and by whom the tax, collected on the expenses during the delivery of digital products and services, will be calculated and declared,
- how to address the matters in question when executing the double tax treaties.

It is evident that the concept of "permanent business establishment" should be replaced with the approach of economic presence, in electronic environments. Therefore, the definition of "digital establishment" ought to be reshaped and made, accordingly. Although tax agreements specify which activities will not be regarded as an "establishment", activity definitions remain incapable, given the varieties of the activities in the electronic environment.

It is required that right amount of income should be taxed in the right country and the right amount when deciding on the taxable income of the associated organisations and therefore an automated data exchange has to be established between the tax offices.

Furthermore, another result that can be inferred from all these remarks is that it will not be a proper approach to consider each website or web server an "establishment". However, the traditional taxation principles and definitions are open to abuse and might create an unfair competitive environment since they remain incapable of comprehending the electronic commerce. On the other hand, the fact that a website or web server should be accepted as an establishment in any case and condition will lead us to a unifactorial and accordingly to uniform taxation. For instance, a matter to be taxed as an element of "agricultural income", without taking the existing taxation rules into account, needs to be taken into account and taxed as a "commercial income", with the establishment approach that is attributed to the websites. With regards to the element to be taxed, the distinctions set out in the current legal regulations will eventually be taxed as a "commercial income", by rendering them down to a single revenue item. Hence, despite what's been achieved so far since 1998, it is evident that more accurate assessments should be made in defining the digital workplace and previous assessments are still insufficient.

Considering that those offering electronic services are based overseas and have no nexus here, it is controversial how to control the applicability and whether or not it is applied. We are in the opinion that the most reasonable proposal that might spring to mind at this point would be that the nexus in such transactions should be connected to "payment", and the responsibility should be conferred to the "banks or similar financial institutions".

Mainly, the point agreed upon in OECD and doctrine is that the requirement that virtual establishment ought to connect its asset to certain thresholds (Income, user, agreement thresholds, spaces allocated to advertising, etc.) is the most concrete proposal at the moment. This matter has to be further discussed comprehensively, and the assessments have to be made based on these considerations. However, it is also essential that the terms such as electronic application, database, online activity area, storage, advertising services, website, user, monthly period, resident, total income and service be redefined.

References

Alptürk, E., (2005). Elektronik Ticaretin Hukuku ve Vergilendirilmesi, Gelirler Kontrolörleri Derneği, İstanbul.

Batun, M., (2014). "OECD Model Anlaşması Çerçevesinde İşyeri: İlişkili Şirketler ve Elektronik Ticaret", Vergi Dünyası Dergisi, Sayı: 393, ss.64–75.

Bird, R.M., Gendron, PP, (1998). "Dual VATs and Cross-Border Trade: Two Problems, One Solution?", International Tax and Public Finance, 5, pp. 429–442.

Budak, T., (2017). "The Transformation Of International Tax Regime: Digital Economy", Inonu University Law Review In ULR, 8 (2), pp. 297–330.

Budak, T., (2018). Dijital Ekonominin Vergilendirilmesi, Oniki Levha Yayıncılık, İstanbul.

Cangir, N., (2000a). "Sanal İşyeri-I", Vergi Dünyası, Sayı:227, ss.52–60.

Cangir, N., (2000b). "Sanal İşyeri-II", Vergi Dünyası, Sayı:229, ss.48–56.

Cangir, N., (2002). "Ottowa'da Kabul Edilen Vergileme İlkeleri Ya Da Sanal Dünyanın Vergisel Vizyonu", Vergi Dünyası, Sayı:250, ss.23–30.

Erdem, T., (2016). "Kaydırılmış Kazanç Vergisi (Diverted Profit Tax)", Vergi Sorunları, Sayı:330, Mart, ss.111–119.

Ertaş, B.L., (2017). "Dijital Ekonomide Yurt Dışından Alınan Hizmetler Bakımından KDV Mevzuatındaki Sorunlar", Vergi Raporu, Sayı:219, Aralık, ss.131–140.

Gençer, Ç.A., (2013). "Elektronik Ticarette Bağlanma Noktası Olan "İşyeri" Kavramı", Vergi Sorunları, Sayı:293, Şubat, ss.18–23.

Gianni, M., (2014). "The OECD's Flawed and Dated Approach to Computer Servers Creating Permanent Establishments", Vanderbilt Journal Of Entertainment & Technology Law, 17 (1), pp. 1–38.

Gülhan, N., Turunç, S., (2015). "Dijital Ekonominin Vergilemesinde Yaşanan Sorunlara Yönelik Son Dönemde Uluslararası Vergi Alanında Yaşanan Gelişmeler", Vergi Dünyası, Sayı: 409, Eylül.

Hoffart, B., (2007). "Permanent Establishment in the Digital Age: Improving and Stimulating Debate Through an Access to Markets Proxy Approach", Northwestern Journal of Technology and Intellectual Property, 6 (1), pp. 105–121.

Hongler, P., Pistone, P., (2015). "Blueprints for a New PE Nexus to Tax Business Income in the Era of the Digital Economy", IBFD, Working Paper, 20 January 2015, WU International Taxation Research Paper Series, No. 2015-15, (http://epub.wu.ac.at/4509/4/SSRN-id2591829.pdf), (16.03.2018).

Işık, H., (2014). Uluslararası Vergilendirme, Oniki Levha Yayıncılık, İstanbul.

Kahraman, A., (2017). "Dijital Ekonomide Vergileme Tercihleri ve Türkiye: Ne Tür Bir "İnternet Vergilemesi", https://www.kpmgvergi.com/Blog/Pages/FullBlog. aspx?article=776, (01.05.2018).

Kahraman, A., (2018). “Dijitalleşen Ekonominin Vergilemesinde AB Teklifi Vergi Korumacılığı mı?”, https://kpmgvergi.com/Blog/Pages/FullBlog.aspx?article =884, (04.06.2018).

Kara, M.C., Öz, E., (2016). “Dijital Vergilendirmeye Küresel Bir Bakış”, Vergi Dünyası, Sayı: 424, Aralık, ss.30–37.

Lexner, K.D., (2010). “Selected Issues in the U.S.-Dk Tax Treaty: Permanent Establishment in Relatıon to E-Commerce Transactions and the Distinction Between Payment for Services and Payment for Intangible Property Rights”, Copenhagen Research Group On International Taxation – CORIT, Discussion Paper No.7.

OECD, (2014a). BEPS Action 1: Address the Tax Challenges of the Digital Economy, 24 March 2014 – 14 April 2014, Public Discussıın Drafts. (https://www.oecd.org/ctp/tax-challenges-digital-economy-discussion-draft-march-2014.pdf), (13.03.2018).

OECD, (2014b). Beps Action 1: Address the Tax Challenges of the Digital Economy, Comments Received On Public Discussion Draft, 16 April 2014, (https://www.oecd.org/ctp/comments-action-1-tax-challenges-digital-economy.pdf), (29.03.2018).

OECD, (2017). Draft Contents of the 2017 Update to the OECD Model Tax Convention, http://www.oecd.org/tax/treaties/draft-contents-2017-update-oecd-model-tax-convention.pdf, (11.07.2017).

Organ, İ. Kara M.C., (2017). “Daimi İşyeri Statüsünden Kaçınmayı Önlemede Yeni Uluslararası Yaklaşım”, Muhasebe ve Vergi Uygulamaları Dergisi Şubat 2017; 10 (1), ss. 1–12.

Pahlsson, R., (2002). “The E-com Strain on Tax Law Concepts”, European Business Organization Law Review 3, pp.195–210.

Payne, D.M., Raiborn, C.A., (2018). “Aggressive Tax Avoidance: A Conundrum for Stakeholders, Governments, and Morality”, Bus Ethics (2018) 147, pp. 469–487, Springer, Netherlands, https://doi.org/10.1007/s10551-015-2978-5.

SBC News, “Kindred Group Wins Belgium Digital VAT Repeal”, (https://sbcnews.co.uk/sportsbook/2018/03/26/kindred-group-wins-belgium-digital-vat-repeal/), (05.04.2018).

“The Impact of BEPS the Digital Economy”, 2018, (http://taxinsights.ey.com/archive/archive-articles/the-impact-of-beps-on-the-digital-economy.aspx).

Turunç, S., (2017). “Dijital Ekonomide İş Yeri Kavramı ve Transfer Fiyatlandırması”, Vergi Dünyası, Yıl: 36, Sayı: 431, Temmuz, ss.50–59.

Uslu, Y., (2017a). “Dijital Ekonomide Vergisel Problemler”, Vergi Dünyası Dergisi, Yıl: 37, Sayı: 436, ss.148–152.

Uslu, Y., (2017b). "Beps Projesi Eylem Planı 7: Daimi Müessese Statüsünden Kaçınmanın Önlenmesi" ve Uluslararası Vergi Hukukundaki Etkisi", Vergi Dünyası Dergisi, Yıl: 37, Sayı: 435, ss.157–164.

Van der Paardt, R.N.G., (2009). "Taxation of internet gaming and gambling in the European Union", ERA Forum 10, pp.525–531, Springer-Verlag, DOI 10.1007/s12027-009-0144-1.

Yaltı Soydan, B., (1995). Uluslararası Vergi Anlaşmaları, Beta Basım Dağıtım, İstanbul.

Yıldırım, H.Ö., (2017). "ÇVÖA'da İşyeri Kavramı ile İlgili Öngörülen Değişiklikler",Vergi Dünyası, Yıl:37, Sayı:434, Ekim, ss.50–55.

Yılmaz, G.H., Değer, A.A., (2018). "Dijital İktisadi Faaliyetlerde İşyeri Paradoksu ve Vergisel Boyutu", (http://www.verginet.net/dtt/18/DijitalIktisadiFaaliyetlerde IsyeriParadoksuveVergiselBoyutu.aspx), (10.04.2018).

Zhu, Y., (2014). "Proposed Changes to the UN Model Tax Convention Dealing with the Cyber-Based Services", Committee of Experts on International Cooperation in Tax Matters, Geneva, 27–31 October 2014, E/C.18/2014/CRP. 9.

Burçin Bozdoğanoğlu[1]

Cryptocurrencies' Low Risk for Money Laundering and High Risk for Cybercrime: Desperation of Tax Administration or New Future of Taxation

Abstract: In this chapter, the main features of cryptocurrencies and virtual money, especially the ones that have emerged recently, were examined and the differences were tried to be explained.

Blockchain and distributed ledger, which are the underlying mechanisms of cryptocurrencies, are explained, and their effects on the tax evasion of the use of this system by the tax administrations are mentioned. Cryptocurrencies are also classified according to the blockchain mechanisms they use. The evaluation of cryptocurrencies as "money" or "asset" is vital regarding taxation. In this context, it has been examined how the definition of cryptocurrencies is done from both economic and legal perspectives. The definitions made by the European Central Bank (ECB) and the IMF regarding the economy and the definitions made by these institutions from the legal point of view are taken into consideration, and the ECJ (European Court of Justice) decision has been examined in detail, especially at the point of taxation. The use of cryptocurrencies involves crimes such as money laundering, cybercrime, terrorism financing, and fraud. These crimes are carried out using browsers such as Darknet, Tor, etc. which are not possible to follow and cryptocurrency shopping. Therefore, it is possible to distinguish between two groups of tax administrators' difficulties concerning cryptocurrencies, such as anonymity feature of cryptocurrencies and also taxation and regulation discrepancies according to countries, and the chapter examines these difficulties.

Keywords: Cryptocurrencies, Taxation, Money Laundering, Tax Evasion

JEL Classification: E42, H20, H26, G18

1 Introduction

In an increasingly globalised world, the emergence of decentralised cryptocurrency systems has allowed individuals to quickly and easily transfer value to each other without the need for a reliable third-party agent. Although this is beneficial for many individuals, society also has a wide range of difficulties, especially concerning governments. Because cryptocurrencies such as

1 Corresponding author.

Bitcoin generally operate anonymously, governments have significant gaps in the regulation of these currencies, and in the monitoring transfers made with them. This anonymity may provide the basis for criminal activity by facilitating the sale of online illegal drugs and weapons, as in the case of Silk Road. Even more important, this situation promotes the activities of money laundering, tax evasion, and terrorism financing, which are included in the scope of financial crime by international organisations.

However, recently, cryptocurrencies have developed like a stock market, and individuals have begun to make deposits without researching the working system to earn money from these currencies. Cryptocurrencies can be obtained through intermediary institutions. As a result of cyber-attacks to internet sites that provide cryptocurrency, some users have reported that some of their virtual money has been stolen. Due to the anonymous nature of the cryptocurrencies, both the delivery of such funds to the owners and the difficulty of providing evidence, this once again showed how convenient these currencies are for tax evasion and fraud (Marian, 2013:39).

In this chapter, firstly the characteristics of the cryptocurrencies will be examined and the classification of these currencies whose numbers are increasing day by day will be done.

The definition of the virtual currency concept, which is an essential point regarding taxation, will be done and the currency characteristics of the cryptocurrencies will be discussed concerning legal and economic aspects. Besides, the Blockchain system, which is the working mechanism of Bitcoin, the first virtual currency, and inspires other virtual currencies, will be explained. Country examples of the Blockchain system on governmental operations such as public administration and taxation are briefly mentioned.

In the fourth part of the chapter, money laundering, cybercrime, terrorism financing and fraud, which are the crime risks brought by the cryptocurrencies, will be examined.

In the fifth part, the problems experienced by tax administrators about the use of cryptocurrencies addressed and especially the difficulties of tax regulations because of anonymity features of these currencies will be analysed. In addition, the use of cryptocurrencies as a ransom by cybercriminals, which has become widespread, will be explained in detail in the chapter. Cryptocurrencies are also used as a fundamental instrument in the use of counterfeit identities, drugs, weapon purchases, and money laundering activities in alternative Internet browsers known as "Darknet" and by this way it has supported the formation of a phenomenon known as the informal digital economy.

In the last part of the chapter, how virtual currencies are defined and regulations about tax in various countries will be explained. Also, the Court of Justice of the European Union (CJEU)'s decision about VAT in bitcoin is examined and the importance of international corporation and coordination in the taxation and regulation of cryptocurrencies are emphasised.

2 Definition and Main Features of Cryptocurrencies

In this section, the definition of virtual currency (VC) and anonymity/pseudonymity concepts, which are known as essential features of cryptocurrencies, rapid international transaction settlement, and decentralisation and contained network will be examined.

2.1 Definition of Virtual Currencies and Cryptocurrencies

Virtual currencies have many definitions made by different international organisations such as IMF, European Central Bank, and the European Parliament.

According to IMF, virtual currencies (VC) are expressed as "digital representations of values derived by private developers in their unit of account" (IMF, 2016:7). Virtual currencies can be obtained, stored, accessed, and processed electronically. However, as long as the trading partners agree to use them, it is possible to use the virtual currencies for various purposes. The concept of virtual currencies includes a broader set of "currencies" ranging from simple issuances such as mobile coupons and airline nations to virtual currencies supported by assets such as gold and "cryptocurrencies" such as Bitcoin. (IMF, 2016: 7)

According to the classification made by the IMF, as digital representations of value, virtual money enters a broader digital currency category than cryptocurrencies. Besides, virtual currencies also differ from other currencies, which are a digital payment mechanism such as e-money. On the other hand, virtual currencies are not measured regarding fiat currency; they have their account units (IMF, 2016:7).

According to the European Central Bank (2015), virtual currency can be defined as "a digital representation of value, not issued by a central bank, credit institution or e-money institution, which, in some circumstances, can be used as an alternative to money."

The term "virtual currency scheme(s)" (VCS) was first used in the ECB report to describe "both the aspect of value and the mechanisms which ensure the processing of transactions." The report proposed putting virtual currency schemes into three categories:

1) closed virtual currency schemes, which have almost no link to the real economy,
2) virtual currency schemes with unidirectional flows, in which units can be purchased using 'real' currency at a specific exchange rate but cannot exchange back, and trading with other users is not allowed; and
3) virtual currency schemes with bi-directional flows, in which units can be bought and sold according to (floating) exchange rates (ECB;2015:23).

VC schemes comprise two essential elements:

1) the digital representation of value or 'currency' that can be transferred between parties; and
2) the underlying payment and settlement mechanisms, including the distributed ledger system (IMF;2016: 15).

VC schemes contain differences regarding the level of convertibility for goods and services in the real world and to national currencies. Also, as will be explained in the following sections of the chapter, VC schemes can operate with centralised, decentralized, and hybrid models depending on the distributed ledger technology.

According to European Union Parliament, Virtual Currency (VC) means "a digital representation of value that is neither issued by a central bank or public authority, nor attached to a legally established currency, which does not possess the legal status of currency or money, but accepted by natural or legal persons as a means of exchange or for other purposes, and can be transferred stored or traded electronically" (Hays et.al, 2017:52).

However, a cryptocurrency has a different definition from a VC. A cryptocurrency is "a digital virtual currency that uses encryption technology (or cryptography) in its creation and to ensure the security of transactions involving its use" (LexisNexis; 2016:1).

2.2 Anonymity/Pseudonymity

Privacy has always been the primary goal of cryptocurrency developers. However, the cryptocurrencies are not entirely anonymous in a uniform structure; instead, there are different degrees of anonymity. The most known cryptocurrency, Bitcoin, has pseudonymity feature. It means that users are identifiable throughout the network by their alphanumeric keys. Users can select a single key for all operations, or they can create a new key for each transaction they will perform.

Most of the existing cryptocurrency is "pseudonymous." While cryptocurrency transactions are publicly recorded, users are known only by their virtual currency "addresses," which cannot be traced back to users' real-world identity (Carlise, 2017:9).

The history of the cryptocurrencies transactions is kept in the blockchain system so that it is possible for all users to have an authorisation for all their transactions. However, blockchain only identifies users with their VC "addresses" by recording their pseudonyms. Since with pseudonyms it is almost impossible to contact real people or the organisation behind it, fraudsters may benefit from this, for example by giving misleading information about the actual beneficiary of payments to the user. Besides, the impossibility of reversing increases the risk of such fraud and therefore increases the likelihood of an increase in VC usage.

This anonymous character of the cryptocurrencies also makes it difficult to insert a mechanism into the circuit that allows for the resolution of vicious or fraudulent transactions. The anonymity feature increases the demand for regulation against them by the governments as it both makes the follow-up of cryptocurrencies difficult and increases the risk of an illegal transaction.

2.3 Rapid International Transaction Settlement

Thanks to the Bitcoin system first created by Satoshi Nakamoto, the technology behind the world's recognised cryptocurrencies allows users to transfer bitcoins (or other cryptocurrencies) quickly compared to the rest of the world. This situation created the expectation that the new payment methods provided by the cryptocurrencies could be made available to the financial system. It can be argued that the blockchain mechanism behind virtual currencies and its underlying distributed ledger technology can provide low-cost micropayments (or small online transactions) and provide quick and unmediated delivery of funds to underdeveloped countries. However, this ability to transact quickly poses risks (Carlise, 2017; 10).

This is an excellent basis for transferring money by partitioning it out of the primary methods of money laundering. Increasingly, money laundering is occurring on an industrial scale. A single organised criminal network is capable of billions of cross-border financial crime. Terrorist organisations operate worldwide and use international financial networks.

Legal forces are concerned that VCs may offer an attractive opportunity to increasingly globalising crime and terrorist groups, which requires unlimited financial channels (Carlise, 2017: 11). From a technical point of view, cryptocurrencies are still a mature system and efforts are made continuously to make mainstream software more efficient. However, more blockchain innovations offer the opportunity to offer a faster and less costly payment plan that goes beyond borders (Evans, 2014: 24).

2.4 Decentralization

In decentralised systems, there is no central institution, such as the central bank, that manages the system or creates cryptocurrency. In decentralised systems, the role of the central office is a chain of internal protocols that regulate the operation of the system and enables operations to be performed by system participants (IMF, 2016:7). Since payments and transactions are made through the system, these participants, called "miners," are rewarded with a "currency" that is newly printed (called the "money creation process" mining) for the payment transaction. This approach serves two purposes: it introduces newly created VCs into the system and allows the VC scheme to operate decentrally. Unlike the fiat currency system, a cryptocurrency does not represent an obligation on everyone (IMF, 2016: 9).

These systems may allow a limited or unlimited number of currencies to be issued. In the majority of such systems, including Bitcoin, the most well-known cryptocurrency unit, there is currently a limit to the currency that is issued. However, new systems are emerging that do not include such borders (IMF, 2016: 10).

In this sense, cryptocurrencies challenge the standardised concept of fiat currencies. The value of current fiat currencies is supported by the credibility of the central bank and the government. While centrally issued VCs are reliant on supporting the credibility of the private issuer, the value of the privately issued currency is historically supported by the credibility and commodity reserves of the private issuer (IMF, 2016: 9). On the contrary, the value of cryptocurrencies does not receive support from any source. They only gain value from the expectation that others will value and use them (IMF, 2016: 9).

Convertible cryptocurrencies are typically purchased or exchanged through a commercial platform or with another cryptocurrency owner, through a cryptocurrency, against fiat currency, or with other cryptocurrencies.

Cryptocurrencies are generally gathered in a "cryptocurrency wallet" through a cryptocurrency wallet software application. In decentralised systems, some keys provide access to a specific account view stored in the Blockchain. These keys can be used in any data carrier, e.g. in a personal computer's disk drive, in paper output, or in the cloud. In most cases, the so-called "wallet" provides a key storage option on a personal device or in the cloud. In this case, it should not be forgotten that the wallet will not hide any cryptocurrency units, but will only have access to the account view stored in the blockchain (ECB, 2015:13).

3 Types of Cryptocurrencies and Blockchain Mechanism

3.1 Classification of Cryptocurrencies

In this section, cryptocurrencies are classified and the differences of altcoins, coins and tokens will be explained. (Gupta et al., 2017: 11.).

Cryptocurrencies are defined as "digital or virtual currencies that are encrypted (secured) using cryptography." Cryptography is a method by which encryption techniques are used to transfer and verify transactions. Bitcoin has Blockchain technology which is registered and approved chronologically with being the first representative of decentralised cryptocurrencies.

Bitcoin has accelerated the expansion of the ecosystem of cryptocurrency, leading to the development of coins and tokens, even though it is not often accepted as "currency" due to its creative process and legal and economic functions.

While all coins and tokens are considered cryptocurrencies, the critical part of the coin does not function as a currency or medium of exchange (Masterthecrypto, 2016).

The most common classification of cryptocurrencies is in the form of Altcoins and tokens. Altcoins are also called alternative cryptocurrency coins, or just coins, and often these names can be used interchangeably. Altcoins inherently contain cryptocurrencies, which are alternatives to Bitcoin. Much of the altcoins have been the result of the differentiation of Bitcoin, which was built using the open source, the original protocol with changes in the base code of Bitcoin. For this reason, an entirely new coin with different sets of features is being designed (Masterthecrypto, 2016).

There are also other altcoins that are not produced from Bitcoin's open source protocol and support their native currency by building blockchain structures with their protocols. The best-known examples are Ethereum, Ripple, Omni, Nxt, Waves, and Counterparty (Masterthecrypto, 2016). The characteristic feature of all altcoins is that they have independent blockchains for transactions related to their coins.

Tokens define as "a representation of a particular asset or utility, which usually resides on top of another blockchain." Tokens can mainly include all kinds of assets from loyalty points and emotions even other cryptocurrencies as much as they are counterparty or commercial.

The creation of the tokens is more comfortable than the altcoins. Because there is no obligation to change the code in a particular protocol or create a blockchain from scratch. It is enough to follow the standard template on the blockchain as it is on Ethereum or Waves platforms to create tokens (Masterthecrypto, 2016). The functionality of creating your tokens has become possible through the use of smart contracts (Masterthecrypto, 2016). With this system, there is no need for any third party to work since it has self-executing programmable computer codes.

3.2 What's Blockchain? Is it Useful for Governmental Transactions such as Taxation?

In this section, the working principle of the blockchain mechanism that emerged with Bitcoin, the first cryptocurrency, will be explained as the basis (RBC, 2017:15).

Distributed ledger technology behind the blockchain mechanism and the possibility of using this technology in financial transactions, money transfers, public administration, e-vote, and tax administration will be examined. It will also refer to examples of countries that use this mechanism for taxation and public administration transactions (WU Global Policy, 2017a: 13).

Blockchain technology can be defined as a collection of digital methods for storing the same data in more than one place. A blockchain can be thought of as a database that stores the number of accounting units held by each user (Hays et al., 2017: 8). With an encrypted password, commonly referred to as a public-private key pair, users can access and expire account units called cryptocurrencies. A blockchain is a collection of information that is not held by a physical entity but is known as a node spread across all computers on the network. Due to a large amount of data storage, the operation of the blockchain system is costly and slow (Hays et al., 2017: 8).

Structurally, a blockchain is a network that assigns timestamps to operations by entering a chain of continuous process groups or blocks each containing a mix of new information plus the previous block. This blockchain is assured by cryptographic evidence using the enormous computing power, distributed servers to verify and process transactions known as "mining" which includes the competition to get paid and complete the process. The blockchain system has been secured both technically and economically with this crypto-economic incentive since everybody who wants to blockchain control override rules must have at least 51 % of the computing power(WU Global, 2017b:7). The final element is the provision of a "consensus" mechanism whereby transactions are validated by coded rules that run on thousands of computers at the same time.

Every computer in the world that stores a copy of the database must accept every change to the database so that the network can process new data entries. Blockchain provides users with unparalleled computing power and security that cannot be provided by any other technology. The essential features of blockchain along with all this technology are trust, transparency, and accountability (WU Global, 2017a:7).

Trust – With blockchain, all parties involved in a transaction have to rely solely on the blockchain without the need for a central authority.

Transparency – As the ledger is distributed, all users in the transaction network can view transactions subject to security rights.

Accountability – Since all parties to the transaction can view the distributed books, anyone can follow how the process progressed and how it was completed.

The Bitcoin blockchain is an example of a peer network node data storage system that continuously grows as transactions are broadcasted and verified by the network. Since Bitcoin is the first application of blockchain technology, people often tend to use "Bitcoin" words in the same sense as blockchain. However, the two concepts are not the same. The blockchain is the underlying technology that protects the Bitcoin transaction ledger.

In short, a blockchain can be defined as a computer network that does not need any central server, each having an identical copy of the database (distributed) and changing its status (records) with a collective agreement based on pure mathematics (WU Global, 2017a:3).

At this point, it is necessary to briefly explain the concept of "distributed ledger" to be able to refer to the smart contracts that constitute the basis of the blockchain technology and which will enable this technology to be used for taxation. Simply a distributed ledger defined as "a database type that is shared, replicated and synchronised among members of a network" (WU Global, 2017b:3). Distributed ledgers record transactions described such as asset or data exchange among participants on the same network. There is a consensus among the participants on the network about the updates to the records in the book. Centralised third-party mediators such as financial institutions or clearing units are not included in this system.

There are three different approaches to distributed ledgers (IMF, 2016: 21).

- Fully public systems: These are decentralised systems that are open to all Internet users such as Bitcoin, Ethereum, and other cryptocurrencies. In this system, participants are known only by nicknames, and it is aimed to verify the transactions, to encourage the protection of blockchain and to give participants of the embedded banknotes in the system.

- Entirely private systems: In this system, a central organisation gives permissions. Database management and auditing that is included in a single company are among the applications of this system.
- Hybrid or consortium systems: In this system, the consent approval process is controlled by preselected individuals or organisations, such as a consortium of financial institutions or customers of a company.

Distributed ledgers' have the technology to change finances by reducing costs and providing broader financial participation. In principle, they can be applied to any area that requires fast, accurate, and secure record keeping independent of a cryptocurrency (IMF, 2016:19). Blockchain and distributed ledger technology have the potential to modernise accounting and tax payments. In the long run, the blockchain can significantly increase tax compliance by guaranteeing real-time, automatic tax payments from the taxpayer to the state budget at the time of the execution of the transaction. This is accomplished by using code fragments of Smart Contracts that are programmed to execute automatically when predefined conditions are met (WU Global, 2017a:7). Smart contracts were first introduced in the early 1990s and defined as "a process that encodes the requirements of the traditional contract into a computer program and conducts them automatically" (Szabo, 1994).

The natural execution process allows unrelated parties to interoperate with one another in the absence of a trusted third party confirming the validity of the process (WU Global, 2017a:7). How smart contracts can be used in the taxation process can be explained as follows: for example, the payroll tax is automatically deducted and can be paid to the treasury during the transfer of salary so that the employer's obligation to act as a withholder will cease. The use of smart contracts for taxation contributes to the benefits of real-time compliance, reducing transaction costs and preventing counterfeit documents.

As it can be understood from this, the most fundamental benefit of this new technology is transparency and accountability that decentralisation takes place at the highest level. However, fully open transparent distributed ledger/blockchain systems may not be compatible with the public sector's requirements and data protection limitations. Therefore private or hybrid blockchain systems could be more appropriate for transactions such as taxation (WU Global, 2017a:7).

It is known that some tax administrators are beginning to use or have prepared for distributed ledger technology infrastructure. Estonia and Finland are the best-known examples of this in Europe (WU Global, 2017b:7). Estonia is currently using widely distributed ledger technology, known as Keyless Signature Infrastructure (KSI), which enables its citizens to access their records kept in government records to verify their integrity. The United Kingdom has advanced considerably in developing a whole of government approach to blockchain, including in the area of taxation. Also, many developing countries are aware that this technology can provide them with "frog jumping" with their peers in developed countries because of the "legacy" of the old technology they have (WU Global, 2017b:7).

Another important country, China, announced that it intends to utilise this technology in social taxation and electronic export issues. China is also the first world country to test the Central Bank-supported cryptocurrency. In Rwanda, the blockchain system was used in the taxation process, especially in the prevention of VAT fraud. As a result, especially VAT compliance and collection increased significantly (Ainsworth& Alwohaibi; 2017:7).

3.3 An Important Point for Taxation: Definition of Cryptocurrencies from Legal and Economic Perspectives

Under this heading, the features expected from the traditional "currency" will be listed first. In this framework, the ability of virtual currencies to be "currency" or "asset" will be discussed in the legal and economic context (Nica et al., 2017). Also, a description of the virtual currency made by the European Central Bank will be included (ECB, 2015: 25).

There are a few questions to ask when considering the role of virtual money as "money."

- Do they satisfy the legal definition of money and fulfil all the economic roles of money (store of value, the medium of exchange, and unit of account)?
- How do they compare to other privately-issued monies that existed historically?
- If they become more widely used, could (or should) these privately-issued currencies substitute for national currencies?

It is possible to answer these questions by looking at the economic and legal definitions of money. Regarding economic recognition, it appears that the ECB has stated that cryptocurrencies do not carry three known characteristics of "money" for various reasons (ECB, 2015: 23).

There are three essential characteristics of money in the economic literature: medium of exchange, store of value, and unit of account as it is known.

Both in the study note prepared by IMF (2016:17) and in the report prepared by the ECB (2015:23), it is stated that cryptocurrencies for the reasons given below did not carry these three essential features of money.

- Cryptocurrencies' high price volatility limits their ability to serve as a reliable value store. Cryptocurrencies are not government debt. However, most cryptocurrencies are not the debts of private organisations. Their prices are of much higher volatility than the national currencies and are following a slightly unstable course.
- The network of accepted small-size and limited cryptocurrencies restrict their use considerably as a means of exchange. Although cryptocurrency-based payments are growing very fast, the number of transactions and volume in cryptocurrencies remain small.
- At the moment there is little evidence that VCs are used as an independent unit of account. In other words, rather than being used directly to determine the value of goods and services, cryptocurrencies indicate the value in the fiat currency in the exchange rate.

When it is considered from a legal point of view, there are evaluations that cryptocurrencies are inadequate to meet the legal concept of currency. With no generally accepted legal currency or currency definition, in the context of the explanations contained in the working note prepared by the IMF (2016: 16), "money" in the legal sense is evaluated as follows:

From a legal point of view, the concept of money relates to the fact that the state creates a legal framework for the centralised issuance of banknotes and coins. The concept of currency in this context means the unit of account and means of exchange for which the law prescribes the unit of account. Quite literally, currency includes banknotes and coins issued by a unit that has "authority exclusively granted by a central authority such as the central bank" to do so.

Currencies are given "legal tender" status under the legal framework of the state. This status usually gives the borrower the opportunity to convert to currency through compulsory acceptance in the jurisdiction of their monetary liability. Therefore, the value and reliability of a sovereign currency are proportional to the state's support of that currency.

- The basis of the "legal tender" concept is that the state has a regulatory power in the money market. In legal terms, money; it is broader and more comprehensive than the currency concept and includes not only banknotes and coins but also quick assets such as demand deposits.

However, when the central bank or private banks create a currency, the currency statement must be issued by a sovereign authority. In this respect, it should aim to be a generally accepted means of change within the state (Procter, 2012:32).

4 Financial Crime Risk is Created by Cryptocurrencies

Cryptocurrencies can be exploited as an instrument for money laundering, terrorism financing, tax evasion, cybercrime, and other forms of illegal activity. In this section, the risk of financial crime created by cryptocurrencies will be examined and classified (UNODC, 2014:10).

4.1 Money Laundering

Money laundering denotes "the process by which criminals disguise the original ownership and control of the proceeds of criminal conduct by making such proceeds appear to have derived from a legitimate source" (Sat et al., 2016: 246).

Cryptocurrencies whose main features are anonymity, fast dealing, and decentralisation make them suitable to money laundering.

In this section, money laundering transactions made through internet browsers, mainly known as the dark web, will be examined. Also, the placement of the underlying mechanisms of money laundering and the use of cryptocurrencies will reveal how money can be realised in online gaming and micro laundering.

Money laundering is an activity that organises criminal organisations in bringing criminal proceeds into legal economies. Almost all criminal groups are obliged to disclose profits from their criminal activities. However, it differs depending on how the money laundering occurs, the level of expertise of organised crime activity, and the frequency and size of money laundering activities (Europol; 2017:18).

Criminal organisations are trying to use cryptocurrencies and their anonymity features, as well as technologies such as DeepWeb, DarkNet, brought by technological developments. Given the limited amount of cryptocurrency environment, money laundering involving virtual currencies can be performed in two general ways (Carlise; 2017:14).

- In the first method, criminals can place dirty fiat money in a bank or financial institution. In the next phase, various virtual money-based transfers and purchases can be made to hide the money's criminal origin.
- In the second method, criminals can sell illegal goods or services in exchange for virtual money. They can then turn them into fiat currencies, finance transactions, and purchases designed to hide illegal sources.

Rapid processing of cryptocurrencies and the proliferation of useful anonymisation tools in the digitalisation process are essential obstacles in the identification of criminals. An increasing number of online platforms and applications offer new ways to transfer money and are not always aligned with traditional financial service providers. Money launderers use a large scale document fraud method to facilitate their activities. Fake documents such as counterfeit bills and counterfeit identification documents are used to hide the source of criminal cash to open bank accounts or set up banking companies. In this context, money launderers serve both organised crime and terrorist organisations (Europol; 2017:19).

New payment methods, such as cryptocurrencies, prepaid cards, online payments, and internet vouchers, are continually emerging and are often subject to less regulation than traditional payment methods. Along with alternative banking platforms, these new payment methods allow the movement of criminal funds in large amounts (Europol; 2017:19).

4.2 Cybercrime

In this section, cybercrime will be defined and classified. Cybercrimes which emerged in the last period and demanded the cryptocurrencies for ransom also will be featured. These crimes known as cyrptoware (ransomware using encryption) is a significant threat to EU and other countries, targeting not only citizens but increasingly public and private sector organisations alike (Europol, 2017: 28).

Cybercrime is not only a European Union problem, but a global phenomenon that affects all countries of the world, and can be a destructive force in any field where the Internet is useful. The attack area of cybercrime continues to grow with the digitalisation of the society, with more individuals, enterprises, public institutions, and devices connected to the internet.

Cyber-dependent crimes are crimes committed using only a computer, computer networks, or other information communication technology. Cyber-related crimes can be examined in five subcategories as malware and ID theft, network attack, cryptoware, payment order fraud, payment card fraud (Europol, 2017: 29).

Malware steals user data such as credit card numbers, login credentials, and personal information, often in infected machines, for later use by fraudulent criminals.

Network attacks: While network interventions that cause private data (data breaches) or illegal access or disclosure of intellectual property are common, the scale is continually increasing, and hundreds of millions of records are globally threatened every year. Sometimes it is not possible to save the result of these attacks. In some cases, hackers may seek ransom in the form of virtual currency to save their data.

Cryptoware: In this system, the user-created files of the victims are encrypted by the hackers, and access to the victim's files is blocked unless they pay a fee to decrypt the passwords. In this process, the ransom for access to the file is in the form of virtual currencies (usually Bitcoin). There is no guarantee that you will not be able to access the file if the desired ransom is paid.

In payment order fraud process, criminals use fraudulent transfer orders to defraud private and public sector entities. Social engineering techniques and malicious software take a significant role in this method.

The characteristic feature of these crimes is the seizure of user information by different methods and the ransom of cryptocurrencies in return (Europol, 2017: 30).

4.3 Terrorism Financing

Although financing terrorism with cryptocurrencies is not considered a significant risk, it is seen as a potential and emerging risk. Security experts are expressing concerns that terrorists are quickly becoming more technologically masters. As this trend continues, cryptocurrencies will become increasingly suitable instruments for financing terrorists' activities. Terrorist groups prefer to use VCs for purchasing illegal firearms or explosives in addition to travel documents or other items in the dark web to facilitate their operations (Carlise, 2017:12).

For example, sales of weapon parts or unarmed weapons are legal in certain countries and are therefore available on the standard website, but when the gun is installed or reactivated, the sale becomes illegal and will be sold in Darknet. Terrorist groups prefer Darknet for such exchanges, and cryptocurrencies are used for the confidentiality of identity information (Europol, 2017:22). According to the definition made by Europol; "Darknet is a distributed anonymous network within the deep web that can only be accessed by software such as TOR, I2P, and Freenet" (Europol, 2017:23). Although the precise scale of the crime on Darknet has not yet been fully defined, it is known that an increasing crime factor, including terrorist groups, is operating on this platform.

Similarly, there are also studies that criminals can use smart contracts to regulate payment for the completion of illegal activities such as drug delivery or assassination (Prisco, 2015:3).

4.4 Fraud

Cryptocurrencies carry a large number of fraud risks. First is the risk of cryptocurrency users committing fraud. To explain this situation, for example, the power of a Bitcoin is the invariance of the process of the blockchain.

In this process, once a transaction is confirmed, it cannot be reversed or terminated as a credit card company or bank may reverse or cancel the transaction. However, this situation exposes cryptocurrency users to risks (Carlise, 2017: 30). As there are no legal regulations in VC networks, purchasers are not protected against failure to deliver goods or against fraudulent or faulty commodities. The anonymity of VCs allows fraudsters to operate under false identities and to mislead themselves in online markets to commit fraud (Carlise, 2017:30).

The second risk factor is direct virtual money exchanges and service providers. Although some of the cryptocurrency stock exchanges working as Ponzi schemes are in good condition, it has been seen that both Bitcoin and many small and later-emerging cryptocurrencies and vendors that supply them have disappeared from their sites. Shopping on the unrecorded Bitcoin market has simply disappeared, and service providers who have acted as intermediaries have closed their internet sites by stealing the deposits of the customers. (FATFA, 2015: 32). According to Chainalysis, it is estimated that in the first half of 2016, approximately 2 % of the global Bitcoin, which is approximately 6 million, is related to fraud or Ponzi schemes (Popper; 2016: 3)

A recent well-known example of cryptocurrency fraud is about NiceHash. Nearly $64m in bitcoin has been stolen by hackers who broke into Slovenian-based bitcoin mining marketplace NiceHash. The hack was "a highly professional attack with sophisticated social engineering" that resulted in approximately 4,700 bitcoin being stolen, worth about $64m at current prices (Gibbs, 2017).

While financial institutions are subject to testing by authorities, users may have a misconception that virtual money and actors playing a pivotal role in it are being regulated or audited (ECB, 2015: 21). This confusion may be due to a significant degree of similarity to the electronic retail payment tools of virtual money in particular. Specifically, the apparent similarity of e-money may lead users to believe that a reimbursement obligation can also be applied to the virtual exchange (ECB, 2015: 21).

For this reason, VCs present important consumer protection issues that require government attention and refer to the benefits of making public regulation of VCs with common rules set by international organizations.

5 Tax Administration Problems about Usage of Cryptocurrencies and Proposals

It's possible to combine the problems of tax administrations on the taxation of cryptocurrencies into two categories. The first problem is about the anonymity feature of cryptocurrencies and second main issue with regulating cryptocurrencies seems to be that it is considered neither to be legal tender nor security or a similar financial instrument but "a hybrid product."

5.1 Anonymity and Monitoring Problem and Its Effects

In this section, the difficulty of monitoring tax administrations on cryptocurrencies due to their ability to perform anonymity and cross-border transactions will be explained. Also, this difficulty which creates a high risk for tax evasion will be examined.

The anonymity of the cryptocurrencies makes it difficult to determine the transactions of the tax authorities with these funds and the gains obtained (Ruppert; 2017:402). In some studies in the literature, it is argued that this characteristic of cryptocurrencies makes it impossible to maintain the tax mechanisms and thus it is argued that cryptocurrencies become "tax havens" for taxpayers (Marian; 2013:39). Because cryptocurrencies have general characteristics of traditional tax havens.

- Gains are not subject to tax: Cryptocurrencies activities occur in cyber accounts known as online wallets and are not taxed in the source because the income from it is not determined by law, difficult to find, and is not subject to any legal regulation (Marian, 2013: 40). In this way, tax collection agents in financial institutions are out of the system in this digitised cyber process.
- The anonymity of the taxpayer's identities is protected: When users want to create or sell cryptocurrency without providing any descriptive information, they do so anonymously as they do so with the online wallet (Marian, 2013:41). If the service provider is not required to identify himself/herself with his / her real identity while creating the online wallet, it will be very tough for the accumulated earnings to return to the service provider in this case. According to current tax laws, this income is subject to taxation for this service provider. However, it is not possible for any tax authority to know the income derived from there unless it is declared voluntarily (Marian, 2013:43). This situation makes cryptocurrencies a financial instrument that has the potential to become "super tax heaven" (Freeman, 2011:63).

In addition to these features, the operation process of cryptocurrencies is not dependent on the existence of financial institutions. Cryptocurrencies can be changed peer-to-peer according to the definition. This characteristic of cryptocurrencies offers tax evaders an essential advantage that traditional tax havens do not have.

With all of these features, cryptocurrencies can potentially lose the partial success of governments' against tax fraud in tax havens.

If cryptocurrencies continue to gain momentum, it can be expected that tax evaders prefer cryptocurrencies to traditional tax havens. While cryptocurrencies are available for legitimate purposes, they are also suitable for supporting illegal activities, as mentioned in previous chapters. From the perspective of tax evasion, which is a criminal offence, the cryptocurrencies and the profits from them seem quite attractive.

Given the current volume of cryptography, it is difficult to estimate the scale and importance of tax evasion. Some evidence suggests that cryptocurrencies can already be used for tax evasion. Many cryptocurrency holders use them like a savings account. This type of wallet is only used for cryptocurrency reception but never sends. The earnings in these wallets are outside the knowledge of tax authorities as long as they are not voluntarily declared (Dorit & Shamir; 2013:21).

Governments are aware of the difficulties of arranging for virtual currencies, including bitcoin, to facilitate tax evasion. Nevertheless, even in developed countries where financial institutions are authorised to apply taxation, the anonymity and traceability aspects of taxation of cryptocurrencies have not been fully resolved. The main difficulty in this regard is the development of mechanisms that allow tax authorities to discover the funds that are stored in the cryptocurrency accounts (Stewart & Johnston; 2012:426).

At this point, it is clear that the traditional methods that are used by governments to prevent tax evasion cannot succeed in the digital-based process of cryptocurrencies. For example, information exchange agreements are not ineffective. Since cryptocurrencies do not operate under the existence of an independent jurisdiction. Governments can use sophisticated statistical analyses to try to identify owners of cryptographical purses as they do in traditional off-shore tax evasion. However, such an approach can only be used in certain situations and cannot be systematically used to solve the problem. As a tax evasion instrument, innovations in cryptocurrency require innovative policymaking.

5.2 Taxation and Regulation Discrepancies about Cryptocurrencies According to Countries

In this section, regulations made in various countries for the taxation of cryptocurrencies will be featured. Each country has its own rules about cryptocurrencies, and some countries have different laws depending on the region (Hays et al., 2017:52). As we mentioned before, the determination of cryptocurrency investments is difficult, or almost impossible, regarding the tax collection units of governments. It is therefore expected that investors will come to cryptocurrency every year and declare their assets honestly. (Hileman & Rauchs, 2017:21).

Virtual money, as a value store or a means of exchange, will have a tax function to the extent that it fulfils an economic function. The structure and functions of VC schemes increase complex issues that require cryptocurrencies should be taxed. While some significant jurisdictions have taken necessary steps to resolve these issues, this is not the case in all countries. The reason for this is that no agreement has been reached between countries on the definition of cryptocurrencies.

The most fundamental point in the taxation of cryptocurrencies is that they will be considered as non-monetary goods such as property or as currency. If the former position is accepted, the use of virtual money for investment or the purchase of goods or services will also require, accounting for gains or losses. In this case, the nature of the gain or loss will depend on the applicable rules in the related jurisdiction (IMF, 2016:30). For example, if it is defined as an entity, such as the length of the asset retention period or the classification of a process as speculation. In the second case, if virtual currency is accepted as a "legal tender" or "currency", foreign exchange gains or expenses will have to be recognised. Also, the tax treatment of the gains arising from the acquisition of newly created VCs through mining and the VAT and sales tax for transactions involving tax treatments and VCs are issues that should be addressed (IMF, 2016: 30).

Cryptocurrencies are not considered to be precisely a formal currency, neither a means of meeting merchandise definition nor a financial instrument. The European Union Parliament qualifies the cryptocurrencies a hybrid vehicle carrying all these qualities (EPRS, 2014:7). Financial analysts claim that cryptocurrencies carry both money and commodity features. The issue whether, for tax law, bitcoin should be treated as a currency or as a property asset remains controversial in tax law. As we mentioned at the beginning of our work, cryptocurrencies are not accepted as legal tender by ECB and IMF.

The countries in Europe are following a decentralised approach to cryptocurrency regulation. Not only the European countries but also US, Japan, and China have differences in classification of cryptocurrencies (Hays et al. 2017:54).

The only common point is related to the VAT. In all EU countries, cryptocurrency sales are exempt from the VAT. The ECJ (European Court of Justice) provided clarification with its decision, in 2015, on the status of bitcoins for the value-added tax (CURIA, 2015:1). In the decision the court accepted the bitcoin as a currency and according to court «bitcoin» means of payment used in a similar way to legal means of payment and the transactions which cover to provide services consisting of Exchange of traditional currency for the bitcoin and vice versa must consequently be exempt from the VAT (EPRS, 2016:1). When examining the details and justification of the court decision, it is understood that bitcoin and other cryptocurrencies are accepted as "currency" status.

The VAT Directive provides that "the supply of goods and services for consideration within the territory of a Member State by a taxable person acting as such is to be subject to VAT." However, some transactions in member states are exempt from VAT; in considering article 135 (1) (e) "currency, bank notes and coins used as legal tender" (CURIA, 2015:1).

David Hedqvist, a Swedish citizen, wants to provide services for the "bitcoin" virtual currency, including transactions involving a change in the traditional currency and vice versa. Before proceeding with these transactions, Hedqvist requested a preliminary ruling from the Swedish Revenue Law Commission to determine whether VAT should be paid for the sale of bitcoin and other virtual currencies. The decision was appealed to the Supreme Administrative Court by the Swedish Tax Office. According to the Swedish Court, "Bitcoins are useful only as a means of payment (medium of exchange). As they serve the same purpose as national currencies, the principle of fiscal neutrality requires that they be treated in the same way."

Also, although bitcoin is not a legal currency, it serves the same purpose as the national currencies i.e. it acts as a means of exchange. For this reason, it justifies the application of VAT exemption for national currencies to bitcoin changes in line with Article 135 (1) (e).

The first legal matter that the EU Court has to deal with is whether the exemption of "transactions concerning currency used as a legal tender" in the VAT Directive applies to the exchange of bitcoins according to the traditional currency (EPRS, 2016:2). At this point, according to Court contrary to the currency exchange service, the representation transfer of real payment instruments such as legal currency is not considered as a taxable transaction. Because pure forms of payment are not the means to be consumed or used as goods.

The second legal regulation is that the SEK exchange transaction for bitcoin, which is a taxable transaction, is still covered by the "exemption from concerning currency transactions." At this point, the court pointed out that "not to impede the convertibility of pure means of payment by levying VAT" and "to ensure that in the interest of the smooth flow of payments the conversion of currencies is as unencumbered as possible" (EPRS, 2016:2).

As a result, the ECJ has argued that "transactions involving non-traditional currencies, in line with the preliminary Court's decision, are financial transactions to the extent that they are accepted as a payment instrument by the parties." On the one hand, CJEU pointed to the similarity between traditional money exchange and, on the other hand, the traditional currency exchange for bitcoin (CURIA, 2015:2). To limit the scope of the exemption to traditional currencies would, according to the Court, "deprive some of the effects of the exemption." However, bitcoins have no other purpose than being a payment instrument (EPRS, 2016:3).

The reason and interpretation of the court order are undoubtedly dynamic as it tries to adapt the VAT Directive to new conditions that are probably not predicted by the drafts. However, the comment by the decision is functioning at the same time because it focuses not only on verbal expression but the exact socioeconomic function of bitcoin and other virtual money. This decision is also a turning point from the fact that it is the only legal document that clarifies the legal status of virtual currencies within the scope of EU law and allows joint action regarding the VAT.

Therefore, decisions in the framework of EU law, which will provide cooperation and coordination on the taxation of virtual currencies, are leading the way concerning countries.

Notably, there is a need for more analysis and debate on harmonisation on legal status and taxation of cryptocurrencies. At this point, legislative and regulatory changes to ensure harmonisation with legal status and taxation can be achieved through the cooperation and coordination of international organisations. Therefore, more global coherence should be achieved on these issues.

6 Conclusion

Cryptocurrencies offer many potential benefits, including higher speed and efficiency, particularly at the point of making payments and transfers across borders and ultimately encouraging inclusion in the financial system. The "Blockchain" mechanism behind some virtual currencies, and the distributed ledger technology – which is a decentralised mechanism that introduces innovations for monitoring transactions on an extensive network – it includes offering potential benefits beyond the realities of virtual currencies. However, cryptocurrencies present significant risks as a potential instrument for money laundering, terrorist financing, tax evasion, and fraud.

It is very complicated to control and regulate the cryptocurrencies as they are in the responsibility of the different institutions from the national point of view and they operate on the global scale. These regulations also include the taxation, and it is observed that the cryptocurrencies are generally evaluated in the "asset" category, and there are countries which are willing to make tax regulations in this framework. However, many virtual currencies are non-transparent and operate outside of the conventional financial system. Units that want to organise the activities of virtual currencies have begun to arrange these difficulties with various approaches that often try in the country by country terms.

Regulations have included clarifying the applicability of practising the existing legislation to virtual currencies, delivering a warning to consumers, licence requirements for virtual currencies to operate on the market, the prohibition of transactions of financial institutions with virtual currencies, the complete prohibition of virtual currencies, and prosecution of infringement crimes (IMF, 2016: 5).

These regulations include initial policy responses to the challenges posed by cryptocurrencies, but they need to be improved. In particular, it is expected that national authorities will design regulations by the risks, without suppressing the innovations contained in the cryptocurrencies. In this context, more cooperation on an international level is needed to facilitate the process of developing and refining policies at the national level. International organisations play an essential role in identifying and discussing the risks posed by cryptocurrencies and possible regulatory responses. International organisations are expected to continue in this role. International standards can be established as experience in regulations is gained. These standards can establish frameworks for cooperation and coordination across the country in areas such as information sharing and the investigation and prosecution of cross-border crimes. However, best practices provide guidance on the most appropriate regulatory responses in different areas, and they can be assessed to promote harmonisation in the jurisdictions.

References

Ainsworth, T.R. & Alwohaibi, M. (2017). "Blockchain, Bitcoin and VAT in the GCC: The Missing Trader Example", Boston University School of Law, Law & Economics Working Paper, No: 17-05, http://www.bu.edu/law/faculty-scholarship/working-paper-series/, (22.02.2018).

Carlise, D. (2017). Virtual Currencies and Financial Crime Challenges and Opportunities, Royal United Institute for Defence and Security Studies, Occasional Paper, March 2017, https://rusi.org/sites/default/files/rusi_op_virtual_currencies_and_financial_crime.pdf, (21.01.2018).

CURIA (2015). "The Exchange of Traditional Currencies for Units of the 'Bitcoin' Virtual Currency Is Exempt from VAT", Court of Justice of the European Union, Judgement in Case C- 264/14, https://curia.europa.eu/jcms/upload/docs/application/pdf/2015-10/cp150128en.pdf, (15.01.2018).

Dorit, R. & Shamir, A. (2013). "Quantitative Analysis of the Full Bitcoin Transaction Graph", https://eprint.iacr.org/2012/584.pdf, (26.03.2018).

European Central Bank (2015). Virtual Currency Schemes – a Further Analysis, Frankfurt, https://www.ecb.europa.eu/pub/pdf/other/virtualcurrencyschemes201210en.pdf, (17.01.2018).

European Parliamentary Research Service (2014). "Bitcoin: Market, Economics and Regulation", Briefing, 11.04.2014, http://www.eprs.ep.parl.union.eu —http://epthinktank.eu, (21.01.2018).

European Parliamentary Research Service (2016). "CJEU Rules Sale of Bitcoin Exempt from VAT", http://www.europarl.europa.eu/RegData/etudes/ATAG/2016/593558/EPRS_ATA(2016)593558_EN.pdf (24.01.2018).

Europol (2017). European Union Serious and Organized Crime and Threat Assessment, Crime in the Age of Technology, https://www.europol.europa.eu/sites/default/files/documents/socta2017_0.pdf, (23.01.2018).

Evans D. S. (2014). "Digital Currency Deep Dive: Is Bitcoin Cheaper and More Efficient than Traditional Payments?", PYMNTS.com, (20.02.2018).

Financial Action Task Force (2015). Guidance for a Risk-Based Approach Virtual Currencies, http://www.fatf-gafi.org/media/fatf/documents/reports/Risk-Based-Approach-Banking-Sector.pdf, (17.01.2018).

Freeman, A. (2011). "Bitcoin: The Ultimate Offshore Bank Account?", Economics and Liberty: Observations From A. Freeman (23.08.2011), http://economicsandliberty.wordpress.com/2011/08/23/bitcoin-the-ultimate-offshore-bank- account, (14.1.2018).

Gibbs, S. (2017). "Bitcoin: $64m in cryptocurrency stolen in 'sophisticated' hack, exchange says", https://www.theguardian.com/technology/2017/dec/07/bitcoin-64m-cryptocurrency-stolen-hack-attack-marketplace-nicehash-passwords, (14.02.2018).

Gupta, S., Lauppe, P. &Ravishankar, S. (2017). "Fedcoin: A Blockchain-Backed Central Bank Cryptocurrency", Yale University, https://law.yale.edu/system/files/area/center/global/document/411_final_paper_-_fedcoin.pdf, (06.01.2018).

Hays, D.K., Stoeferle, R.P.& Valek, M.J. (2017). Cryptoresearch Report, Vontobel Incrementum, December 2017, https://cryptoresearch.report/wp-content/uploads/2017/12/Incrementum-Crypto-Research-Report-Edition-1-English-Version.pdf, (15.02.2018).

Hileman, G. & Rauchs, M. (2017). Global Cyrptocurrency Benchmarking Study, University of Cambridge Judge Business School, https://www.jbs.cam.ac.uk/fileadmin/user_upload/research/centres/alternative-finance/downloads/2017-global-cryptocurrency-benchmarking-study.pdf, (25.01.2018).

International Money Fund (2016). *Virtual Currencies and Beyond: Initial Considerations*, https://www.imf.org/external/pubs/ft/sdn/2016/sdn1603.pdf, (23.01.2018).

LexisNexis (2016). Taxation of Virtual Currencies, http://www.taxchambers.com/wp-content/uploads/2016/12/Taxation-of-Virtual-Currencies.pdf, (16.02.2018).

Marian, O. (2013). "Are Cryprtocurrencies Super Tax Havens?", Michigan Law Review First Impressions, Vol:112, September 2013, pp.38–48.

Masterthecrypto (2016). "Coins, Tokens & Altcoins: What's the Difference?", https://masterthecrypto.com/differences-between-cryptocurrency-coins-and-tokens/, (15.02.2018).

Nica, O. &Piotrowska, K. & Schenk-Hoppe, K.R. (2017) "Cyrptocurrencies: Concept and Current Market Structure", University of Manchester, FinTech working paper No: 1, https://papers.ssrn.com/sol3/Delivery.cfm/SSRN_ID3059599_code231140.pdf?abstractid=3059599&mirid=1, (14.01.2018).

Popper N. (2016) "How China Took Center Stage in Bitcoin's Civil War", https://www.nytimes.com/2016/07/03/business/dealbook/bitcoin-china.html, (21.02.2018).

Prisco, G. (2015) "The Future of Smart Contracts: Positive Social Innovation or Criminal Activity?", https://bitcoinmagazine.com/articles/future-smart-contracts-positive-social-innovation-criminal-activity-1440020288/, (14.04.2018).

Procter, C. (2012) "Mann's Legal Aspect of Money", Oxford University Press.

RBC Wealth Management (2017). "Cryptocurrency and Blockchain: Ready for Prime Time?", A Special Report by the Portfolio Advisory Group, https://us.rbcwealthmanagement.com/delegate/services/file/364303/content, (11.01.2018).

Ruppert, P. (2017). "Privacy, Tax Evasion, and the Development of Cryptocurrencies", Georgetown Law Technology Review, April 2017, Vol: 1, No: 2, pp. 401–415.

Sat, M.D.& Krylov, O.G.& Bezverbnyi, E.K.& Kasatkin, B.A.& Kornev, A.I. (2016) "Investigation of Money Laundering Methods Through

Cyrptocurrency", Journal of Theoretical and Applied Information Technology, Vol: 83, No: 2, pp. 244–254.

Stewart, D. D. & Johnston, S. S. (2012). "Digital Currency: A New Worry for Tax Administrators?", Tax Notes International, http://www.taxhistory.org/www/features.nsf/Articles/C1A7ED502DD2B84685257AAF0056A2A2?OpenDocument, (25.01.2018).

Szabo, N. (1994) "Smart Contracts", http://www.fon.hum.uva.nl/rob/Courses/InformationInSpeech/CDROM/Literature/LOTwinterschool2006/szabo.best.vwh.net/smart.contracts.html, (21.04.2018).

United Nations Office on Drugs and Crime (2014). Basic Manual on the Detection and Investigation of Laundering of Crime Proceeds Using Virtual Currencies, June 2014, https://www.imolin.org/pdf/imolin/FULL10-UNODCVirtualCurrencies_final.pdf, (11.01.2018).

WU Global Tax Policy Center of Vienna University of Business and Economics (2017a). "Blockchain 101 for Governments", The Committee of Experts on International Cooperation in Tax Matters, Fifteenth Session, 17–20 October, Geneva, Institute for Austrian and International Tax Law Vienna WU Global Policy Center, http://www.un.org/esa/ffd/wp-content/uploads/2017/10/15STM_Blockchain-101.pdf, (04.01.2018).

WU Global Tax Policy Center of Vienna University of Business and Economics (2017b). "Blockchain: Taxation and Regulatory Challenges and Opportunities", First Meeting in the Multi-stakeholder Series, Vienna, 15–16 March 2017, WU Global Tax Policy Center of Vienna University of Business and Economics, https://www.wu.ac.at/fileadmin/wu/d/i/taxlaw/institute/WU_Global_Tax_Policy_Center/Tax___Technology/Backgrd_note_Blockchain_Technology_and_Taxation_03032017.pdf, (12.01.2018).

Şafak Ertan Çomaklı[1] and Murat Uzun

The Main Obstacle for the United States of Europe Goal: Delegating The Power of Taxation

Abstract: It is certain that the European Union, which shows an advanced integration internationally today, has a political roadmap in addition to the goals of living together in peace and economic union. However, the ultimate destination of this union is expressed in various forms and viewpoints. According to some, there is nothing further than an economic union for the European Union which is regarded as a chain ring connected to each other with a silk thread. On the other hand, according to some, it seems inevitable that the member states of the European Union will come together to form the United States of Europe. However, whatever the case, it is a remarkable matter that the European Union is a community which consists of "independent free states" that aims to protect its material interests by living together in peace. This can be seen from the fact that countries with a peaceful environment, states that will not force them to expand economically and especially those that can bring new commercial areas to have the preponderance as a candidate member of the European Union. It should not be forgotten that although there are many members with historical affiliations, each one has an independent political organisation. In this study, the aim is to discuss the issue of delegating "the power of taxation", which is possessed to "be able to be a state" in relation with the United States of Europe goal. In this context, the political mechanisms and priorities necessary "to become a united state" will be briefly examined.

Keywords: Taxation, European Union, State, Constitution, Sovereignty

JEL Classification Codes: *H-20, H-70, K-34*

1 The Capability to Be a State

A State is a political organisation that created with the willingness of humankind to live together along with the people who want to govern them. This organization has essential elements for "sovereignty"; "army" (military force), "flag", "owned land", "administrative organization and center" (administration and capital), "the power of coinage", "the power of taxation" (financial organization power) and "foundation contract" (constitutional text). These are indispensable conditions as prerequisites of being a state. There is one more important subject here; the said elements must exist only "*on their own*" to be in the "*sovereign*"

1 Corresponding author.

structure. That is a single army, a single flag, a single country, one capital, single currency, one constitution and single power of taxation. Naturally, it is clear that there will be no existence of the state in the absence of "human" existence.

The main core units of states are historically shaped on the army and the finance at the beginning. Accordingly, having a "military power" and "taxation authority for financing monetary needs" emerged as the main elements of state sovereignty. In the spirit of the state concept, the army and the finance maintain their characteristic of being the main element in the human development and change process. However, in the last century, developed societies have included components of the modern era, such as constitutions in the political system.

It is unthinkable for the states to be reduced to the elements mentioned above alone. This is because the political organisation with state legal personality can be reached as the integral of the mentioned elements. According to this, it is possible to say that the mentioned elements do not mean anything to be a state alone. Even though the principle of "less state more law" (Selçuk, 1998: 17) is tried to be absorbed today, the state cannot be constituted without having the elements in question – with less law or with more law. This reveals the "European Union", the clearest example of modern times, which our country has been trying to integrate for years.

The European Union is an organisation that defines the international societal creation of the economic, financial and political spheres based on state. Although this structure comes from a technical skeleton, it observes the "*political unity society*" regarding the policies and targets it is trying to implement. Many agreements have been made in this direction. Along with this, the negotiations and the ideas that have been formed have been tried to emphasise many things which are called "unity", that is to say, " *being together as a single unit* " which is sanctified of humanity.

However, the point to be reached in the perspective of the European Union is the "alliance", but the possibility of being a "state" at the end of the road is also being discussed. Is the goal to be reached at this point be "the state"? Alternatively, is it to have a land that can live together in peace?

The desire to live peacefully and to have territorial integrity is, of course, a point that the European Union will want to achieve as integration at an advanced level. However, is the capability of being a "state" possible for the "Union"? In this chapter, the validity of the elements of being a state in the process of development of the European Union in the process and the end is tried to be examined. Firstly, the approaches of some member states of the United States of Europe is tried to be given, and then the developments of the elements mentioned above in the European Union regarding being the United States is elaborated.

2 Approaches to the Idea of the United States of Europe

If we should consider the idea historically, the idea of the United States of Europe was seen by Kautsky as a unification of European states under a universal economy-trade policy, a federal parliament, a federal government and a federal army of forces to prevent wars (*Die Neue Zeit*). On the other hand, in the "Is the time ripe for the slogan: 'The United States of Europe'" article of Leo Trotsky in 1923, this expression takes its place at the same historical level with the 'One Government for the Proletariat and Peasantry" (Troçki, 1923). Unlike Kautsky, according to Trotsky, the creation of "the United States of Europe" should be the existential struggle of the proletariat class, not the capitalist class. Aside these, it is seen that the idea of "the United States of Europe" which W. Churchill has mentioned in his speech in Zurich in 1946 "About the Tragedy of Europe", expresses a war prevention approach inside the geographical borders of Europe (The Churchill Society London, 1946). According to this, Churchill is aiming for the United States of Europe as a "peace project". If we look at it today, the point that the European Union has overstepped for half a century is the view that a peaceful atmosphere has been established among all the member states, especially the constituent states.

As a result, the German-French Coal and Steel Community, the idea of which was developed by the Minister of Foreign Affairs Robert Schuman and Jean Monnet to control the coal and steel production, was proposed on May 9, 1950 and the European Coal and Steel Community was founded with the participation of Italy, Belgium, the Netherlands and Luxembourg along with Germany and France. The goal was to provide peace and security in Europe by controlling coal and steel production which is essential for the military industry. Undoubtedly, the influence of the two totalitarian systems behind the economic and political union idea in Europe, Marxism-Leninism and National Socialism cannot be underestimated. Thus, the dream of an idea of a union in Europe which lived for years is put into action (Özaşık,2011).

Even though the expressions of the United States of Europe are used, it is not possible to say that the member states of the European Union today formally express their aims of being "United States" as a future-oriented wish[2].

---

2 It will be correct to examine the idea of the United States of Europe by analyzing the historical process. However, the main subject of the study, instead of explaining the mentioned subject, it will be more suitable to put the explanations in this situation as annotations. It should be stated that it is for sure that the idea of the United States of Europe has been taken into consideration and expressed by many philosophers (even if the concept is not directly expressed) in politics and political history areas.

Because, at present in the European Union, priority is given to monetary union and continuation of "ensuring unity in financial law". In this issue, as Simon Heffer points out in his article in the Daily Mail newspaper (Heffer, 2011), there is no doubt that in monetary union, "one economic policy, one taxation system, one social security system, one public debt system, one economy and one minister of finance" is an important issue to overcome.

In this direction, the Union has to have the required outfit firstly for the economic union starting from the goals which it has signed under the Treaty of European Union for the organisation in itself and future planning. This approach is also intended to be expressed in the "aims" contained in Article 3 of the relevant agreement. In other words, the European Union member states recognise that this can only be possible with "the strengthening of the materialistic benefits and guaranteeing them" if they want to achieve the prospective United States goal. At this point, the main element that has to be emphasised is that benefits are "being guaranteed". Because a state does not accept any integration without securing the "*protection of the power of taxation*", which allows for its existence, from the perspective of the future of its political organisation. This situation requires the meeting on a joint constitutional base rather than some constitutional arrangements. Shortly, although states can strengthen their economic benefits through trade and various agreements, they do not want to lose the power of the political organisation that has created these expediencies.

In this regard, especially the point of view of the UK towards the United States of Europe is also facing towards the economic events. It is seen that shortly of England as a powerful state, has no intention to join Euro which is the indicator of monetary union in the present situation (Chapman & Brummer, 2011).

As it can be seen in the statements of German ex-minister of Foreign Affairs Joschka Fischer, about the United States of Europe goal, if the European Union cannot proceed towards a "United State", it will not be possible to preserve the influence of the Union. In this respect, it is possible to deduce from the statements made in the European Parliament that they are not too optimistic about the target. (Willis, 2011).

Romanian President T. Basescu has statements in newspapers, saying that it is necessary to form the "United States of Europe" to oppose the power/effect which will be created against globalisation (Ciocoiu, 2011). At this point, it is seen that the idea of the United States of Europe is seen as a defence mechanism against globalisation along with being only political and economic power.

It is still difficult to predict how far the European Union will record on the road to political integration. It seems very difficult to establish a "United States of Europe" that federalists want. However far the institutions and applications go on this direction, can "being European" as an upper identity take the places of national identities of the European citizens living in the Member States, or can it be more important than national identities? Today, the answer to this question is "no". It is not anticipated that such a transformation will take place shortly. However, a politically integrated Europe will continue to be a part of the Union as a long-term goal.

Nonetheless, the attempts of Germany and France to create an "Economic Government" or in other words an "Economic State" in the European Union is started to be perceived as progress towards the United States of Europe (The American Dream, 2011). However, the important thing here is to put what the United States of Europe means for the member states on the table with all its consequences. Because no state at this point would like to put its political union in a province position for the United States of Europe Goal where they cannot fully see the consequences of their political union.

3 The Sufficiency of the Present Elements for the European Union to Be the United States of Europe

The European Union, the twenty-eight European States with their expressions of member states, refers to "a one economic and political partnership" (Basic Information on the European Union). In this context, it will not be difficult to say that the Union is organised with the capability of being a state although the goals of peace, stability, wealth, rising living standards, creating a common market, etc. are expressed (EU Foreign and Security Policy, 2011).

It is possible to say that the European Union has an army concerning being a state. The Union has an army organisation according to the 42nd article under the title of the Common Security and Defense Policy in the Second Section of the Treaty of Maastricht (Treaty on European Union, 1992), although it does come from the states with the existing military regimes. According to Article 42§ 1, "The common security and defence policy shall be an integral part of the common foreign and security policy. The common security and defence policy provide an operational capability based on civil and military capabilities of the Union ". Again, pursuant to Article 42§ 2, "This policy becomes a common defense if the European Union Summit decides by unanimity," and likewise in Article 42§ 3, "Member States shall make civilian and military capabilities available to the Union for the implementation of the common security and defense policy, to contribute to the objectives defined by the Council. Those member states which together establish multinational forces may also make them available to the common security and defence policy." and "The "European Defense

Agency" in the field of defence capabilities development, research, acquisition and armaments shall identify operational requirements, shall promote measures to satisfy those requirements, shall contribute to identifying and where appropriate, implementing any measure needed to strengthen the industrial and technological base of the defense sector, shall participate in defining a European capabilities and armaments policy, and shall assist the Council in evaluating the improvement of military capabilities."

Besides this, according to article 42§ 6, "Those member states whose military capabilities fulfil higher criteria and which have made more binding commitments to one another in this area to the most demanding missions shall establish permanent structured cooperation within the Union framework." Moreover, according to article 42§ 7 which comes after, "If a Member State is the victim of armed aggression on its territory, the other Member States shall have towards it an obligation of aid and assistance by all the means in their power, by Article 51 of the United Nations Charter." Along with this, the European Defense Council is created, and its duties are listed in article 43. Also, in parallel to the economic power that is independent of NATO and other foreign influences, an armed forces union in the shape of the "European rapid reaction force" which is currently not expressed as an army (EU Foreign and Security Policy, 2011) was created (Reid, 2004: 2). As it can be understood, like it is stated in the Treaty on European Union that is signed, the Union has an army. The said European Rapid Reaction Force consists of 60 thousand people with the military power contributions of the member states. It is decided that military force will be taken respectively from Germany, France, Italy, Spain, the Netherlands, Greece, Finland, Sweden, Belgium, Ireland, Portugal and Luxembourg (Brown, 2001). In other words, it can be said that the United States of Europe aims to provide an agreement on the concept of an army.

Besides, another factor that the European Union has in the way of being the United States is the "flag". There is a twelve-star "European emblem" expressing integrity on the blue ground as the European Union has agreed. This Emblem is the flag of the European Union. In order to make the European Emblem usable, the user of the Emblem should have no possibility to be confused for either the European Community or the European Council, and the Emblem should not be used in relation to goals or activities that are not in accordance with the goals and policies of the European Community or the European Council. This emblem is used in the form of "flag" as a sign of the symbol of a state organisation and union (The European Symbols, 2011).

The European Union has an institutional structure that can serve the benefits of the member states (EU Institutions and Other Bodies, 2011). As of today, the

Union has a capacity of a total of twenty-eight states. This situation also means that the different systems of these twenty-eight states are included in a single and joint system. According to this, the European Union has an institutional structure which can serve for the benefits of the member states (EU Institutions and Other Bodies, 2011). These institutions, when article 13 of the European Union is looked upon, are the European Parliament, European Commission, the Council of European Union, the Summit of European Union, Court of Justice of the European Union, the European Court of Auditors, European Central Bank and other institutions, organs and agencies. According to article 10/2 of the Treaty of European Union, the expression of, "Citizens are directly represented at Union level in the European Parliament. Member States are represented in the European Council by their Heads of State or Government and in the Council by their governments, themselves democratically accountable either to their national parliaments or their citizens." take place. Via this, it is seen that the integration created by twenty-eight member states has a parliament on the representation level and when gone into detail, many other institutions with constitutional characteristics.

In this context, it should be expressed that the European Union has a legal system, too. The European Union legal system consists of a double structure of Primary and Secondary sections. While the main foundation principles make up the Primary Legislation order, the decisions, directives and applications that are taken about these main principles make up the Secondary Legislation (Decision-making in the European Union, 2011).

These institutions are the European Parliament, European Commission, European Union Council, European Union Summit, the European Court of Justice, European Court of Auditors, European Central Bank and other institutions. Among the three leading institutions of the European Union, which are the European Union Commission, European Union Council of Ministers of the European Union and European Parliament, the majority of the official organs of the first two institutions are located in Brussels. When these are taken into consideration, Brussels is expressed as the capital of the European Union. It is possible to say that a joint city is used as a centre and the capital is physically existing in the present conditions concerning the capability to be the United States.

Even though money appears historically as a market product, it continues to exist as a reflection of the economic sense of existence and power of a state. That is because the essential element which reveals the economic power of the state is "money". In this context, as the result of long-standing talks and studies, the European Union has agreed on "euro" as the monetary unit in order to make its power felt economic. Among the twenty-eight European Union member states, nineteen states are using Euro as the official monetary unit. (The Euro Monetary Union, 2011). Although in many non-euro countries such as Sweden, Poland, and the Czech Republic public opinion is against joining the single currency, accepted Euro as the official monetary unit (Dale, 2017). According to this, the European Union seems to have gone beyond a political union with economic dimension about "single monetary unit" to be the United States. The European Union seems to have transcended the political union of the "one currency" to become the United States of Europe.

However, it can be said that the most significant obstacle for the European Union on the way to be a "United State" is the delegation of "the power of taxation" and in this context signing the "foundation contract" (constitutional text). That is because the European Union is comprised of states countries which have the power of taxation in their states and do not want to leave their constitutional power which acts independently even though they have excellent integration characteristics and shows policies related to them. The most important thing for the member states is keeping the "power of taxation ", which symbolises sovereignty. Today, the states take their "power of taxation" from the constitutions, and most of the member states do not want to meet on a joint constitutional text which doesn't include this power which is accepted as a sign of power. In other words, none of the states wants to give up its "power of taxation", which is a sign of being a state. This is the major obstacle to the European Union's goal of becoming the "United States of Europe".

4 Conclusion

The European Union carries the characteristics of the most advanced interstate integration of our time. It appears that the economic and financial policies of the European Union have many commonalities in the political climate. On the other hand, the efforts to find a solution by discussion and the mutual logic level with its institutions when faced with a different situation can be expressed as an indicator of being developed. However, it is obvious that the European Union's future steps to become "the United States of Europe" will be set back by the problems of the "delegation of the power of taxation" and signing the "foundation contract" (constitutional text). It is possible to say that the most substantial example of this can be said in the preparation and acceptance process of the common "European Constitution". In detail, the preparation process of the European Union Constitution began in December 2001 at the Laeken Summit. The draft which was prepared was presented in Thessaloniki in 2003. However, no agreement on the draft has been reached in the same year in the Conference among Governments in Rome and later in the Brussels Summit dated December 12–13, 2003. However, in 2004 an intergovernmental agreement was reached. According to this, while the European Union Constitution was signed on September 29, 2004 with a ceremony that took place in the same room where the Treaty of Rome was signed, by the government or state heads of twenty-five member states at the time, the final act was also signed by Turkey, Bulgaria and Romania who had "candidate state" status along with the member states. It was predicted that the member states would approve the constitution mentioned above until May 2006 and put into effect at the beginning of 2009.

In respect of this, while sixteen-member states saw this Constitution fit to be approved in their national parliaments, most European Union countries announced that they would hold a referendum for the European Constitution. According to the principle, even one state rejecting this constitution will prevent it to be put into effect. Moreover, France and the Netherlands, had "no" as answers in referendums made in 2005. At this, after the meeting among the Ministers of Foreign Affairs of EU member states, it was stated that "they share the common vision of clarifying the legal base of the Union in 2009".

Along with this, another subject that hurts the said goal for the European Union states to be the united states is the prediction of the constitutional transfer of the power of taxation and getting reduced to one of the united states even though they satisfy other elements that are mentioned above. That is because, some states in the European Union are collecting tax from many land parts or countries inside their land integrity, economically even if not materially. On this subject, even if it is not expressed today, one of the main reasons can be shown as the presence of states inside the European Union which have colonies in the modern sense and these countries not leaving their strong positions by getting reduced to one of the united states for the *benefit* of the goal of "the United States of Europe". This situation shows that a resistance point is present against the transfer of "the power of taxation" in its spirit.

Although the European Union takes a number of steps regarding the development of its integration in terms of its benefits, if it is considered that tax collection is among the most important powers for the State, it is possible to interpret the idea of the United States as "the European Union trying to take over the basic sovereignty right of the member states" in this direction (Çomaklı, 2006). Besides, when we consider the risks of losing their power of taxation which the member states are very afraid of, due to its inevitable hardships that it can carry, the European strategy until today has refused the total taxation and financial integration of the Union (EU Tax Law). As it is stated, no European Union state seems to be on the side of transferring the said power to protect its political power and independence. In this context, the state mainly means tax. Because the indicator of being a state power, to have full sovereignty, collecting tax from the public, being recognised by other states and sending ambassadors, employing military force and being able to protect its borders, not being under the control of another political authority and protection.

As Reid has stated, the United States of Europe can be taken as the conceptual definition of more people, more wealth and more trade than a political union and a military power like the United States of America (Reid, 2004:1). Ultimately, the Constitution of the European Union represents the most important step taken by the member states towards forming a political union. However, the fact that the European Union, which aims to be a "United States", fails to reach a consensus in the constitutional text, is inevitably an obstructive target. Insofar as it is expressed, being a "United States of Europe" will only stay as a dream unless the member states accept delegating "the power of taxation" which is a power indicator of being a sovereign state.

References

Basic Information on the European Union. (2011). http://europa.eu/about-eu/basic-information/index_en.htm (01.10.2011).

Brown, Derek. (2001). "*The European Rapid Reaction Force*" April 11, http://www.guardian.co.uk/world/2001/apr/11/qanda.derekbrown (05.10.2011).

Chapman James ve Alex Brummer. (2011). "*Why Eurozone Should Become United States Of Europe, By David Cameron*", http://www.dailymail.co.uk/news/article-2034521/Why-Eurozone-United-States-Europe-David-Cameron.html#ixzz1YZj5k46T, (21.09.2011).

Ciocoiu Paul. (2011). Romania's Basescu Backs "United States of Europe", *Southeast European Times*, http://www.setimes.com/cocoon/setimes/xhtml/en_GB/features/setimes/features/2011/08/30/feature-04 (29.09.2011).

Çomaklı Şafak E., (2006). "Shadow Economies in European Union Countries And, in This Context, Evaluation of Tax Avoidance And Tax Evasion in Turkey in Process of Negotiations", International Symposium on the Changes and Transformations in the Socio-Economic and Political Structure of Turkey Within the European Union Negotiations, Dumlupınar University, 16–18 March 2006, Kütahya.

Dale, Reginald. (2017). "Not the United States of Europe", Atlantic Council, http://www.atlanticcouncil.org/blogs/new-atlanticist/not-the-united-states-of-europe (03.03.2018).

Decision-making in the European Union. (2011). http://europa.eu/about-eu/basic-information/decision-making/index_en.htm (02.10.2011).

"Die Neue Zeit, 1911 (On War N.B.) Moreover, 1912 (Inter Alıa, On A United States Of Europe)". Lenin: Notebook 'ι' ("Iota"). Lenin Internet Archive. http://www.marxists.org/archive/lenin/works/1916/ni-iota/neuezeit.htm (30.09.2011).

EU Foreign and Security Policy. (2011). http://europa.eu/pol/cfsp/index_en.htm (04.10.2011).

EU Institutions and Other Bodies. (2011). http://europa.eu/about-eu/institutions-bodies/index_en.htm (04.10.2011).

EU Tax Law, http://www.laweuropa.com/English/index.php?d=vergi&mod=Ab_Vergi_Introduction (03.10.2011).

Heffer, Simon. (2011). Rise of the Fourth Reich, How Germany Is Using the Financial Crisis to Conquer Europe, http://www.dailymail.co.uk/news/article-2026840/European-debt-summit-Germany-using-financial-crisis-conquer-Europe.html#ixzz1YZXflrAO, (19.09.2011).

Özaşık, Adem. (2011). AB'nin Yeni Anayasası "Reform Anlaşması", Türkiye Bilim Sitesi, http://www.genbilim.com/content/view/6277/88/ (03.09.2011).

Reid, Thomas R. (2004). *The United States of Europe – the New Superpower and the End of American Supremacy*, The Penguin Press.

Selçuk, Sami, (1998). *Zorba Devletten Hukukun Üstünlüğüne*, Ankara, Yeni Türkiye Yayınları.

The American Dream. (2011). "*The United States Of Europe: A Proposed "Economic Government" Would Integrate Europe To A Degree Not Seen Since The Roman Empire*" http://endoftheamericandream.com/archives/the-united-states-of-europe-a-proposed-economic-government-would-integrate-europe-to-a-degree-not-seen-since-the-roman-empire (21.09.2011).

The Churchill Society London. (1946). "*Winston Churchill Speaking In Zurich*", http://www.churchill-society-london.org.uk/astonish.htmlhttp://www.churchill-society-london.org.uk/astonish.html (03.10.2011).

The Euro Monetary Union. (2011). http://europa.eu/about-eu/basic-information/money/euro/index_en.htm (03.10.2011).

The European Symbols. (2011). http://europa.eu/about-eu/basic-information/symbols/flag/index_en.htm (01.09.2011).

Treaty on European Union. (1992). https://europa.eu/european-union/sites/europaeu/files/docs/body/treaty_on_european_union_en.pdf (02.03.2018).

Troçki, Lev. (1923). *"Avrupa Birleşik Devletleri Sloganı İçin Uygun Zaman mı?"*, http://www.marksist.com/ceviriler/avrupa_birlesik_devletleri_slogani_icin_uygun_zaman_mi.htm (03.09.2011).

Willis, Andrew. (2011). "*Joschka Fischer: United States Of Europe Is The Only Way To Preserve EU Influence*" http://Euobserver.com/18/31634, (21.09. 2011).

Hamza Erdoğdu and Esra Siverekli

An Econometric Analysis of the Relationship between Economic Growth and Tax Revenues: An ARDL-Bounds Test Approach

Abstract: The aim of this study is to investigate the relationship between gross domestic product, a general measure of the growth of the country's economy, and tax revenues, the output of taxation which is the main action of governments' fiscal policies, in the period of 2006–2017 in Turkey using monthly data. The ARDL/Bounds Test method is applied to examine the long-run cointegrating relationship between the series. The main findings of this study are that the series of tax revenues and gross domestic product are positively high correlated. There exists a long-run or equilibrium relationship between variables. An increase of 1% in economic growth leads to an increase of 2.92% in tax revenues. The tax system in Turkey is buoyant to lead to reductions in the deficit ratio potentially. The empirical results of the study help the policymakers in the better assessing of the relationship between tax revenues and gross domestic product to formulate tax policies.

Keywords: Tax Revenues, Tax Buoyancy, Economic Growth, ARDL-Bounds Test

JEL Classification Codes: E62, H21, H29

1 Introduction

Tax revenues, which form the basis of the most critical public financing instruments of the governments, have great importance in ensuring social continuity by financing public services. Taxes have been the most essential and primary source of income from the period when the states, the most significant political organisation, first emerged. With different applications, taxes have come up today by bringing the rule of law of taxation. During this period of progress, the tax has come out of its financial aim and has begun to fulfil its economic, regulatory functions in different forms. Thus, the function of providing economic growth together with the financing of public services has become one of the essential functions of the tax.

The meaning and basic functions of the tax, together with the regulatory function that it has in the economy will be related with the literature and will constitute the literature section. In this section, achievement of economic growth, one of the functions of tax, and reciprocal relationship between taxes from the point of bi-directional view in the literature will be evaluated and thus the theoretical base will be established for the econometric analysis in terms of economic growth-tax revenues and tax revenues-economic growth relation which will be addressed in the subsequent chapters. In this study, specific effects of economic growth on tax revenues are analysed.

Starting with the literature part, the first chapter, which is the basis for the study by establishing the relationship between economic growth and tax revenues by theoretical and applied econometric methods, will be the basis of methodology and data section. In the following sections, the relationship between tax revenues and economic growth in Turkey will be analysed from 2006 to 2017 using ARDL approach, and the impact of tax revenues, selected from Central Government Budget Revenues items within Budget Realizations, on economic growth will be introduced in the result section. This study, determining whether there exists a relationship between tax revenues and economic growth in the long term in Turkey, a country having an ongoing process regarding economic growth and development, is essential.

2 Literature

Sayar (1975) argues that tax expresses unrequited value given to the government by the taxpayers as a contribution to public expenditure. Akdoğan (2005) defines taxes as payments in the form of cash, taken from natural and legal persons according to the power of sovereignty, in order to meet the expenses required by public services and the burdens of public debts. Depending on the increasing roles and functions of the government, the decision-making unit of the public economy, over time, the non-financial objectives of the tax have also been included in addition to financial purposes. Thus, according to Ataç (1999), especially after the 1950s, economic growth and development have gained importance in fiscal policy. He suggests that economic growth and development are long-term goals of fiscal policy, as well as the amount and composition of public revenues, are the essential tools for reaching the objectives of the fiscal policy.

Solow (1956), developed the neo-classical economic growth theory, claims that tax policies have no significance regarding growth, in other words, tax policies have no effect on long-term growth.

Unlike the neo-classical growth model, the tax is considered as an essential policy tool in the endogenous growth models. With the government tax instrument, the government has adopted an active role in the economic structure by encouraging AR-GE and technology transfers, offering education and health services, protecting property rights and targeting competition.

The effects of taxes on economic growth and development are based on the economic effects of taxes. Thus, according to Türk (2005), the effects of taxes on economic life are considered as the effects on production, consumption, income distribution, different movements and full employment. The effects of taxes on the economy and thus on the economic growth and development, Siverekli (2003) urges that tax types be evaluated in two ways: taxes on income and taxes on expenditure. This study shows that taxes on income will provide growth and development in the country's economy via tax cuts that encourage work and lead to an increase in production and national income, and structures in tax administration and tax incentive mechanisms. The study also reveals that the taxation of spending can provide economic growth and development by reducing luxury consumption and encouraging savings. Similarly, Musgrave (1958) explained the concept from another perspective, the multiplier mechanism, by specifying that the changes to the budget, which tax revenue does not depend on income level, based on lump-sum tax and the changes to budgets based on income tax cause changes in national income at different levels.

Reflecting the relationship between economic growth and tax revenues from a broader perspective, the concept of tax buoyancy refers to the sensitivity of the change in tax revenues to change in national income. In other words, the concept of tax buoyancy is a broader concept that aims to calculate changes in tax revenues versus discretionary changes, such as changes in tax rates, tax bases, regulations and governing effectiveness, as well as automatic changes in tax revenues against changes in GDP. Leuthold (1986) defines that a tax is buoyant if its revenues increase by more than 1% for a 1% increase in national income or output. Akar and Şahin (2015) find that the tax system is less automatically stabilising in the short term if the tax buoyancy is smaller than 1, while in the long term the growth increase positively affects the financial sustainability. Dudine and Jalles (2017) claim that the situation, when the main components of tax buoyancy are taken into account, reduces fluctuations that will emerge and inflation as well as increase human capital.

Daniel (2013) explains the growing relationship between economic growth and tax revenues as the transfer of the national income increase to the public sector through taxation. Also, he points out that every 1% increase in GDP leads to a 0.22% increase in national income by ensuring that the increasing rate of national income is transferred from the private sector to the public sector as tax revenue.

Demir ve Sever (2017) study the relationship between tax revenues and economic growth of OECD countries using panel data analysis. They find that in the long term, a unit increase in direct taxation resulted in a decrease in the income level of 0.13 units, however, in the short run, the total income, direct tax and indirect taxes negatively affect income level. They also point out that in the short term, one unit increase in total taxation resulted in a decrease of 0.17 units in income level and a unit increase in direct and indirect taxes resulted in a decrease of 0.02 and 0.008 units in income level respectively.

By the central budget classification, a study on tax revenue elasticity was conducted by Akar (2013), using monthly tax revenues and industrial production index data from the period of December 2012 to January 2007 in Turkey. It indicated that in the long run, total tax revenues grew faster than GDP and the overall tax revenues did not converge based on the error correction model in the long run. It was also determined that regarding tax types, tax revenues on earnings and income, property, domestic goods and services were elastic in the long term and unstable in the short term. Indeed, Johansson et al. (2008) reported that the most effective and adverse effect on growth in the corporate income tax, followed by personal income tax and the tax on expenditures. On the other hand, wealth taxes have the least effect on growth. Hyman (1999) emphasises that corporate tax has the most significant adverse impact on growth due to corporate profits and thus negatively affecting tax revenues via abandoning institutional investment decisions because of high taxation.

Using the annual data for the period 1975–2013, Eren et al. (2018) perform a study investigating the impact of tax revenues on development analysed with different causality tests. They find that direct taxes have more influence on the development process in the short-term in Turkey, however, in the medium and long-term, this effect has disappeared. Finding a long-term relationship between per capita income and indirect tax revenues shows that development process forms a tax structure that indirect taxation is more weighted.

Durkaya and Ceylan (2006) investigated whether the series of total direct and indirect tax revenues and GDP had unit roots from 1980 to 2004. The study revealed that there was a bi-directional causal relationship between direct tax and economic growth, on the other hand, there was no causal relationship between indirect taxation and economic growth.

Siverekli (2003) claims that as public revenue, taxes, used in the financing of a significant portion of public goods and services, lead to private sector activities become more productive. Taxes fulfil this especially when income distribution is restored, and economic growth is inadequate with tax incentive mechanisms. Mostly depending on the volume of investment, the tax has a significant effect on the process of economic growth and development. Thus, when taken over income, taxes affect consumption and saving volume. The reduction in the savings volume through the taxes, leading to adverse effects on accumulation of capital and investments, prevent the planned speed of economic development by narrowing the investment volume of the private sector. If the funds are transferred from the private sector to the public sector through taxes, investment volume and growth process are not affected negatively, in the case of channelling investments into the public sector. However, for this, it is essential to use the methods which influence the total saving volume at least in determining tax rates and selecting tax resources. The relationship between taxation and economic growth can be positive, if the reasonable tax rates, which will not cause the above negatives for society, are determined. As stated in the theory of Laffer curves, in order to not lead to negative consequences of tax rate increases on the economy and taxpayers after a certain point, it is necessary to determine the respective tax rates based on countries' economic development levels, natural wealth, community values, habits, cultural structure, etc.

When considered essential functions and effects and the literature examples are given before, it is possible to say that the effect of the tax on economic growth creates different results regarding tax types and short and long periods. On the other hand, assessing tax revenues on monthly or annual periods is another factor affecting the relationship. Finally, it is essential to emphasise that the analysis methodology used in the study is also an essential factor. Moreover, the relationship between tax revenues and economic growth is based on a mutual relationship that, on the one hand, changes in tax revenues affect economic growth, on the other hand, changes in economic growth lead to changes in tax revenues. In the analysis of the related relationship, it is also essential to determine the starting point of the interaction. However, the relationship between economic growth and tax revenues is a relationship that interacts and affects each other in a bi-directional way.

3 Data and Econometric Methodology

3.1 Data

Monthly electricity consumption as a proxy variable to represent the monthly gross domestic product (GDP) and monthly tax revenues (*taxrev*) in the central government budget realisations are used from January 2006 to June 2017. It would be possible to model shorter-term effects by preferring monthly data instead of annual or quarterly data. Both variables are measured in natural logarithmic and deseasonalized data: electricity consumption obtained from the official sources of Turkey Electricity Transmission Company and tax revenues

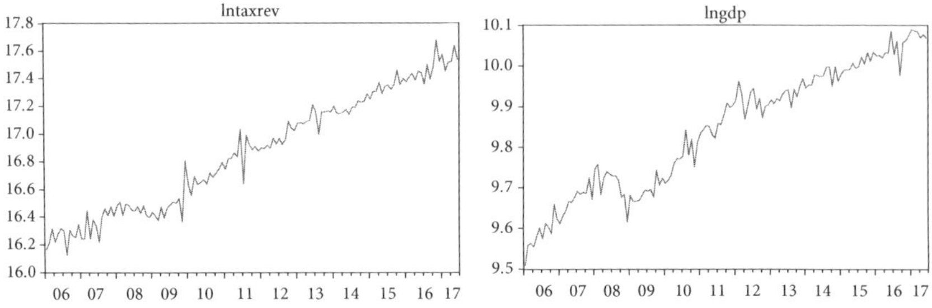

Fig 1. The Natural Logarithm of the Series, 2006–2017. Kaynak: General Directorate of Budget and Fiscal Control and General Directorate of Budget and Fiscal Control.

obtained from the official sources of General Directorate of Budget and Fiscal Control (BÜMKO). The variables are presented in Fig 1.

3.2 Econometric Methodology and Model

Developed by Pesaran and Shin (1998) and Pesaran et al. (2001), the ARDL-bounds test approach determines if there exists a long run relationship among variables. The methodology has some advantages compared with other conventional cointegration tests. The first and most important is that it can be performed if the variables in the models are I(0), I(1) or a mixture of both. The second, it is constructed as a single-equation giving simplicity of application and interpretation. The third, it allows different optimal lag lengths to be assigned for different variables in the equation.

In the first step of the ARDL-bounds test approach, an unrestricted error correction model is established. This model is as follows:

$$\Delta \ln taxrev_t = \beta_0 + \sum_{i=1}^{p} \beta_{1i} \Delta \ln taxrev_{t-i} + \sum_{i=0}^{q} \beta_{2i} \Delta \ln gdp_{t-i} + \delta_3 \ln taxrev_{t-1} + \delta_4 \ln gdp_{t-1} + \varepsilon_t, \qquad (1)$$

$\ln taxrev_t$: the natural log of tax revenues, $\ln gdp_t$ the natural log of electricity consumption, Δ: difference operator, p,q: the lag lengths, ε_t :error term, and abbreviations of the variables used in the study.

To test for the existence of a cointegrating relationship between variables, abound test based on the F test statistic is applied after the lag length p,q in equation (1) is determined. The null hypothesis $H_0 : \beta_3 = \beta_4 = 0$ implies that there exists no long-run relationship between variables. The F calculated test

Tab 1. The Results of Unit Root Tests

Variables	**Level**	**First Difference**		
	t-statistic	**Probability**	**t-statistic**	**Probability**
$\ln taxrev_t$	0.022	0.958	-17.66	0.000
$\ln gdp_t$	-1.278	0.639	-20.599	0.000

statistic value is compared with the lower and upper critical values of the table in Pesaran, Shin and Smith (2001). If the calculated *F* test statistic value is less than the critical value, the null hypothesis that no cointegration occurs is accepted. If the *F* test statistic value is larger than the upper critical value, the null hypothesis is unacceptable, which means that cointegration occurs. By determining the existence of cointegration, long and short-term relationships between variables are investigated by establishing lagged autoregressive models. If the null hypothesis of no cointegration is rejected, the following unrestricted error-correction model (ECM) is estimated, Pesaran et al. (2001):

$$\Delta \ln taxrev_t = \beta_0^* + \sum_{i=1}^{p} \beta_{1i}^* \Delta \ln taxrev_{t-i} + \sum_{i=1}^{q} \beta_{2i}^* \Delta \ln gdp_{t-i} + \lambda ECT_{t-1} + u_t \quad (2)$$

Where ECT denotes the error correction term and λ denotes the speed of adjustment parameter. The coefficient on error correction term indicates short-run deviations from the long-run equilibrium after a shock. A negatively significant coefficient on error correction term ensures that the system is converging to the long run equilibrium and estimated model is stable.

3.3 The Unit Root Tests

The time series used in the econometric analysis must be stationary. Granger and Newbold (1974) state that spurious regression problems can be encountered if the series is not stationary. The Augmented Dickey-Fuller (ADF), suggested by Dickey and Fuller (1979), unit root test to check the stationary properties of the time series variables was applied. Tab 1 presents the results of the test.

The results of the unit root tests display that both series are nonstationary in levels. The first differences of two series, the seasonally adjusted and log-transformed monthly $\ln taxrev_t$ ve $\ln gdp_t$ series become stationary at first differences, called I(1) series.

To test the existence of a possible long-run relationship between gross domestic product and tax revenues, an unrestricted error correction model is

Tab 2. The Results of the ARDL(6,0) Model Estimation

Regressor	Coefficient	Std. Error	Statistics	Probability
$\ln taxrev(-1)$	-0.047236	0.087070	-0.542502	0.5884
$\ln taxrev(-2)$	0.223264	0.089008	2.508357	0.0134
$\ln taxrev(-3)$	0.309565	0.090444	3.422722	0.0008
$\ln taxrev(-4)$	0.076124	0.089611	0.849501	0.3972
$\ln taxrev(-5)$	0.112117	0.087544	1.280692	0.2027
$\ln taxrev(-6)$	0.184938	0.087611	2.110893	0.0368
$\ln gdp_t$	0.412265	0.201552	2.045452	0.0429
C	-1.645357	0.813308	-2.023042	0.0452

Tab 3. The Results of the Bound Test

k^*	*F- statistics*	**Critical Values at %1 Significance Level**		**Critical Values at %5 Significance Level**	
		Lower limit	**Upper limit**	**Lower limit**	**Upper limit**
1	8.558803	4.94	5.58	3.62	4.16

**k*represents the number of independent variables in equation (1).

first established. For this purpose, based on the Akaike Information Criteria (AIC) model selection criterion, the autoregressive lagged distributed model is obtained, given in Tab 1 below.

3.4 The ARDL/Bounds Test

The results in Tab 2 suggest that the autoregressive lagged distributed model in which the tax revenues is estimated as a dependent variable is ARDL (6,0). The model implies that the tax revenues variable is explained by the current values of the economic growth variability as well as the lagged values of up to six months starting from one after the other.

After determining that the error terms of the model do not have autocorrelation problems, the Bounds test is applied. The test results, based on the ARDL (6, 0) model, are provided in Tab 3 below.

The value of the calculated test statistic for the bound test is 8.56 which exceeds the upper critical bounds values at the 1% and 5% significance levels. The test results show that there is an equilibrium relationship between tax revenues and economic growth.

Tab 4. The Estimated Long-Run Cointegrating ARDL Model (6,0)*

Regressor	Coefficient	Std. Error	t-statistic	Probability
$\ln gdp_t$	2.919	0.303	9.642	0.0000
C	-11.650	2.935	-3.969	0.0001

*The model was selected automatically based on Akaike Information Criterion (AIC).

3.5 The Estimation of Long-Run Coefficients

After determining that there exists an equilibrium relationship between tax revenues and economic growth, the long-run coefficients of the cointegrating ARDL model are estimated and provided in Tab 4.

The coefficient $\ln gdp_t$ is signed as expected and statistically significant at the 5% level. The regression results of the log-linear tax revenue function show that the regression coefficient of log income [tax buoyancy] is about 2.92. It can be inferred that a 1% increase in national income leads to increase the tax revenue by 2.92% per annum. Jalles (2017) states that a tax buoyancy greater than one (2.92) would increase tax revenue by more than gross national product and have the potential to lead to reductions in the deficit ratio.

3.6 The Estimation of Error-Correction Model

The estimation results of the error-correction model are given in Tab 5.

Tab 5. The Results of the Error-Correction Model

Regressor	Coefficient	Std. Error	Statistics	Probability
$\Delta \ln taxrev_{t-1}$	-0.904	0.080	-11.227	0.0000*
$\Delta \ln taxrev_{t-2}$	-0.681	0.113	-5.979	0.0000*
$\Delta \ln taxrev_{t-3}$	-0.369	0.127	-2.897	0.0044
$\Delta \ln taxrev_{t-4}$	-0.295	0.117	-2.514	0.0132
$\Delta \ln taxrev_{t-5}$	-0.184	0.085	-2.163	0.0324
$\Delta \ln gdp_t$	0.470	0.190	2.476	0.0146
ECT_{t-1}	-0.138	0.026	-5.221	0.0000*

* indicates significance at the 1% level.

ECT_{t-1}

The error correction term is negative (–0.138) and statistically significant at the 1% significance level. The coefficient, specifically, refers that about 14% of any disequilibrium level of tax revenues will be adjusted in the current period. In other words, by adjusting nearly 14% of any disequilibrium, the system converges to the long run equilibrium level every month.

3.7 The CUSUM and CUSUMSQ Tests

Finally, to test the stability of the long-run and short-run coefficients estimated by the ARDL model, cumulative sum (CUSUM) and the cumulative sum of squares (CUSUM Square) Tests are applied. Proposed by Brown et al. (1975), the tests are applied to the recursive residuals of the ARDL (6,0) model. The plots of both CUSUM and CUSUM of Squares are displayed in Fig 2.

The results of the CUSUM and CUSUM of squares tests also confirm that the residual variance of the ARDL (6,0) model is somewhat stable since the plots of CUSUM and CUSUM of squares generally stay within the critical 5% significance boundaries.

4 Conclusion

This study attempts to investigate the long-run relationship between tax revenues and economic growth for Turkey. In the first step, the ADF test is used to confirm both the variables are stationary and integration orders. Then the ARDL/Bounds test methodology is conducted to explore the long-run relationship between tax revenues and gross domestic product.

The main findings of this study are:

(1) The variables, tax revenues and gross domestic product are positively high correlated with each other.

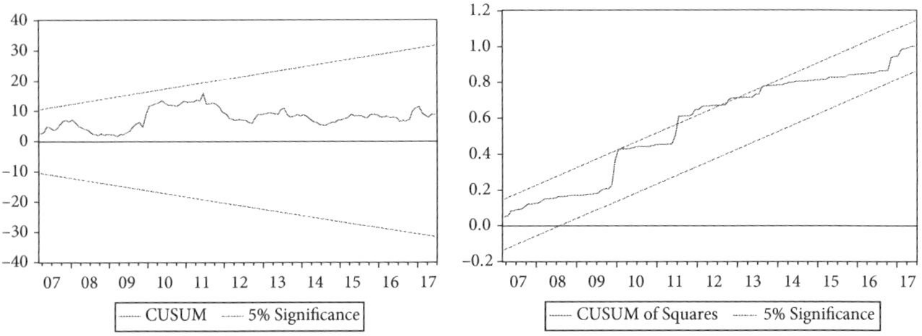

Fig 2. The Plots of CUSUM and CUSUM of Squares

(2) There exists an equilibrium relationship between tax revenues and the gross domestic product consistent with Akar& Sahin, 2015:11.
(3) An increase of 1% in economic growth leads to an increase of 2.92% (called the tax buoyancy-coefficient) in tax revenues.
(4) The tax system in Turkey is buoyant to lead to reductions in the deficit ratio potentially.

The empirical results of the study help the policymakers in better assessing of the relationship between tax revenues and gross domestic product to formulate tax policies. Even though an increase of 1% in economic growth leads to an increase of about 3% in tax revenues, it is not an economically and socially appropriate solution in the short term to target the increase in the tax rates.

Although the right to taxation belongs to the governments, the basic policy to increase taxes should concentrate on economic growth. For this, especially in the middle and long-term, emphasise on policy implementations that will focus on increasing production by avoiding policy changes frequently. Rather than tax increase applications that would prevent production growth, the following should be adopted as the primary objectives: new innovative products, incentive mechanisms to encourage domestic production, and increasing entrepreneurship-based economic activities.

If inevitably tax increases are to be made, it should be done at least during the periods when the economy is growing. Attention should be paid to the fact that tax increases do not have a restrictive effect on the production capacity of taxpayers, especially for manufacturers. While this is done, focusing on the taxes on spending tax increases disturbing justice in the distribution of income should be avoided. Instead of the idea that the increase in tax revenues will only be achieved by increasing taxes, practices, such as tax inspections, that will eliminate tax losses should be taken into account and tax compliance of taxpayers must be carefully revised.

For the further studies, ARDL-Bounds Test method can be applied correctly for the following taxes: Corporate Income Taxes, Personal Income Taxes, Social Security Contributions, and Taxes on Goods and Services.

References

Akar, S. (2013), "Vergi Gelirlerinin Esnekliği ve İstikrarı: Merkezi Bütçe Sınıflandırmasına Dayalı Ampirik BirAnaliz", *Maliye Dergisi*, 165: 27–37.

Akar, S. & Şahin, Uysal, Ö. (2015). "An Analysis of Tax Buoyancy in Turkey", *Journal of Economics, Finance and Accounting – (JEFA)*, 2 (1): 29–43.

Akdoğan, A. (2005). *Kamu Maliyesi*, 10. Baskı, Ankara: Gazi Kitabevi.

Ataç, B. (1999). *Maliye Politikası*, Genişletilmiş 5. Baskı, Eskişehir: Anadolu Üniversitesi Eğitim, Sağlık ve Bilimsel Araştırma Çalışmaları Vakfı Yayınları; No:118.

Brown, R.L., Durbin, J. & Evans, J.M. (1975). "Techniques for Testing the Constancy of Regression Relations Over Time", *Journal of the Royal Statistical Society*, 37: 149–163.

Daniel, J. K. (2013). "The Relationship between Tax Revenue and Economic Growth in Kenya", *A Research Project, School of Business, University of Nairobi*, D61/67843.

Demir, M. & Sever, E. (2017). "Vergi Gelirleri Ekonomik Büyüme İlişkisi: OECD Ülkelerine İlişkin Panel Veri Analizi", *Aksaray Üniversitesi İktisadi ve İdari Bilimler Fakültesi Dergisi*, 9 (2): ss. 51–66.

Dickey, D. A. & Fuller, W. A. (1979). "Distribution of The Estimators for Autoregressive Time Series with a Unit Root", *Journal of the American Statistical Association*, 74(366): 427–431.

Dudine, P. & Jalles, J. T. (2017). "How Buoyant Is the Tax System New Evidence from a Large Heterogeneous Panel", *IMF Working Paper*, WP/17/4.

Durkaya, M. & Ceylan, S. (2006). "Vergi Gelirleri ve Ekonomik Büyüme", *Maliye Dergisi*, 150: ss. 79–89.

Eren, M. V., Ergin, Ü. A. & Aydın, H. İ. (2018). "Türkiye'de Vergi Gelirleri ile Ekonomik Kalkınma Arasındaki İlişki: Frekans Alanı Nedensellik Analizi", *Doğuş Üniversitesi Dergisi*, 19(1): ss. 1–18.

Granger, C.W.J. & P. Newbold (1974). "Spurious Regressions in Economics", *Journal of Econometrics*, 2: 111–120.

Hyman, D.N. (1999). "Public Finance: A Contemporary Application of Theory to Policy", New York: The Dryden Press.

Jalles, T. J. (2017). "Tax Buoyancy in Sub-Saharan Africa: An Empirical Exploration", *African Development Review*, 29(1): 1–15.

Johansson, A., Heady, C., Arnold, J., Brys, B. & Vartia, L. (2008). "Tax and Economic Growth", *Economics Department Working Paper No.620*, ECO/WKP 28, 2–85.

Leuthold, J. H. & Guessan, T. N. (1986). "Tax Buoyancy and Elasticity in Developing Economy", *Bureau of Economic and Business Research*, Faculty Working Paper No. 1272; University of Illinois, Urban Campaign.

Musgrave, R. A. (1958). *Kamu Maliyesi Teorisi-Kamu Ekonomisi Alanında Bir İnceleme*, (Çev: Orhan ŞENER-Yaşar METHİBAY), Ankara: Asil Yayın Dağıtım.

Pesaran, M. H. & Smith, R. J. (1998). "Structural Analysis of Cointegrating VARs", *Journal of Economic Surveys*, 12: 471–505.

Pesaran, M. H., Shin, Y. & Smith, R. J. (2001). "Bounds Testing Approaches to the Analysis of Level Relationships", *Journal of Applied Econometrics*, 16: 289–326.

Sayar, N. S. (1975). *Kamu Maliyesi: Kamu Gider ve Gelirleri Prensipleri*, C. 1, 5. Baskı, İstanbul: İ.İ.T.İ.A. Nihad Sayâr Yayın ve Yardım Vakfı Yayınları No: 256, Sermet Matbaası.

Siverekli, E. (2003). "Vergilendirmenin Ekonomik Büyüme ve Kalkınmaya Etkisi", *Erciyes Üniversitesi İktisadi ve İdari Bilimler Fakültesi Dergisi*, 21: ss. 97–116.

Solow, R. M. (1956). "A Contribution to the Theory of Economic Growth", *Quarterly Journal of Economics*, 70: 65–94.

Türk, İ. (2005). *Kamu Maliyesi*, Mevzuattaki Değişikliklere ve Son İstatistik Verilerine Göre Güncelleştirilmiş 5. Bası, Ankara: Turhan Kitabevi.

Gonca Güngör Göksu

Relationship between Economic, Social and Cultural Rights with State Budget: Human Rights Budgeting

> "Budget analysis should be a potent instrument in the struggle for human rights."[1]

Abstract: The budget on which the resources needed for the delivery of public services are classified became an essential tool in achieving socio-economic/socio-cultural goals in the late 20th century. Human rights budget designed for this goal is a quite effective tool in supporting women, children, elderly and disadvantaged groups. This budgeting approach is considered among the social budgeting arrangements and aims to transfer more resources and improve the conditions of citizens having trouble accessing fundamental rights such as education, health, food and shelter. Within the scope of the study, human rights budgeting have been examined, and the analysis examples of human rights budgeting from various countries have been presented. The aim of the study is to analyse the relationship between human rights and state budget and to find out what changes human rights budgeting practices cause on state budgets. It is also targeted to determine the points to be considered while analysing human rights budgeting in the study.

Keywords: State Budget, Economic, Social and Cultural Rights, Human Rights Budgeting and Analysis

JEL Classification Codes: H5, H61, K38

1 Introduction

Human rights, also known as economic, social and cultural rights, have gained more and more importance, with the International Covenant on Economic, Social and Cultural Rights adopted by the United Nations in 1966. When human rights are mentioned, education, health, fundamental rights are the first to come to mind. These fundamental rights are specific to all humanity, regardless of nationality, place of residence, sex, national or ethnic origin, colour,

---

1 Thomas Hammarberg, Swedish diplomat and human rights advocate. He served as European Council Human Rights Commissioner in Strasburg.

religion, language. Every person in the world should have equal rights without being exposed to any discrimination. For this reason, there are more duties and obligations to the state in the provision of human rights.

Government budgets are an effective instrument in providing public services. So government budgets consulted to meet socio-economic and socio-cultural needs are primary resources. Incomes obtained from taxpayers are used for many important areas such as education, health, public security, transportation and infrastructure. Nowadays, government budgets are related to every individual in society and affect them. Although the government budget in a country affects all citizens, minority groups such as elderly, children, women, persons with disabilities can be more sensitive to decisions on the allocation of public resources. Because these people who are in a disadvantaged situation live in hard conditions, the smallest changes in public financial resources cause significant differences in their lives.

The main topic of study is human rights budgeting. Human rights budgeting has increasingly gained importance as a result of the changes in the context of social budgeting regulations. In providing obligations of human rights, government budgets have critical tasks. Especially, human rights budgeting, which is used to support special groups, includes the processes of preparing, approval, implementation and audit of state budgets. Besides, human rights analysis is performed to determine whether budgets are implemented or not according to the human rights norms. In the scope of the study, related budgeting approach is evaluated comprehensively, and the analysis examples done in different countries are examined. However, according to the limits of the study, it is not possible that all analysis examples in literature are examined. For this reason, the different examples from only eight countries (Guatemala, Argentina, Canada, Brazil, Mexico, South Africa, Northern Ireland and India) are presented. Also, the main steps, which should be followed, are emphasised while performing an analysis related to human rights budgeting.

2 The Concept of Human Rights and Legal Legislation for the Protection of Human Rights

Human rights concern, human dignity, and the fights for human rights are based on recognition and respect for this honour. Even though human rights definitions are not included in the legal manuscripts in the past, human rights have always existed throughout history. Today, states have undertaken some engagement willingness to ensure an adequate standard of living, the provision of education/health services, and the protection of the economic welfare, social and cultural rights of children, women, and minorities. These legal rights are guided within the guidelines specified below (FLAC, 2014):

- Dignity,
- Equality,
- Non-discrimination in the use of human rights,
- It is the provision of an ongoing dialogue across the community on the political preferences and legal, human rights obligations that must be included in the budgeting process.

Up to now the most critical step towards the protection of human rights is the convention that has been accepted in 1966 by the United Nations *"International Covenant on Economic, Social and Cultural Rights"*. The various articles of this convention, which entered into force in 1976, are of great importance regarding human rights. According to the International Convention on Economic, Social and Cultural Rights, individuals have access to the highest standards of health-regarding working conditions, social security facilities, same living standards, education and health services, and physical and mental health (Fundar, 2004: 20). In the first article of the International Covenant on Economic, Social and Cultural Rights, the following expressions of human rights are emphasised (United Nations, 1966):

"The States Parties to the present Covenant:

- *Considering that, by the principles proclaimed in the Charter of the United Nations, recognition of the inherent dignity and the equal and inalienable rights of all members of the human family is the foundation of freedom, justice and peace in the world,*
- *Recognizing that these rights derive from the inherent dignity of the human person,*
- *Recognizing that, by the Universal Declaration of Human Rights, the ideal of free human beings enjoying freedom from fear and want can only be achieved if conditions are created whereby everyone may enjoy his economic, social and cultural rights, as well as his civil and political rights,*
- *Considering the obligation of States under the Charter of the United Nations to promote universal respect for, and observance of, human rights and freedoms,*
- *Realizing that the individual, having duties to other individuals and to the community to which he belongs, is under a responsibility to strive for the promotion and observance of the rights recognised in the present Covenant."*

Provisions relating to the protection of human rights are stated in the first 15 articles of the contract. The first 15 articles of the related contract are: (i) The right to self-determination of rights, (ii) The application of the Convention in domestic law and the prohibition of discrimination, (iii) Gender equality, (iv) Limitation of rights, (v) Prohibition of abuse of rights, (vi) Right to work, (vii) Fair and appropriate working conditions, (viii) Trade Union rights, (ix) The right to social security, (x) The protection of family, mother, children and young people, (xi) The right to life standard, (xii) The right to health standards, (xiii) The right to education, (xiv) Obligation to provide compulsory primary education and (xv) Regulations on the right to participate in cultural life. Other commitments to the protection of human rights under the United Nations include: *(i)Convention on the Elimination of All Forms of Discrimination against Women, (ii)Convention on the Rights of the Child, (iii) Convention on the Elimination of Racial Discrimination and (iv)The Convention on the Rights of Persons with Disabilities*".

3 Investigation of Economic, Social and Cultural Rights and Budgetary Relations

Human rights are often a matter of work by lawyers and judges. For this reason, many lawyers and judges have made essential contributions to this field. However, in recent times the interest of other disciplines and actors in the field of human rights has increased considerably (O'Connel, 2017:83). Because, if the protection of human rights is required in society, governments have to carry out economic and financial policies effectively in this direction. At the beginning of the 1990s, with the end of the Cold War, issues such as democratisation, local administration, and management reform began to be given priority. Thus, human rights policies have begun to be examined more at the macroeconomic level (Hatchel and Rebhan, 2008:2).

When the historical process is assessed, revolutionary movements, especially at the end of the 18th century, and public financing are significant regarding the rising voice of human rights (O'Connel, 2013:119). Governments must use public financing in order to effectively achieve optimal social benefits (FLAC, 2014:3). Because the violation of civil and political rights by states means increasing socioeconomic inequalities among social groups. The minority is the most affected by current income inequalities. Accessing the fundamental human rights necessary for these groups to live a dignified life is very difficult (Manion et al., 2017: 2). For this reason, states are also responsible for making decisions and producing policies for minority groups (FLAC, 2014:2).

Over the past 20 years, many academics and practitioners have been working on human rights budgeting (Kuosmanen, 2016:248). There are many types of research on human rights within the United Nations. One of these researches was prepared in 2014 by Magdalena Sepúlveda CARMONA who is the United Nations rapporteur. According to the prepared report, "*Participation, accountability, transparency, and access to information are critical human rights principles that must be observed throughout the policy cycle, such as the design of budget and tax laws, budgeting of expenditure and the implementation of the budget, which also applies to fiscal policies.*" According to the researcher, the human rights budgeting system and governments have to ensure that rights are maintained, supported and realised through budget processes.

3.1 The Theory of Human Rights Budgeting

Social budget is covering expenditures about education, health, safety, social aids, etc. (Şeker, 2011:22), which is preferred in order to improve the social services in terms of equality, income distribution, poverty, employment and social integration in the direction of public services and allows these individuals to be affected positively in disadvantaged situations. In the preparation and implementation of the social budget, it is essential to eliminate the basic needs of people. Thus, it is aimed to increase the quality of life of the individuals constituting the society (Özcan, 2016:123). In recent years, social welfare state concept has been included in country constitutions, and social welfare has been given more importance to the concept of the social budget in order to increase follow-up of social expenditures and public services (Özcan, 2016:78). Nowadays, social budgeting applications are evaluated in five groups. These groups are: sex-sensitive budgeting, participatory budgeting, citizen-focused budgeting, child-friendly budgeting, and human rights budgeting (Çiçek and Dikmen, 2016: 137).

Under the state budget, it is important to know two parallel processes in order to better understand the economic, social and cultural rights of individuals. In these processes, human rights are the budgetary means. First, it is necessary to examine what the human rights budgeting approach expresses in the true nature. Human rights budgeting: the development and implementation of the state budget to be sensitive to human rights standards and human rights obligations. This process aims to reach a budget designed to achieve effective human rights (Blyberg, 2015:4). Thus, within the scope of human rights, citizens are allowed to make optimum use of essential public services such as poverty, health and education (Çiçek and Dikmen, 2016:137). In this budgeting system, socio-economic and socio-cultural classification of public resources is envisaged, and budget allocations are offered to citizens who cannot benefit from essential services. Thus, essential public services (education, health etc.) and non-basic public services (defence, diplomacy etc.) can be compared (Meriç, 2013:159–160).

In other words, human rights budgeting is a powerful tool to monitor whether the state, local governments or affiliates use existing resources to provide human rights. The human rights budgeting system applies not only to education and health rights but also to similar rights such as the right to marriage, the right to water, the right to adequate food, the right to work and the right to social security (GTZ, 2010:2). There are two linkages between the preparation and implementation of public budgets and human rights. First of all, the resources required for human rights are needed to pass on the imagination. Second, the realisation of human rights is not a policy option that exists under the condition of scarce resources. On the contrary, it constitutes a legal framework for human rights, economy and finance policies. For this reason, the government that has prepared a budget compatible with human rights is not benevolent government acting in good faith, but a government that fulfils its legal obligations (Kuosmanen, 2016:248).

Another name for human rights budgeting is the civil society budget. Because this budgeting system is an application based on human values that civil society organisations value (Meriç, 2013:160). There are two critical issues in the context of human rights budgeting. The key to these issues is the *efficient use of* available *resources*. In other words, spending should have an essential influence on reaching the rights of individuals. Another important point is that the *resources* allocated for the realisation of economic, social and cultural rights are not *transferred to other public spaces* (Blyberg and Hofbauner, 2014:5–6).

Human rights budgeting involves some strategic objectives. These objectives include informing parliament, committees, local councils, and audit institutions, strengthening public finance skills in ministries and local governments, to support the strengthening of the representation capacity of non-governmental organizations, in particular minority groups, and creating a critical discussion environment through the public and media public hearings on the budget (German Institute, 2010:4). Also, this budgeting system is balanced fiscal power between citizens and the state by applying the income derived from the people still being offered opportunities to be spent for the public; participation is increasing, accounts are encouraged to be given a democratic environment (Meriç, 2013:160).

Human rights budgeting should include transparent, efficient and fair tax policies and support the fight against corruption. In order to achieve this, the contributions of non-governmental organisations and other stakeholders are necessary (German Institute, 2010:3). The United Nations Development Fund, the United Nations Children's Fund, the World Health Organization and the Food and Agriculture Organization, etc. some human rights-related practices are prioritised in United Nations' sub-agency policies and programs (Elson, Radhika and Heintz, 2011:32). These sub-organisations also emphasise the use of state budgets in order to encourage the application of economic, social and cultural rights (Nolan, 2013:42–43). However, it may be difficult to identify areas of economic, social and cultural rights. It is natural to transfer expenditures directly to areas such as health, water, food and education. However, spending on areas such as road construction or tourism may indirectly relate to human rights budgeting. For example, road-building farmers can more easily bring their products to markets. Thus, there is an indirect effect in meeting the need for food. The development of tourism areas is also creating post-employment, thus contributing to the right to work (Blyberg and Hofbauer, 2014:3). Important points regarding human rights obligations during the budgetary budget are as follows (OHCHR, 2017:111):

- Government policies, programs and plans should be developed and implemented in a way that reflects human rights obligations and best suits human rights.
- Some rights must be fulfilled. Any restriction on resources is not a valid reason to allocate funds or limit expenditures to realise these rights. For example, basic health, primary education right, etc.
- According to the International Covenant on Economic, Social and Cultural Rights, it is necessary for governments to give priority to the realisation of economic, social and cultural rights in their policies, programs and plans, and that this priority should be reflected in the government's budget allocations.
- The deduction of budget allocations for programs, projects and economic, social and cultural rights will affect people's rights in the negative.
- Governments should conduct regular analyses to assess the impact of budget allocations on different groups.

Fig 1 shows the human rights budgeting process step by step. According to the graph, there are four stages of the implementation of state budgets in line with human rights. The first stage is to prepare the state budgets by human rights. At this stage, it is necessary to form policies and plans that are sensitive to human rights and to design the budget in this direction. The second step is the stage in which the budget is discussed and approved by the decision-making body. At this stage, decision-making bodies are eyeing the budget and can make changes to the budget if they see it. The third step is the execution phase. At this stage, the collection of public incomes, making expenditures, monitoring and analysing income-expenditure are included in the scope of human rights. The final step is the stage of audit and evaluation. At this stage, there is an audit of income and expenditure in the framework of human rights and the review of the audit report.

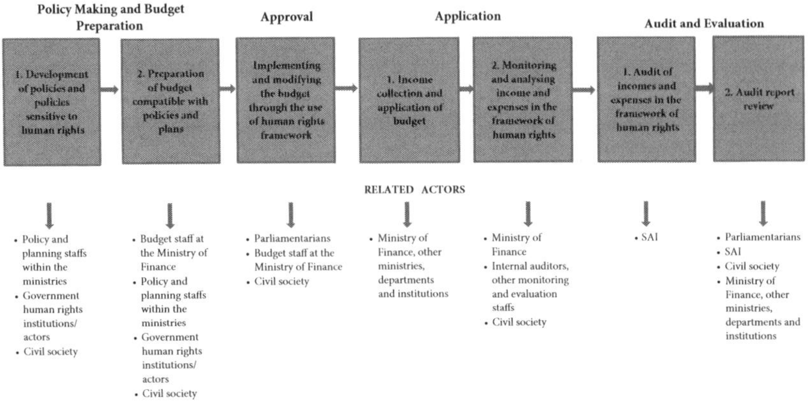

Fig 1. Human Rights Budgeting Process
Reference: *Blyberg, 2015:16.*

3.2 Human Rights Budgeting Analysis

Another important process that needs to be considered when analysing the relationship between economic, social and cultural rights and state budgets is human rights budgeting analysis. The design and implementation of state budgets to comply with human rights norms and standards are not sufficient to ensure that human rights are effectively achieved. The analysis of human rights budgeting requires that the policies and plans be handled together with the process of monitoring and evaluating the budget. This helps to determine whether the results achieved are below their targets and how they can be improved in the short term (Blyberg, 2015:4). Human rights experts are developing new strategies and methods to meet the needs of the disadvantaged. In other words, human rights budgeting, economic analysis, social and cultural rights budget analysis is an improved analytical technique in this direction. This analysis technique is a powerful tool for the development, monitoring, evaluation and defence of economic and social rights. Understanding and analysing state budgets is necessary to determine whether governments use their existing resources to the most significant extent on economic and social rights in the framework of international human rights legal obligations and policies (Manion et al., 2017:2). This method of budget analysis aims to analyse the relationship between state failures and human rights in order to fulfil human rights obligations.

Approaches to economic, social and cultural-based budget analysis may vary. First of all, such analyses can be thematic and group-based, or both. A group of analysts can analyse state budgets only from the perspective of specific rights such as housing, education or health. Other group analysts focus on the impact of budget decisions on a particular group, for example, children (Nolan, 2013:43). The human rights budgeting analyst needs to be well aware of the critical components of a particular economic and social segment, how these components are expressed on the budget, the methods used to allocate budgets, and how the budget relates to economic and social rights. Thus, budget analysts can assess governments' budget policies and provide viable alternatives (Manion et al., 2017:5). The necessary steps that an investigator should follow when conducting a human rights budgeting analysis are (Allen et al., 2016:15):

1) legal obligations as measurement tools[2] consider,
2) choose a method of budget analysis,
3) use quantitative methods to analyse budgets,
4) define the process, and
5) examine the budget analyses that have already been done on the subject.

Human rights budgeting analysis methods are divided into three groups. The first method of analysis is income-based analysis, the second method of analysis is the analysis of budget appropriations (how budget allocations are distributed); and the final analysis method is the analysis of budget expenditures (expenditure allocated) (Manion et al., 2017:6). Income-centric analyses focus on governments' taxation authorities and examine total public revenues. Analyses made in this direction may lead to changes in income collection methods, or to fight against tax evasion. However, researchers analyse different ways of collecting income to analyse what they will contribute to the minority population and low-income individuals (Allen et al., 2016:10). Within the budget analysis of budget allocations, researchers compare spending patterns to see whether governments fulfil their obligations. For example, the balance between national security and education expenditures can be looked at, or the variation in per capita health expenditures between the districts can be examined. Public expenditure analysis deals with the relation between current expenditures and budget appropriation allocations. In this context, it is examined whether expenditures are more or less than expected (Elson, 2006:24). In the analysis of public expenditures, the central budget allocation for economic, social and

2 The related obligations are explained one by one under 3.2.1 the heading.

cultural rights and their share in GDP are taken as a basis (Elson, Radhika and Heintz, 2011:22).

In all the three analyses, the numerical data on the state budget can be used in four ways (Allen et al., 2016:11–12):

- **International Comparative Budget Analysis:** Expenditures in one area of a country are compared to expenditures in the same areas of other countries. For example, a researcher might want to compare the share of public spending on women in India and Nepal. Comparisons are made between countries with similar economic conditions.
- **National Level Budget Analysis:** State revenues, expenditures and appropriation allocations are examined at the national level. For example, at a particular time analysing the changes under the constraints of educational expenditures in Turkey.
- **Local Government Budget Analysis:** In this context, data are provided for comparison between any two local governments in a country. For example, expenditure on health services at the regional level may be the subject of analysis. Analysts often use analyses of local government besides the central government to ensure that states fulfil their obligations to the minority.
- **Comparative Budgetary Analysis among Sectors:** When making an intersectorial budget analysis, income and expenses are compared. For example, the situation of sex-based expenditures in sectors related to women such as health industry, education system or agriculture can be examined.

Examination of the analytics regarding the time limit is in two forms. The first is a static analysis. In a static analysis, the state budget for a specific period is analysed. Within the scope of dynamic analysis, which is another form of analysis, the current year budget is compared with the past year budget. Thus, the changes in incomes, expenditures and allocations in differentiated periods are examined. Dynamic analysis is particularly critical in assessing the extent to which governments fulfil their obligations in decisions regarding economic, social and cultural rights to the maximum use of available resources (OHCHR, 2009:13). Human rights budgeting analysis can be explained with an example. First, it must be decided which human rights stream should be analysed. For example, you want to analyse your right to education in the first instance. In the second step, the method of analysis should be determined. According to this, the researcher can choose the budget allocations and expenditures allocated to the education service. In the third step, the researcher should determine what numerical data to use. Suppose, for example, that the budget analysis at the local government level has been selected. Thus, the right to receive primary education services in two

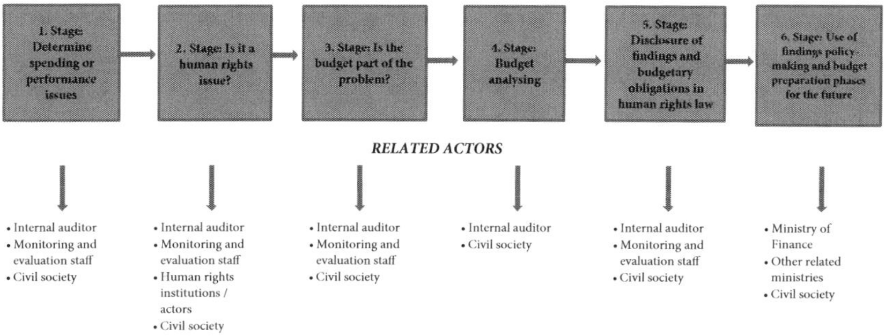

Fig 2. Human Rights Budget Monitoring and Analysis Process
Reference: *Blyberg, 2015:20.*

different regions at the national level can be examined. The final stage is processed constraint (static or dynamic). If continued through the same example, a comparison can be made between specific years (last ten years) by selecting a dynamic analysis technique. As a result, researchers, the recent 10-year period in which the fundamental right to education allowances allocated from the budget and spending in order to provide the primary services in two districts close to each other regarding development in Turkey is aimed to compare.

Fig 2 shows the stages for evaluating the state budgets regarding human rights analysis. Here is an example of a fundamental right to health in order to better understand the steps that need to be followed:

Stage 1: Determining Spending or Performance Problem or Performance Problem: In the course of health care delivery, the Ministry of Health receives complaints from hospitals that pandemic prevention vaccines are not being delivered or the number of deliveries is less than needed.

Stage 2: This is a Difficult Manifestation Human Rights Issue: Every individual has the right to access health care. The lack of adequate vaccination against child palsy weakens the quality of health care. Therefore, this hurdle is a question about the right to health.

Stage 3: Is this a habitual budgetary problem? There is a need to do more research to answer this question. Firstly, there may not be enough information about why less vaccine was delivered than needed or that vaccine delivery was not planned as planned. However, if the Ministry of Health's interviews with local health departments reveal that the public resources allocated to the hospitals are insufficient to purchase the full of needed vaccinations, this issue points to a potential budgetary element.

Stage 4: Budget Analysis: At this stage, the Ministry of Health may determine that the cost of the vaccines is higher than anticipated when preparing the budget, or the Ministry may identify some deficiencies in the procurement process as closer scrutiny is made. For example, it can be determined that the vaccination unit sale price is determined to be unnecessarily higher than the previous year when the vaccination purchase contract was awarded to a different partner from the cooperation.

Stage 5: Disclosure of Findings in Human Rights Law and Budget Obligations: If the government fails to obtain surpluses at the best possible price, the result is that the available resources cannot be used to the maximum so that individuals can access the right to primary health care.

Stage 6: Use of Present Findings for the Future Budget: The Ministry of Health takes the necessary precautions to overcome the deficiencies that may occur during the next year's auction process in order to get the best possible feather purchases and to solve the problems in allocating the budget appropriations.

3.2.1 The Obligations Included in Human Rights Budgeting Analysis

Under this heading of the work, some obligations must be noted in the human rights budgeting analyses, as outlined in the United Nations Convention on the Protection of Human Rights. Relevant obligations are (Allen et al., 2016:15):

(i) Maximum Available Resources,
(ii) Progressive Realization,
(iii) Non-Regression,
(iv) Minimum Core.

In 2007, the United Nations Committee on Economic, Social and Cultural Rights adopted the so-called *"An Evaluation of the Obligation to Take Steps to the 'Maximum of Available Resources' Under an Optional Protocol to the Covenant"*, which states that each Contracting State has the right to fully fulfil the rights recognised in the Convention, including individual, economic and technical cooperation "Maximum Available Resources" (United Nations, 2007). Thus, the maximum use of available resources within the framework of human rights budgeting has become an outstanding obligation. The maximum available use is to use all the means to mobilise all resources within the country in order to achieve a government's gradual economic, social and cultural rights (Blyberg and Hofbaur, 2014:2). As a result, governments must take care to use public resources to provide economic, social and cultural rights (Blyberg, 2015:4).

With the maximum use of available resources, resources are used as effectively as possible. Governments must guide the maximum use of resources in allocating and producing resources to allow human rights to be realised (Hofbauer, 2014). Under this obligation, it is not possible to use the appropriations allocated to support human rights under the state budget in other areas. Moreover, the maximum use of resources can be applied not only within the context of state budget policies but also in the fields of taxation, state development assistance, public expenditure policies (Elson, Radhika and Heintz, 2011:16–17). The maximum use of available resources by States has three major influences. Firstly it is considered legal to investigate whether states reach the maximum level of available resources. It is also questioned whether other influential states give priority to resources for the realisation of these rights over other projects not directly related to economic, social and cultural rights. Finally, in the realisation of the respective rights, the resources should not be directed for other purposes, not allocated or returned to the central court (O'Connel, 2017:88).

The second critical human rights obligations related to budgeting and analysis is *Progressive Realization*. The progressive realisation of human rights does not mean that governments have no obligation to the rights concerned until a specific economic development is achieved. The progressive realisation, the government of continuous advancements, will be made regarding the status of human rights, and therefore the state of the urgency to take necessary measures, also in the future economic development of all kinds relating to the provision effectively social and cultural rights implies (Clarence, 2000). The respective expression is included in the 1st paragraph of Article 2 of the International Covenant on Economic, Social and Cultural Rights, in Article 4 of the Convention on the Rights of the Child and 1st paragraph of Article 4 of the Convention on the Rights of Persons with Disabilities (OHRCH, 2018). Progressive realisation can sometimes be interpreted as the fact that states do not have to protect economic, social and cultural rights until they have adequate resources. On the contrary, however, this obligation represents an urgent necessity to take appropriate steps towards the full realisation of economic, social and cultural rights. Sufficient resource inadequacy does not justify the lack of measures or inaction for the implementation of these rights (OHRCH, 2008:14).

Budgeting appropriate with human rights and other important obligations is not a negative thing. Therefore, the current economic situation should not be allowed to misuse social and cultural rights unless there is a strong justification (PWESC, 2015:2). The budget revenue limitations or against fiscal austerity measures even states should allocate the highest possible allowance to ensure full implementation of economic, social and cultural rights, i.e. a specific and ongoing obligation to support economic, social and cultural rights of states. The final obligation for human rights budgeting is *Minimum Core*. Within this obligation, a threshold is set for each of the existing rights. Accordingly, States are obliged to ensure that, regardless of the source level, each of the economic, social and cultural rights of people living in their jurisdictions are protected at least at a determined threshold. For example, hunger protection, primary education, emergency medical services, housing needs and protection services are among the minimum requirements for individuals to be able to lead a dignified life, and states are always obliged to provide these rights (Chapman and Russell, 2002).

3.2.2 Examples of Human Rights Budgeting Analysis in Various Countries

Some examples of human rights budgeting analysis exist in various countries. For example, Queen's University reviewed public spending in Northern Ireland using economic and social rights-based budget analyses under the Belfast Budget Analysis Project (QUB, 2010). A research organisation named FUNDAR conducted a survey in 2004 on federal health programs in Mexico. IDASA (The Institute for Democracy in South Africa) has conducted case studies for the Provincial Organization (IDASA, 2004) and the Center for Economic and Social Rights (CESR) in South Africa. Human rights in Ireland have also been analysed during the economic crisis (Corkery, Way and Otero, 2012).

Tab 1 presents some examples of the studies on human rights budgeting analysis in different countries. Some of the relevant examples are examined at the next stage of the study. However, since it is not possible to examine all the analysis made by the constraints of the study, the selected analysis examples are evaluated.

3.2.2.1 Example 1: Income-Based Analysis and Budget Appropriation Analysis Performed by the Economic and Social Rights Center in Guatemala

In 2009, a study was conducted jointly by the Center for Economic and Social Rights (CESR) and Instituto Centroamericano de Estudios Fiscales (ICEFI) (Allan et al. 2016:12–13). The purpose of this analysis was to examine whether the government fulfilled its commitments on health, education and nutrition rights. In the scope of the research, income-based analysis and budget appropriation analysis methods were preferred. In addition, international comparative budget analysis, national budget analysis and inter-sectorial comparative budget analysis were used to determine numerical data related to the analysis. In the content of the analysis:

Tab 1. The Some Examples of Human Rights Budgeting Analysis

Analysis Name	**Publication Institution**	**Authors**	**Year**
Health Care: A Question of Human Rights, Not Charity	Fundar	Fundar	2002
Dignity Counts: A Guide to Using Budget Analysis to Advance Human Rights	Fundar, International Human Rights Internship Program (IHRIP), International Budget Partnership (IBP)	Helena Hofbauer and Ann Blyberg	2004
Budgeting for Women's Rights: Monitoring Government Budgets for Compliance with CEDAW	United Nations Development Fund for Women	Diane Elson	2006
A Human Rights Budget Analysis of the Northern Ireland Housing Executive's Current Plans to Clad the Seven Towers Flats	The Seven Towers Residents Group	Participation and Practice of Rights Project	2006
Budgeting to Advance the Right to Food	Food & Agriculture Organization (FAO)	FAO	2009
Guatemala: Assessing Fiscal Policies from a Human Rights Perspective, Methodological Case Study on the Use of Available Resources to Realize Economic, Social and Cultural Rights in Guatemala	Center for Economic and Social Rights (CESR)	Allison Corkery and Maria Jose Eva	2012
Applying an International Human Rights Framework to State Budget Allocations	Rory O'Connell, Aoife Nolan, Mira Dutschke, and Eoin Rooney	Rory O'Connell, Aoife Nolan, Mira Dutschke, and Eoin Rooney	2014
Article 2 & Governments' Budgets Handbook (Including case studies from Brazil, Tanzania, and several other countries)	International Budget Partnership (IBP), Global Movement for Budget Transparency, Accountability and Participation	Helena Hofbauer and Ann Blyberg	2014
The Right To Food In South Africa: An Analysis Of The Content, Policy Effort, Resource Allocation And Enjoyment Of The Constitutional Right To Food	Studies in Poverty and Inequality Institute (CESR) and Asia Pacific Forum (APF)	CESR & APF	2015
Alternative Federal Budget	Canadian Centre for Policy Alternatives (CCPA)	CCPA	2016

Reference: Allen et al. 2016:33–34.

- Size of the Guatemalan state budget and the overall size of the economy (GDP) are compared,
- It has been understood that tax revenues generate most of the state budget resources,
- How the taxes were collected (income and sales tax) and which groups were taxed at the highest rates were researched.

When the results of the analysis are evaluated, it is noticed that there is a high level of unfairness when the tax revenues are obtained. The share of direct taxes in total tax revenues is quite low, whereas the share of indirect taxes such as value-added tax is very high. Findings show that the value-added tax collected at high rates is a decisive factor regarding human rights and has a very negative impact on the poor, especially women, especially the minority. The analysis also revealed that the tax cuts applied were much higher than the corporate tax collected from businesses. In other words, the Guatemalan government has given up valuable opportunities to mobilise more resources and fulfil human rights obligations. At this point, the CESR has stated that Guatemala does not fulfil its obligations for adequate health, education and nutrition. The wealthy and influential groups in the country have ensured that tax policies are directed at their interests and deprive the remaining groups of their access to human rights.

3.2.2.2 Example 2: The Analysis of the Impact of Tax Reform on Social Policies in Brazil

In Brazil, the Socioeconomic Institute Study (Estudi Instituto Socioeconômicos-INESC) has analysed the impact of tax reform on social policy funds in the country and obtained critical technical notes. The INESC has for many years examined the budgetary and revenue issues that determine programs and expenditures related to the realisation of human rights. After reviewing the Brazilian government's tax reform proposal, the organisation concluded that the effects of this reform would be detrimental to the poor of the community. INESC has created more than 100 non-governmental organisations, bringing together the Social Rights Defense Movement under the threat of tax reform. Analyses made suggest that the proposed tax reform will put social rights, especially the poor, at risk. The Defenders of Social Rights advocated that the proposal should not be submitted to vote without the necessary changes. Analysis of the tax reform of the health policy revealed that the resources would be reduced by the US $ 6.7 billion. As a result, the lengthy negotiations with government officials have dropped the final tax reform proposal (Blyberg and Hofbauner, 2014: 12–16).

3.2.2.3 *Example 3: An Analysis of the Conviction in Northern Ireland*

An interesting example of human rights budgeting analysis was made in Belfast, Northern Ireland. The Northern Ireland Housing Authority has afforded low-cost housing to citizens living in this area. The Northern Irish Housing Administration, the Social Development Department service delivery centre, is responsible for the construction of the state-owned housing in Northern Ireland. A group called the Seven Towers Residents Group has been participating in the "Participation and Practice of Rights" Project (PPRP) and are using a human rights-based approach to the issues identified that is related to the right to adequate living standards. It was analysed whether the right to marriage was implemented gradually under the project using indicators and criteria (PPRP, 2011:2). The analysis carried out has the following objectives:

- Increase the quality of health and ensure the safety of buildings,
- An accommodation that meets the needs of the community,
- To protect existing investments,
- Complete and support the Northern Belfast Housing Strategy,
- Reducing the costs of future interventions on the exterior,
- Securing roof areas in order to remove vandalism from the middle, thus reducing future maintenance of roofs.

When the results of the survey were evaluated, the existing proposals on housing that were hot and not humid by the housing contract indicated that they could not afford the residents' rights. The result shows that the implementation violated the obligation to improve the situation. As a result, Northern Ireland Housing Administration has violated international human rights law obligations.

3.2.2.4 *Example 4: An Analysis of Poor Income in India*

An analysis of economic, social and cultural rights in India was conducted by the Center for Budget and Governance Accountability (CBGA). It is primarily focused on the disadvantaged and discriminatory situation of children and women among the indigenous peoples (Dalits and local tribes) living in the North Eastern part of the country. The Indian national budget covers 16% of the total appropriation amount of each ministry related to the central budget by Dalit and the local public. According to the analysis results, serious scepticism emerged in practice, and it was understood that only half of the targeted budget was allocated. For this reason, in 2008–2009, CBGA, Dalits and local tribes called the boycott "The government has stolen 8% of us" (Hentschel and Rebhan, 2008:2). According to another analysis by the same organisation on the

Social Sensitive Budgeting in the country, only 3.6% of the total state budget was allocated to gender equality, and only 7% of women in the country benefited from public expenditures (Hentschel and Rebhan 2008:3).

3.2.2.5 Example 5: An Analysis of Public Expenditures in South Africa

The Studies in Poverty and Inequality Institute (SPII) focused on economic situation in the country, social and cultural rights in the development process of the budget analysis to follow the policy analysis including the development of economic indicators. In the study is used analysis focused on revenue, budget allocations and expenditure allocation (Allen et al, 2016:14). SPII governed sectorial comparative budget analysis within the context of food rights. It also analysed the National School Nutrition Program through budget appropriations analysis. It examined the adequacy of the amounts allocated to the National School Nutrition Program to determine whether there was a significant increase or decrease in budgetary allocations over a five year period. In this context, a measurement method called Five Targeting (Quintile targeting)[3] was used in the study.

According to the results of the analysis, although there is extensive information about food programs in the country, the state does not always draw attention to the obstacles encountered when applying for the programs. Because the coordination and implementation of various food programs in the country are responsible for more than one state, the data can be recorded differently to measure the effects of their implementation. This situation significantly affects the quality and results of the data. Incorrect financing management and detailed financial tables cause shortcomings in the suppliers 'and suppliers' food supply records.

In South Africa, The Imali Ye Mwana Network (MYMN) has surveyed children. The group aims to draw attention to increasing public spending and the effectiveness of expenditures for the protection of children's rights. In making this analysis, the investigative institution recalled that the useful resources would fulfil the maximum usability and gradual fulfilment obligations. According to the results of the survey, when civil society movements related to children's rights are not promoted, it is challenging to promote child rights budgeting alone.

3 Five-point targeting is a statistical value of a data set that represents 20% of a given population. For example; the first five represent the lowest income data five (1–20%); the second five represent the second lowest data (21–40%). The fifth (81–100%) represents the highest income group. A household is often used to create cut-off points for a specific population (www.investopedia.com).

However, it has been stated that achieving children's rights budgeting is much more successful if it is linked to a broader support campaign (Hentschel and Rebhan, 2008:3).

3.2.2.6 Example 6: An Analysis of Water and Sanitation in Canada

In 2016, a study carried out by the Canadian Center for Policy Alternatives (CCPA) revealed that there were increasing inequalities among the Canadians. The organisation analysed the budget about the water supply to the Canadian people through income-focused, and budget appropriations analyses. The Canadian government legally accepted water and sanitation services in 2012. According to the analysis, a total of $ 575 million is allocated to water and cleaning services, while only $ 61 million is allocated to sanitation. Also, the CCPA also recommended the creation of a national public water and wastewater fund (CCPA, 2016:144), which encourages the state to ensure that the right to water and sanitation is achieved in the context of maximum availability of available resources.

3.2.2.7 Example 7: An Analysis Related to Education in Argentina

Center Association for Equity and Justice (ACIJ) in Argentina is an organisation, slums of socio-economic discrimination and seeks the strengthening of civil society in the city of Buenos Aires. According to an analysis they conducted in 2006, more than 6,000 children did not attend school. According to the results, more than 70% of the violations of the right to education have occurred in the poorest regions of the city. Analysis of the local government budget has concluded that the government has made the less public expenditure in the poorest region (Hentschel and Rebhan, 2008:4).

3.2.2.8 Example 8: An Analysis of the Right to Health in Mexico

Center for Analysis and Research (A Centro de Analisi e Investigacion (Fundar)) in Mexico has been working as an independent, interdisciplinary and pluralistic organisation for many years on issues related to democracy and citizen participation. This organisation has addressed the health system in Mexico and analysed whether the state is entitled to health care. First of all Fundar's fundamental principles are (www.fundar.org.mx):

- To expand and strengthen citizen participation,
- To make a call for transparency and accountability,
- To contribute to the rule of law,
- To promote equality,
- To secure human rights.

Fundar's significant contribution to the budget process in Mexico is to simplify and disseminate budget information, encourage budget transparency, and increase the capacity and awareness of budgetary issues among other non-governmental organisations. Fundar's initial research in 2001 revealed that despite the highest maternal mortality rates in the state of Oaxaca, it had the lowest budget share in the country. Fundar's findings and advocacy work in partnership with other non-governmental organisations led to a significant increase in budget allocations of 600 million Pesos for public health interventions in 2003 to prevent maternal mortality (Robinson and Vyasulu, 2006:12).

Another analysis by Fundar about health implies that the Finance, Tourism and Foreign Departments spent more than the budget allocated, in other words, when extra resources were available, these resources were not allocated to health programs. Moreover, when viewed from buildings or significant infrastructure investments, the Department of Defense spent 17% more than the budget allocated, while the Department of the Navy spends about 25% more than the appropriations allocated from the budget. Conversely, the Ministry of Health has spared less than half of the budget allocated for capital investments (Fundar, 2004:37–38). As a result, when the results of Fundar's work on the right to health were assessed, it was seen that the government violated the right to health.

4 Conclusion and Evaluation

Human rights, which have been increasing in importance since the 18th century, are a matter that has been sensitively addressed by the United Nations. In the context of the organisation, protecting human rights is accepted as an essential aim and a guiding principle. Nowadays, the member states have more roles to ensure the protection and continuity of human rights. Human rights budgeting is a matter that the United Nations cannot ignore. Mainly because the implementations of human rights budgeting take an active role in improving the living standards of disadvantaged citizens.

In the context of human rights budgeting, the protection and ensuring continuity of fundamental rights such as education, emergency health, food, etc. are given priority in designing state budgets. But it is not enough to determine the policies and plans relevant to economic, social and cultural rights in the budget preparation process. At the end of the budget period, an examination and analysis of the implementations' effectiveness are needed. Because not analysing the results of a budget compatible with human rights is a significant lack. At the end of the analysis, the successful and unsuccessful areas should be identified, and the precautions to be taken in the next budget term should be determined.

Also, following the steps of such an analysis correctly, allows the research to give more accurate results.

When the examples of analysis in different countries are examined, it is understood that fiscal and political decisions about human rights have not been effectively implemented in some countries. For example, in Canada, the decision of water and sanitation rights was taken to parliament in 2012. However, when the policy results were analysed, the results were not directly proportional to the decisions made by the government. In other words, water and sanitation measures were inadequate. In Guatemala, it seems that the government did not obey the obligations of basic health, education and food according to the results of income-based analysis and budget appropriation analysis. Even though the human rights budgeting analysis shows the effectiveness of implementation results, it helps to estimate the results of some political decisions before applying them. For instance in Brazil, a tax reform suggestion was planned to propose during Lula's government period. However, human rights analysis showed that if new tax reforms were accepted and implemented, it would have risked social rights and notably, the disadvantaged groups in the country, and it would have reduced the resources of health policies to as much as 6.7 million US dollars. For this reason, the new reform was cancelled.

To protect and support citizens and to meet their needs are among the main tasks of states. Because maximising social utility is one of the priorities of the state administration. Consequently, by implementing human rights budgeting, it is enabled that the civil society audits public expenditures and that social welfare increase is possible through effective use of resources throughout the country. On the other hand, it is also possible to avoid wasting public resources by establishing a more transparent and accountable public financial management.

References

Allen, I., M. Manion, T. Matthews, and R. Ralston (2016). *Human Rights Watch Advisory Project Report*, Humphrey School of Public Affairs, University of Minnesota, USA.

Blyberg, A. (2015). *Human Rights Budgeting and Budget Analysis*, The Scottish Human Rights Commission (SHRC), http://www.scottishhumanrights.com/media/1706/human-rights-budgeting-and-budget-analysis-oct-2015-vfinal.doc, (30.01.2018).

Blyberg, A. and Hofbauer, H. (2014). *Article 2 and Governments' Budgets*, International Budget Partnership, https://www.internationalbudget.org/wp-content/uploads/Article-2-and-Governments-Budgets.pdf, (30.01.2018).

Carmona, M. S. (2014). *Report of the Special Rapporteur on Extreme Poverty and Human Rights*, A/HRC/26/28, Human Rights Council, http://www.ohchr.org/EN/Issues/Poverty/Pages/AnnualReports.aspx, (30.01.2018).

CCPA (Canadian Centre for Policy Alternatives) (2016). *2016 Alternative Federal Budget*, ISBN 978-1-77125-269-0, https://www.policyalternatives.ca/, (30.01.2018).

Charman, A. R. and S. Russell (2002). Core Obligations: Building a Framework for Economic Social and Cultural Rights, Intersentia, Antwerp.

Clarence J. D. (2000). "Towards Effective Monitoring of Compliance with Obligations and Progressive Realisation of ESCR", Second Global Forum on Human Development, 9–10 October, Rio de Janeiro, Brazil.

Corkery, A., S. A. Way and V. W. Otero (2012). *The OPERA Framework: Assessing Compliance with Obligations to Fulfill Economic, Social, and Cultural Rights*, Center for Economic and Social Rights, The New Horizons in Economic and Social Rights Monitoring Meeting, Canada.

Çiçek, Ş. E. and Dikmen, S. (2016). Child-Friendly Budget as an Instance of Social Budgeting, *The International Journal of Economic and Social Research*, 12(2), 131–147.

Elson, D. (2006). *Budgeting for Women's Rights: Monitoring Government Budgets for Compliance with CEDAW*, United Nations Development Fund for Women (UNIFEM).

Elson, D., B. Radhika, and J. Heintz (2011). "Public Finance, Maximum Available Resources and Human Rights", *Human Rights and Public Finance Budgets and the Promotion of Economic and Social Rights*, Aoife Nolan, Rory O'Connell and Colin Harvey (Eds.), Oxford and Portland, Oregon.

FLAC (The Free Legal Advice Centres) (2014). *A Human Rights Approach to Budgeting*, https://www.flac.ie/publications/briefing-human-rights-approach-to-budgeting/, (30.01.2018).

Fundar (2004). *Dignity Counts A Guide to Using Budget Analysis to Advance Human Rights*, International Human Rights Internship Program, International Budget Project, ISBN 0-9707700-4-9, Fundar – Centro de Análisis e Investigación, Mexican.

German Institute of Human Rights (2010), *Human Rights Budgeting*, http://www.institut-fuer-menschenrechte.de/uploads/tx_commerce/e-info-tool_hr_budgeting.pdf, (22.01.2018).

GTZ (Deutsche Gesellschaft für Technische Zusammenarbeit) (2010). *Human Rights Budgeting*, http://www.institut-fuer-menschenrechte.de/uploads/tx_commerce/e-info-tool_hr_budgeting.pdf, (30.01.2018).

Henstschel A. K. and Rebhan C. (2008). *Social and Human Rights Budgeting-Budget Monitoring, Participatory Budgeting and Human Rights*, Conference Report, Berlin.

Hofbauer, H. (2014). Budgeting for Human Rights: Using the Maximum of Available Resources, http://www.rightingfinance.org/?p=954, (30.01.2018).

IDASA (The Institute for Democracy in South Africa) (2004). *Comparative Provincial Housing Brief*, IDASA Budget Information Service Budget, Brief No. 145, Cape Town, South Africa.

Kuosmanen, J. (2016). Human Rights, Public Budgets, and Epistemic Challenges, *Human Rights Review*, 17, 247–267.

Manion, M., R. Ralston, T. Matthews, and I. Allen (2017). Budget Analysis as a Tool to Monitor Economic and Social Rights: Where the Rubber of International Commitment Meets the Road of Government Policy, *Journal of Human Rights Practice*, 9(1), 146–158.

Meriç, M. (2013). "Transformation and Change in Budget Systems", *Kamu Bütçesinde Yeni Yaklaşımlar*, Figen Altuğ, Ahmet Kesik, Murat Şeker (Eds.), ISBN:978-975-02-2372-3, Seçkin Publication, Ankara.

Nolan, A. (2013). "Putting ESR-Based Budget Analysis into Practice: Addressing the Conceptual Challenges", *Human Rights and Public Finance Budgets and the Promotion of Economic and Social Rights*, Aoife Nolan, Rory O'Connell ve Colin Harvey (Eds.), Oxford and Portland, Oregon.

O'Connel, R. (2013). "Recovering the History of Human Rights: Public Finances and Human Rights", *Human Rights and Public Finance Budgets and the Promotion of Economic and Social Rights*, Aoife Nolan, Rory O'Connell and Colin Harvey (Eds.), Oxford and Portland, Oregon.

O'Connel, R. (2017). "Human Rights and Fiscal Oversight: A Case Study of the Northern Ireland", 2011–15 Budget", *Journal of the Institute of Public Administration*, 65(3), 83–99.

OHCHR (The Office of the United Nations High Commissioner for Human Rights) (2008). Frequently Asked Questions on Economic, Social and Cultural Rights, Fact Sheet No. 33, United Nations Office at Geneva, Switzerland.

OHCHR (Office of the United Nations High Commissioner for Human Rights) (2009). *Report of the High Commissioner for Human Rights on Implementation of Economic, Social and Cultural Rights*, E/2009/90, United Nations Office at Geneva, Switzerland.

OHCHR (The Office of the United Nations High Commissioner for Human Rights) (2017). *Realizing Human Rights through Government Budgets*, HR/PUB/17/3, United Nations Office at Geneva, Switzerland.

OHCHR (The Office of the United Nations High Commissioner for Human Rights) (2018). *Fundamental concepts on ESCRs – What Are the obligations of States on Economic, Social And Cultural Rights?*, United Nations Office at Geneva, Switzerland.

PPRP (Participation and Practice of Rights Project) (2011). A Human Rights Budget Analysis of the Northern Ireland Housing Executive's Current Plans to Clad the Seven Towers Flats, https://www.pprproject.org/sites/default/files/BUDGET%20ANALYSIS%20JUNE%202011.pdf , (30.01.2018).

PWESCR (Programme on Women's Economic, Social and Cultural Rights) (2015). *Human Rights for All International Covenant on Economic, Social and Cultural Rights A Handbook*, Programed on Women's Economic, Social and Cultural Rights, The Netherlands.

QUB Budget Analysis Project (2010). *Budgeting for Social Housing in Northern Ireland: A Human Rights Analysis*, QUB School of Law, Queen's University Belfast, Ireland.

Robinson M. and Vyasulu V. (2006). *Democratizing the Budget: Fundar's Budget Analysis and Advocacy Initiatives in Mexico*, The Research Project: Lessons from Civil Society Budget Analysis and Advocacy Initiatives, The International Budget Partnership, https://www.internationalbudget.org/, (30.01.2018).

Özcan, G. (2016). *Sosyal Bütçeleme Anlayışı Gelir Dağılımını Sağlamadaki Rolü Türkiye Analizi*, ISBN:978-605-66475-3-6, KitapAna Basım Yayın Dağıtım, İzmir.

Şeker, M. (2011). *Yerel Yönetimlerde Sosyal Bütçeyi İzleme Raporu*, Tesev Yayınları, İstanbul.

United Nations (2007). *An Evaluation of the Obligation to Take Steps to the 'Maximum of Available Resources' under an Optional Protocol to the Covenant*, E/C.12/2007/1 Committee on Economic, Social and Cultural Rights, Switzerland.

United Nations, (1966). *International Convention on Economic, Social and Cultural Rights*, Accepted Date: 16 December 1966, Implemented Date: 3 January 1976.

http://fundar.org.mx/english/#.U82Zbai2264, (30.01.2018).

http://www.investopedia.com/terms/q/quintile.asp?layout=infini&v=5B&orig=1&adtest=5B, (30.01.2018).

Aslıhan Özel Özer[1], Buğra Özer and Pelin Mastar Özcan

An Evaluation of the Share of Turkish Central Government Expenditures within GDP between 1924 and 2016 in the Background of the Concept of "Minimal State"

Abstract: Liberalism sets the object of minimal state in its historical trajectory of evolution since its emergence. In the contemporary times, neoliberalism has also vigorously maintained the minimal state objective and retrenched the state by new global realities since the mid-1970s. Neoliberalism emerging on a background of a coalition with conservatism against the Keynesian welfare state implementations comes to redefine the state by economically defined criteria including effectiveness and efficiency. In order to be able to put into practice the ideal of the minimal state, the neoliberal project has effectively used the tool of public expenditures, with endeavours attempting to keep the mentioned expenditures on its minimum scale. This work attempts to shed light on whether primary institutions of public sector keep up with the minimal state objective in Turkey, henceforth, the effort strives to measure and evaluate whether this tendency has been in effect for public expenditures and government budget expenditures for the Turkish case in her historical, political economy development.

Keywords: Minimal State, Liberalism, Neoliberalism, Public Expenditures, Turkey, GDP

JEL Classification Codes: H10, H50, H6.

1 Introduction

Liberalism sets the object of minimal state in its historical trajectory of evolution since its emergence. In the contemporary times, neoliberalism has also vigorously maintained the minimal state objective and retrenched the state by "new global realities" since the mid-1970s. Neoliberalism emerging on a background of a coalition with conservatism against the Keynesian welfare state implementations comes to redefine the state by economically-defined criteria including effectiveness and efficiency. In order to be able to put into practice the ideal of the minimal state, the neoliberal project has effectively used the tool of

1 Corresponding author.

public expenditures, with endeavours to keep the mentioned expenditures on its minimum scale.

Given such a theoretical background, the study endeavours to problematize to which Turkish experience in liberalism fits the minimal state understanding. As for the case of Turkey, the Turkish experience of the minimal state presents no different case as the neoliberal winds of change began influencing the country in the late 1970s – at the formal point when Turkish governments had to negotiate a comprehensive restructuring of the Turkish State with the notorious 1979 IMF Standby agreement. (Ramazanoğlu, 1985). The minimal state has always been the buzzword of right-wing governments throughout the Republican Era starting with the ascension of the Democrat Party into power by 1950 (Kongar, 2002: 357–361).

Indeed, since the 1950s, right-wing governments characterised by a strong liberally characterised orientation for their economic policies have championed and vowed for the ultimate liberal state. A flashback to the infamous January 24th, 1980 dated Austerity Measures Package, despite the overwhelming support of the Turkish Industrialists and the military. The attempts by political authorities to stabilise the system and to alleviate the crisis were far from successful; on the contrary, the programs exacerbated the on-going crisis (Kongar, 2002:411–422).

The neoliberal experience a la Turca came into light in the heydays of the second Cold War by the early 1980s under the circumstances of chaos i.e. the Russian occupation in Afghanistan and the Islamic Revolution in Iran. It was a world of different neo-liberal projects aiming for the minimal state at the rhetoric level via the programs imposed directly and indirectly via the IMF and the World Bank (Boratav, 1997. Confronted with the instability of the political system to implement the brand new neoliberal agenda, the military took in charge for a neoliberal overhaul of the State thoroughly by – a next to be of the zeitgeist – export-led-growth model. (Keyder, 2004:67–68)

The subsequent civilian governments ardently declared their enthusiasm to undertake the neoliberal agenda with all means available to them in Turkey in the post-1980s. In fact, as for the following two decades in Turkey having abruptly moved to the export-led growth models from the 1960s' and 1970s' developmental models i.e. import substitute industrialization models (Keyder, 1987a and Keyder 1987 b), the minimal state debates have come to be located in an environment embedded against a liberalization and deregulation of the economy coupled with the reduction of tariffs and a financial liberalization (Bayar, 1996: 779) observes that "The year 1980 was the beginning of the radical transformation of Turkey's political economy from its ISI orientation to a more open system. Reform of the trade regime was the core of the programme.

The first element of the reform was the devaluation of the TL and a commitment to a flexible exchange rate policy. The second element was the promotion of exports through tax rebates, export credits, and other subsidies. The third element of the trade reform was imported liberalisation. The import regime was changed radically at the end of 1983 with the announcement that any item other than those specifically banned or subject to licensing could be imported freely. Quantitative restrictions were removed, and tariffs were lowered from an average of 19% to 12%."

In a parallel fashion Keyder (2004: 67–68) evaluates this new era of liberalism for the Turkish case in his own words such that "At the same time, market liberalization unleashed entrepreneurial energies at every level; traders and merchants were suddenly permitted to do things for which they would have served jail sentences a few years earlier. The industrial structures of the developmental era had been characterised by the oligopoly of a few multi-tentacled holding companies, through which the import-substituting bourgeoisie of Istanbul, with their privileged access to policymakers in Ankara, had been able to maintain an iron grip over the economy. With liberalisation, a new breed of entrepreneurs emerged who had to compete in globalised markets, and indexed their behaviour to commercial and consumer signals rather than bureaucratic decisions; hence their dependence on policy was less direct."

Given the background experience of Turkey in minimal state discussions, this work attempts to shed light on whether primary institutions of public sector keep up with the minimal state objective, henceforth, operationally speaking, the effort of the study strives to measure and evaluate whether this tendency has been in effect for public expenditures and government budget expenditures. The plan of the work shall be such that the first section will juxtapose the theoretical underpinnings of the minimal state as a project of neoliberalism. Subsequently, the work will empirically deal with an analysis of public expenditures within government budget expenditures as a share of gross domestic product (GDP). Finally, the concluding remarks of the work will wrap up the discussion by reiterating that minimal state debates remain at a rhetorical level similar to the global experiences shared among the industrialised cases of countries that went through similar neoliberal transformation processes.

2 Minimal State as the Objective of Neoliberalism

This section will devote itself to a discussion of the terms neoliberalism and minimal state. In line with the objective mentioned above, it is incredibly significant why a minimal state as a term matters for the project of neoliberalism. In such regard, the paper starts with a brief kick-off discussion on neoliberalism to be coupled with a systematic analysis of the term minimal state.

2.1 Understanding Neoliberalism

Neoliberalism emerges as the economic project of the New Right Movement that has been a final movement of thought of the restructuring of the Western World with its kick-off triggered by the mid-1970s petrol crisis. By the early 1980s, neoliberalism championed the remaking of the state and related public mechanism along with the requisites of the markets. In the words of Simon et al. (2016:2) neoliberalism is defined as such at a more euphemistic level: "we are generally referring to the new political, economic and social arrangements within society that emphasise market relations, re-tasking the role of the state, and individual responsibility. Most scholars tend to agree that neoliberalism is broadly defined as the extension of competitive markets into all areas of life, including the economy, politics and society."

In such regard, privatisation, austerity, deregulation, and free trade came to be the tools of neoliberal projects and started to be implemented in many sections of the world on a global scale in line with an all over embracing tide of economic liberalisation. Teeple (2000:81) reiterates about the making of neoliberalism that "*neoliberal policies, variously labelled as Thatcherism, Reaganism, neo-conservatism, and the New Right Agenda, were discernible by the mid-1970s and had become formal government policy in many countries by the end of that decade. They are the policy side of the "new reality;" they represent the political requirements of capital internationalised, highly centralised, and global in perspective. They also represent the last national policies to be promulgated, the final act of the independent nation-state, because with their acceptance the economic and political barriers to production and distribution around the world will have been minimised. With their adoption, they will have in effect harmonised the national with the global economy.*" Indeed, neoliberalism also foresaw in reductions of public expenditures while assuming a dominant role for the private sector with the ultimate aim of leaving many public provision of goods and services to their private counterparts. Indeed, neoliberalism was also an important economic project to challenge the Keynesian welfare state against which it coalesced with neo-conservative elements. While the project is located within the scheme of neoclassical economics, at an ideological level, the term has come to be more and more quoted with the notion of minimal state referring to a position that government leaves many fields of public provision of goods and services thereby being limited to very fundamental services of a minimal state. Teeple (2000:105) explains succinctly with a more left fashion as such in relation to the downsizing of the government: "Downsizing in this sense means the abrogation of government responsibilities for the social and economic well-being of society; it means the redefinition of public duties by the state or the reshaping of the boundaries between civil society and the state, so that intervention by the state in the affairs of civil society are hereafter constitutionally or legally restricted. Hence the importance of the constitutional enshrinement of the rights of private property. Social and economic reforms are to be reduced to a minimum and the state prevented from re-establishing them. The objective is the minimal state on the one side and the mythical market on the other – the "market" being simply another name for the unrestrained power of private corporate property. The autocracy of private property is the utopia of the neo-liberal."

2.2 Minimal State: Theoretical Underpinnings of the Term

The minimal state of the libertarian thought also known as a "night's watchman state" can be understood regarding propositions of the neoliberal project that became the model state understanding by the mid-1980s. At a theoretical level, the minimal state is a government which limits itself with the police, military, and court services. Indeed, it is a call for recessing back to the preservation of the ideals of classical liberalism with emphasis on basic inalienable rights of individuals. For an overall theoretical elaboration, the minimal state can be understood in a general theoretical framework of libertarianism. From such a perspective the work will give an overview of the minimal state using subscribing to two liberal thinkers, namely Nozick and Hayek. For a start, the libertarianism sets the ground for the minimal state for a contextual reading. In the words of Garner (2009:1) it is such a context in which: "Individuals' rights are best understood as being property rights, and people have full or pretty full property rights over themselves, as self-owners, and over any land not already owned that they are the first to use and mix their labour with. These rights can be transferred by voluntary agreement or fulfilment of debt, thus granting to recipients also full ownership of these things or their derivatives. Further, people have a right to do with their property, or that of consenting others, what they wish. The Only legitimate use of force is to ensure this ability, by enforcing these property rights against force, fraud or theft. Any violation of these rights and any other use of force are called "aggression," or "the initiation of force," and are illegitimate. Force used in defence against aggression, or in retaliation to it, may be called legitimate." Henceforth libertarianism is a general framework which defines the term liberty as the absence of coercion.

One of the greatest champions of the minimal state, namely, Robert Nozick's approach succinctly puts forth the dimensions of the minimal state. The inalienability of essential trilogy of liberal rights is of utmost importance, leaving no room for the state intervention, whereby Nozick (1974: ix) states as follows: "Individuals have rights, and there are things no person or group may do to them (without violating their rights). So strong and far-reaching are these rights that they raise the question of what, if anything, the state and its officials may do. How much room do individual rights leave for the state?"

The fundamental propositions of the libertarian minimal state understanding hinge upon "the separateness of each person, the existence of inviolable rights, and the side constraint that these rights impose on the behaviour of others" (Patterson, 2005: 168). Accordingly, morality, rational agency and free-will are the most defining characteristics of the individuals. Along with such traits Patterson (2005:168) quotes Nozick such that "(a person) a being able to formulate long-term plans for its life, able to consider and decide on the basis of abstract principles or considerations it formulates to itself and hence not merely the plaything of immediate stimuli, a being able to limit its in accordance with some principles or picture it has of what an appropriate life is for itself and others and so on."

The very assumptions of the minimal state are inextricably linked to the concept of spontaneous order more worked out by the 20th-century political economy thinker Friedrich von Hayek. Spontaneous order can be defined as a by-product of the unintended platform of many individual interactions, aiming not for the service of common aims but at particular results for individuals. Pursuing their purposes, the related agents do not target and end up in promoting an overall pattern of order. Nonetheless, a learning process to conform to the shared norms and constraints will emerge out of the processes. This will bring forth an orderly, effective, and efficient interactions and exchanges (Friedman, 2008: 1–10).

Human action produces spontaneous order but not the human design. It is not a willed, created order. Hayek argues that there are no rooms left for the centralised will to design social order, while the divine will as the source behind social order is not a matter of concern. Henceforth the source of order can be tracked to the physical world (Kley, 1994: 111; 119–120).

Spontaneous order for an economic system is of paramount importance in which the very dynamics of economics such as market prices along with social norms come to be elucidated within the emergence happening as a result of many human interactions. Decentralized decision-making in spontaneous orders thus shall avoid interventions into economic and social systems whose aftermaths take its toll on unintended consequences, which are often quite the reverse of what is intended (Hayek, 1969: 97–99).

2.3 Minimal State from a Public Finance Perspective

The very functions and duties of the state have been debated as the state has come out of the needs of the collective action for the organisation of the society. Economic functions of the state have changed over time based on economic, social, and political reasons, thereby leading to more active participation in economic life for the state. More and more questions have been raised about the inefficiencies due to the intervention of the state into economic life. The minimal state understanding limiting its sphere of activities to a very confined terrain pronounced rhetoric by neoliberalism has been the primary reference point for the new era of neoliberalism. This limits the state to its essential functions of justice, national defence, security, and law. (Tayyar & Küçük, 2013:113).

In the minimal state understanding, it has been argued that the intervention of the state into economic life shall lead to low growth levels, unjust wealth distribution. Realizing the market failures of competitive markets, the market approaches are considered to be more effective than government intervention. Henceforth, market mechanisms are not perfect, yet they are more active so to speak. The following critiques have been directed to government intervention (Zafir; 2009:70): First and foremost, government infrastructure investments are not productive and effective. Second, the direct participation of government in the production processes lead to the under capacity functioning of the private sector coupled with the problem of employment. Such losses will lead and contribute to deficits in public finance mechanism. Third, rent-seeking politicians pursue to maximise their interests along with the close circles, thereby attaining personal gains. While this affects the credibility of politicians, it brings forth the overspending problem.

From the post-1990s perspective more and more critiques have been oriented to the minimal state. Indeed, a somewhat transformation to quasi-welfare state configuration has been on the rise. In such a context, public expenditures as shares of the GNP have risen significantly. In other words, the government's involvement in national economies has increased, thereby leading to the expenditures that lead to welfare gains. Public expenditures' shares as the ratio of GNP have reached a very high level though they have maintained decreased or rendered constant (Sandalcı & Sandalcı; 2016:414). The regulatory state has been the type above of state by World bank reports starting as of 1997.

Tab 1. Average Public Sector Size Shares in Selected Countries 2000–2014

France 54,06	Portugal 47,05	Japan 39,7
Denmark 53,87	Germany 45,54	USA 38,09
Switzerland 53,65	Iceland 44,93	Ukraine 34,78
Greece 52,18	The Netherlands 44,77	Turkey 37,45
Sweden 52,17	Australia 44,55	South Korea 30,24
Belgium 51,60	Norway 43,83	Jordan 30,05
Finland 51,39	UK 43,75	Egypt 28,94
Austria 51,26	Czech 42,64	Latvia 27,94
Hungary 49,42	Spain 41,62	Brazil 24,55
Italy 49,11	Luxembourg 41,59	Armenia 19,76

Source: (Sandalcı &Sandalcı; 2016:418)

Regulatory state as a form of state-directed through markets and civil society has been charged with the management of the transformation to the innovative and entrepreneurial economy. Within this contextual reading the profile of the state has changed with the three main categorical functions of the state put respectively (Zafir; 2009:75–76): First minimal functions referred to the supply of pure public goods. Intermediary Functions come onto the stage secondly referring the internalisation of negative externalities, the deregulation of natural monopolies, asymmetric information problem's remedy, and social security services. Activist functions, lastly, are regarding those redistributive functions and coordination of private sector coordination.

It is observed that even in the most notoriously liberal known countries, shares of public expenditures as of GNP have risen. According to the table, the ratio of increase in developed countries has surpassed those ratios of the developing countries. This situation may be owing to the presences of more consolidated welfare state structures in developed countries and is not an only determinant factor. The experienced financial crises also contribute to the increasing role of the public sector. For example, with the 2008 Financial crisis' aftermath, the rise has been more than observable, Ireland being the most significant one whereby public expenditures have skyrocketed to 67 %. The rises have surpassed more than 50 % for countries like Denmark, France, Finland, Belgium, Sweden, the UK, the Netherlands, and Portugal (Güngör, 2017:272). In the aftermath of 2008 Financial Crisis, ratio of share of public expenditures as share of GNP has recorded falls, remaining at an average of 40,9 % for the OECD countries in the year of 2015 (OECD, 2017:73).

Tab 2. The Growth of General Government Expenditure, 1870–1996 (Percent of GDP)

Years	1870	1913	1920	1937	1960	1980	1990	1996
The ratio of general government expenditure to GDP (%)	10,8	13,1	19,6	23,8	28,0	41,9	43,0	45,0

Source: Table produced with data drawn by authors (Tanzi and Schuknect, 2000: 6)

Tab 3. The Ratio of Total Expenditure to GDP (%)

The ratio of total expenditure to GDP (%)	1980–1989	1990–1999	2000–2010	1980–2010
World	30,70	27,30	26,90	28,30
Developing countries	21,10	18,60	20,90	20,20
Developed countries	33,80	31,50	31,00	32,00

Source: Table produced with data drawn by authors from (Yu et al., 2015: 356)

The focal point of discussion of the current debate, in the light of data depicted in Tab 1 is to be related to the effectiveness, efficiencies and quality of public expenditures, rather than the simple ratio of public expenditures as shares of GNP.

The results of a study carried out by Tanzi and Schuknecht for the growth of the general government expenditures for Australia, Austria, Canada, France, Germany, Italy, Ireland, Japan, New Zealand, Norway, Sweden, Switzerland, United Kingdom, United States, Belgium, Netherlands, and Spain have been shown in the Tab 2.

In the examined countries, the ratio of general government expenditure to GDP (%) has tended to increase over the years; in particular, it has reached extraordinarily high rates in the post-1980s perspective.

A study realised by Yu et al. (2015) examined the ratio of total expenditure to GDP thereby reaching the results in Tab 3.

The present study has reorganised the table drawn by the authors from The Statistics on Public Expenditure for Economic Development (SPEED). Accordingly, the ratio of total expenditure to GDP (%) was subjected to the classification of developing countries and developed countries and compared along decades.

While the world average decreased along the years, the average of the developing countries decreased over the 1990s, yet increased between 2000 and

2010. The case for developed countries decreased over the years along the world average yet resulting around a 31%.

3 Trajectory of the Expenditures of General Budget Institutions within the GDP: The Case of Modern Turkey

The present section evaluates the trajectory of development of public expenditures' share within the GDP between 1924 and 2015 in Turkey. According to a theoretical definition, "public expenditures refer to those budgetary allocations granted to the institutions and organizations of general and annexed budgets on a narrow basis, while broadly speaking, it may come to point at the state's expenditures realized by public legal personalities in regard to welfare, public entrepreneurship, local administrations, funds organized outside the budget and other related fields" (Muter et al., 2012:45). According to Legislation Number 5018 Public Financial Management and Control, Law stipulates that general budgetary units are those institutions subject to the legal personality of the government specified within those budgets of governmental units. The first list of the legislation released from this definition will be analyzed according to different time periods: First and foremost 1924–1938 Era which is inclusive of governmental budgetary expenditures aiming to privatize and encourage the foreign direct investment with the advent of Izmir Economic Congress; 1930–1938 Era characterized by post-1929 statist-oriented economic planning oriented years in the aftermath of the Great Depression; Second, 1939–1945 Era a time of WWII period; third, 1949–1960 Era an period of passage to and multi-party politics; fourth, 1961–1980 an era of planned economy and industrialization in the aftermath of the 1960 Coup d'état; 1980–2001: a fifth phase of launch of neoliberalism; and finally 2001–2016 an ultimate stage whereby the role of the state came to be transformed into a regulatory and supervising body with the data available for the relevant time periods.

3.1 The Share of Public Expenditures of General Budget Institutions within GDP between 1924 and 1929

Along with the resolutions of İzmir Economic Congress, plans for the formation of the sui-generis market economic structure were put forth along with the need of government to intervene into economics due to prevailing circumstances of the time (Hafızoğulları, 2000: 302). Two definitive characteristics of Turkish political economy setting for the period above. Étatism and protectionism have characterised this era which may qualify as the first era of industrialisation from the perspective of the implementation of economic policy (Boratav, 2007:321). The Turkish experience between 1924 and 1930 present no clear performance along with the targets of fast "economic growth" and "economic independence" (Kepenek and Yentürk, 2000: 61). On such grounds, statist policies came to be implemented in line with financing, thanks to the general budget. The following table has been produced using the data between 1924 and 1939.

In the specified period between 1924 and 1938, the very share of general budget governmental units was realised around 10,83%, thereby gaining momentum to increase yet with a fluctuating rate. The lowest level of this share came to materialise around 10,22 % in the year of 1929 due to the impact and the effects of the Great Depression. The very 10,83% realization in 1926, notwithstanding the decreases within the budgetary figures can be explained thanks to the plummeting figures of GDP with an 8,13 % relative to the previous year (The "Muhassasatı Zatiye" expenditure classification was omitted from the budget within the same time interval accompanied with the added units of expenditures known as "Varıdatı Mahsusa", "Harita Müdüriyeti Umumiyesi" and "Limanlar

Tab 4. Share of General Budget Institutions within the GDP- Change of GDP in percentage relative to the previous year- Percentage Change of General Budget relative to the previous year between 1924 and 1938

	General Budget/GDP	Change in GDP	Percentage Change in GDP
1924	10,83	-	-
1925	13,16	-26,5	53,77
1926	10,38	8,13	-14,77
1927	13,44	-10,83	15,47
1928	12,24	10,66	0,84
1929	10,22	26,95	5,97
1930	13,21	-23,58	-1,25
1931	14,88	-12,32	-1,22
1932	18,04	-15,77	2,14
1933	17,99	-2,81	-3,1
1934	18,77	6,74	11,38
1935	19,75	7,79	13,4
1936	15,65	29,22	2,44
1937	17,17	6,6	16,89
1938	16,58	4,86	1,29

Source: Table produced with data drawn by authors from BUMKO, 2018 and TUİK, 2018

İdaresi"). The highest percentages in this period belong to the year of 1935 which can be explained regarding the increases in the GDP with a 7,79% relative to the previous year as realised in the National Economy Ministry's share in 1925.

3.2 The Share of Public Expenditures of General Budget Institutions within GDP between 1939 and 1945

Turkey located herself as a neutral state using non-aggression pacts and treaties as a non "non-belligerent" country in the World War II (WWII) years (Ortaylı, 2018: 89). Defence expenditures soared, henceforth increasing the expenditures of general budgeted units despite the neutral status of the country. The war regulations on the economy were imposed before the War and interventions, and active controls on the economy were implemented with the active hand of government, therefore paving the way for a perfect war economy (Şahin, 1997:75). An analysis of this period would demonstrate as follows:

In an era of World War II whose impact became more than apparent all around the world, the lowest share was realised around 11,05% in 1945 while the highest rate of share remained around 22,68% in 1940. A great deal downturn is more than visible for the GDP and other budgetary figures for 1945. The high rate of realisation in 1941 may be explained with an increase in expenditures of the Ministry of National Defense accompanied by a low rate of GDP. GDP and budgetary allocations recorded a significant decrease for 1945. In particular, the year of 1942 witnessed increases in figures as the Ministry of National Defense shares including ground, naval, air, and gendarmerie forces expenditures units

Tab 5. Share of General Budget Institutions within the GDP- Change of GDP in percentage relative to the previous year- Percentage Change of General Budget relative to the previous year between 1939 and 1945

	General Budget/GDP	Change in GDP	Percentage Change in GDP
1939	19,09	8,85	25,34
1940	22,68	16,65	38,56
1941	19,55	24,48	7,3
1942	14,81	106,8	56,63
1943	11,22	48,94	12,92
1944	16,18	-27,58	4,41
1945	11,05	-18,16	-44,13

Source: Table produced with data drawn by authors from BUMKO, 2018 and TUİK, 2018

soared incredibly. The continuation of the war led to the fluctuations in the economy rendering also volatile shares.

3.3 The Share of Public Expenditures of General Budget Institutions within GDP between 1946 and 1960

The increasing burden on Turkey as land claims in the post-WW2 perspective has contributed to the increasing costs of defence and delayed the return to the state of peace (I. Beş Yıllık Kalkınma Planı, 1963:10). Liberalization policies initiated by Democrat Party aimed to limit the intervention of government with strong incentives to support private sector (Kongar, 2006:358). In a de facto sense, DP governments preferred to foster the private sectors by the very hand of the public sector (Tunçay, 1997:180). In this new brave world of the post WW2 setting and a new political economy setting the analysis would show the following findings for Turkey as such:

In the aftermath of the introduction of multi-party politics, the highest rate of realisation appeared around 20,8 %. The underlying reason behind this jump is

Tab 6. Share of General Budget Institutions within the GDP – Change of GDP in percentage relative to the previous year – Percentage Change of General Budget relative to the previous year between 1946 and 1960

	General Budget/GDP	Change in GDP	Percentage Change in GDP
1946	14,9	25,54	69,3
1947	20,8	9,98	53,53
1948	15	25,8	-9,28
1949	17,64	-4,64	12,19
1950	15,39	7,09	-6,57
1951	13,94	20,1	8,76
1952	17,16	15,02	41,6
1953	15,06	16,52	2,24
1954	16,53	2,05	12,04
1955	17,69	20,25	28,68
1956	16,16	15,39	5,39
1957	14,45	32,99	18,97
1958	14,47	19,35	19,53
1959	15,74	24,97	35,91
1960	16,02	6,95	8,86

Source: Table produced with data drawn by authors from BUMKO, 2018 and TUİK, 2018

due to 20,80 increase of general budget owing to increases of state debts by 200% henceforth paving the way to increases in the general budget with a 53,53% increase, recording a 9,98 increase in GDP. The lowest realisation emerged as 13,94% in the year 1951. Favourable climate conditions, intensification of agricultural production, mechanisation of agricultural sectors, increases in inputs yielded up to a 9,93% increase annually, therefore being the most determinant factor the GDP growth between 1947 and 1953 (Temel et al., 2002:51).

3.4 The Share of Public Expenditures of General Budget Institutions within GDP between 1961 and 1980

In the post-1960s Turkish political economy setting new planning, era kicked off for the Turkish economic policymaking. The first five-year-developmental plan was put into implementation between 1963 and 1967 including investment policies (Boratav, 1997:326). The reduction in purchasing power due to the economic crisis, suggestions for Turkey to put public expenditures and investments into a program by foreign creditors in particular and internal and external dynamics paved the way to the making of a planned economy era for Turkey (Kepenek and Yentürk, 2000:141–142). Keynesian policies became the motto of the day along with the fact that public economic planning and democratic planning became the preconditions of growth and development. (Şahin, 1997: 116–117). The developments are depicted in Tab 7.

Following the 1960 coup d'état, the highest share of general budget institutions' shares within the GDP reached up to 23,33% in 1961, which can be explained owing to the low increase in GDP with a 6,07% and a sudden increase in expenditures around 54,44%. While a low rate emerges around 13,35% for the mentioned share in 1968 because exact opposite circumstances versus 1961 emerged in the problematized year. That is to say, increases in GDP elevated to 61,60% while the public expenditures of general budget institutions took an increase of 5,09%.

3.5 The Share of Public Expenditures of General Budget Institutions within GDP between 1981 and 2000

Notwithstanding the end of Keynesian policies, the rise of petroleum prices, development of international trade, the internationalising characteristic of inflation, and problems of balance of payments made it imperative for governments to intervene in the economy (Oktayer and Susam, 2008:146). Economic liberalisation having kicked off with the withdrawal of government from interventions into the market economy paves the way to the rationalisation of public service deliveries

Tab 7. The Share of General Budget Institutions within the GDP – Change of GDP in Percentage Relative to the Previous Year – Percentage Change of General Budget Relative to the Previous Year between 1961 and 1980

	General Budget/GDP	Change in GDP	Percentage Change in GDP
1961	23,33	6,07	54,44
1962	16,17	16,15	-19,49
1963	17,93	15,61	28,2
1964	19,36	6,83	15,36
1965	19,42	6,94	7,27
1966	19,48	18,75	19,12
1967	20,53	11,47	17,45
1968	13,35	61,6	5,09
1969	14,19	11,77	18,78
1970	16,31	12,48	29,27
1971	18,66	24,08	41,95
1972	17,42	19,53	11,57
1973	17,55	25,79	26,77
1974	15,65	35,61	20,9
1975	17,49	29,64	44,92
1976	18,63	27,12	35,37
1977	22,61	27,95	55,29
1978	21,97	48,87	44,65
1979	22,02	74,63	75,09
1980	21,67	83,49	80,58

Source: Table produced with data drawn by authors from BUMKO, 2018 and TUİK, 2018

all-round the way and a general retrenchment of the government. While the new reality set the target of market economies for the whole capitalist system, global markets were integrated, thanks to the liberalisation of free mobility of commodities, services, and capital on a background of globalisation. (Kazgan quoted by. Oktayer and Susam, 2008:146). In the aftermath of 1970s crisis, austerity measures of January 24th, 1980 were implemented to minimise the state along with the devaluation of Turkish Lira, liberalising foreign trade and imports on a gradual basis, granting financial incentives for export. In the light of these developments, Tab 8 demonstrates as follows for the era between 1981 and 2000:

Yet another military takeover in 1980 introduced a new economic system in Turkey with the problematized share fluctuating around 16,58% in 1982 and

Tab 8. The Share of General Budget Institutions within the GDP – Change of GDP in Percentage Relative to the Previous Year – Percentage Change of General Budget Relative to the Previous Year between 1981 and 2000

	General Budget/GDP	Change in GDP	Percentage Change in GDP
1981	20,41	51,05	42,23
1982	16,58	32,8	7,87
1983	20,95	32,53	67,46
1984	18,97	85,19	43,28
1985	17,87	59,55	50,29
1986	17,84	45,54	45,3
1987	18,84	46,29	54,48
1988	18,73	72,94	71,88
1989	19,82	75,91	86,22
1990	20,58	72,91	79,54
1991	24,14	60,31	88,03
1992	20,23	73,52	45,42
1993	24,43	81,26	118,8
1994	23,02	95,19	83,93
1995	21,96	100,66	91,46
1996	26,51	90,3	129,71
1997	27,72	95,2	104,11
1998	22,03	143,46	93,48
1999	26,62	48,9	80,11
2000	27,83	59,33	66,6

Source: Table produced with data drawn by authors from BUMKO, 2018 and TUİK, 2018

27,83 in 2000. While the same per cent recessed back to 17,87% in 1985, the rate fluctuated around 16,58 % and 19,82 % with the exceptions of the years of 1981 and 1983. The percentage that never went under 20,5% in the 1990s reached 27,83% in 2000. This may be explained under the circumstance of the 1999 Financial Crisis whose impact proceeded until 2000. Fiscal and monetary policies implemented in Turkey since the 1990s created an unstable economic growth environment, thereby bringing high inflation, increasing public debts, interest expenditures contributing to an ever fragile economy. The 1994 Financial Crisis, on the other hand, resulted in the reduction of the concerned rate to 21,96%

3.6 The Share of Public Expenditures of General Budget Institutions within GDP between 2001 and 2016

A severe banking crisis followed by a devaluation of the national currency in Turkey against the other had a devastating effect thereby bringing along a new package of remedies for economic and social recovery. The following principles have shaped the economic policymaking of the governing Justice and Development Party since 2001 as such in their party programs (http://www.akparti.org.tr/site/akparti/parti-programi#bolum, (10.05.2018)): "Our party subscribe to the following principles: The supremacy of free market economy with all rules and regulations, Giving no room for government for the economic involvement in market affairs, The regulatory and auditory role of the government in free markets." In the very same text, the party has vowed for a general reform of expenditures as soon as possible. In such a context, our analysis would yield the following findings for 2001 and 2016.

Tab 9. The Share of General Budget Institutions within the GDP – Change of GDP in Percentage Relative to the Previous Year – Percentage Change of General Budget Relative to the Previous Year between 2001 and 2016

	General Budget/GDP	Change in GDP	Percentage Change in GDP
2001	33,38	44,14	72,87
2002	32,8	45,9	43,37
2003	30,67	29,76	21,33
2004	24,9	22,92	-0,19
2005	22,14	16,08	3,2
2006	23,09	16,87	21,85
2007	23,74	11,18	14,35
2008	23,36	12,73	10,91
2009	32,23	0,21	38,27
2010	26,23	15,35	-6,14
2011	23,66	18,1	6,54
2012	24,96	9,18	15,18
2013	25,35	10,62	12,34
2014	24,84	11,54	9,31
2015	21,03	33,8	13,26
2016	21,82	11,52	15,71

Source: Table produced with data drawn by authors from BUMKO, 2018 and TUİK, 2018

The 2000s brought about overwhelming changes to the Turkish state structure whereby government came to assume a more regulating and supervising role. In the period above, the highest rate appeared around 33,38% while expenditures of general expenditures recorded an increase of 72,87%. The lowest rate stayed around 22,14%, due to the increase in expenditures by 3,20%. The rates realized over 30% was reduced to 20% in 2004 while the lowest rate stayed around 22,14% as general budget expenditures of such institutions increased by 3,20%. The very rate at its lowest level in 2005 as 22,14% climbed up 25,35 % in 2013 and then was contracted to 21,82% as for the year of 2016.

There were many governmental defined as general budget institutions between 2006 and 2011 including a wide array of governmental units, to mention a few such as: Directorate of Family and Social Research, State Personnel, Press and Genera Info, State waterworks, State Highways, Council of National Security, National Revenue Management Directorate, which came to be excluded from general budget classifications in 2012. There were more and more units integrated into such a classification such as the Ministry of Youth and Sports, Public Health Office, Meteorological Directorate, Turkish Public Health Office, etc.

4 Conclusion

The study carries out an analysis which shares of public expenditures of general budget institutions within the GDP regarding their trajectories, with a rate kicking off in 124 with a rate of 10,24% approaching up to 25,19% in the year of 2015. The difference between the early years of the republic and the modern times may be explained in terms of differences between the changing economic circumstances and economic and financial crises that Turkey suffered from. The rises in public expenditures have been used as fiscal policy tools with the aim of income redistribution, economic stability, economic growth, and development in a general framework of Keynesian welfare state. Yet the return of the neoliberal agenda back to the global stage has once again put the minimal state as an ideal. When looked from general budget expenditures the minimal state discourse is less than applicable. 1994 and 2001 Turkey's, 1992 Asia's, 2000 Russia's, 2008 USA's financial crises have contributed to the increases in the public expenditures of general budget governmental units all over the related cases of countries and governmental interventions into the economy.

Indeed, there exists a vast difference between the discourses of a minimal state and the resulting phenomenon that the ideal minimal state was too far to be realised. In other words, the minimal state has always been rhetoric that came odds with the reality. Compared with the American counterpart and other and given the finding of the share of public expenditures remained around 19,5%, the Turkish case represents herself as a terrain where minimal state ideal object was never able to be implemented. This may very well present a point of convergence for Turkey's counterparts which will beg for further work.

References

AK Parti Programı. http://www.akparti.org.tr/site/akparti/parti-programi#bolum_, (10.05.2018).

Bayar, Ali. (1996). "*The Developmental State and Economic Policy in Turkey*". Third World Quarterly, 17(4), 773–785.

Boratav K. (1997). İktisat Tarihi (1908–1980). Tunçay M. (Ed.). *Türkiye Tarihi 4 Çağdaş Türkiye (1908–1980) içinde*. Cem Yayınevi, ss. 265–353.

Boratav, K. (2007). *Yakınçağ Türkiye Tarihi, 1908–1980*, İstanbul: Milliyet Kitaplığı.

Bütçe ve Mali Kontrol Genel Müdürlüğü. (2018). Bütçe Gider-Gelir Gerçekleşmeleri (1924–2016), http://www.bumko.gov.tr/Eklenti/10761,2butcegiderlerixls.xls?0 (09.02.2018).

Doğan, K.C. (2016). "*Küreselleşme ve Neo-Liberal Kuşaklar Çerçevesinde Devleti Konumlandırma Sorunsalı: "Minimal Devlet'ten Düzenleyici Devlet'e*", Uluslararası Sosyal Araştırmalar Dergisi, 9(43), 1795–1803.

Friedman, J. (2008). "*Hayek's Political Philosophy and His Economics*", Critical Review,11(1), 1–10.

Garner, R.A: (2009). "Minarchy Considered", Libertarian Papers 1, 1–61.

Güngör, K. (2017). "*Avrupa Birliği Ülkelerinde Kamu Harcamaları ve Refah Devleti Bağlamında Küresel Krizin Analizi*", Afyon Kocatepe Üniversitesi Sosyal Bilimler Dergisi, 19(2), ss. 267–285.

Hafızoğulları Z. (2000). "İzmir İktisat Kongresi Görüşler ve değerlendirmeler", *Atatürk Araştırma Merkezi Dergisi*, Cilt: XVI, ss. 289–311.

Hayek, Friedrich A. (1969). Studies in Philosophy, Politics and Economics. Touchstone. p. 97.

I. Beş Yıllık Kalkınma Planı (1963). Kalkınma Bakanlığı. http://www.kalkinma.gov.tr/Lists/Kalknma%20Planlar/Attachments/9/plan1.pdf, (22.05.2018).

Kepenek, Y. & Yentürk N. (2000). *Türkiye Ekonomisi*, İstanbul, Remzi Kitabevi.

Keyder, C. (1987a). "*Economic Development and Crisis*" *Turkey in Transition: New Perspectives*. (Ed.) Schick, II and Tonak, A. New York, Oxford University Press.

Keyder, C. (1987b). *State and Class in Turkey: A Study in Capitalist Development*, London, Verso.

Keyder, C. (2004) "*The Turkish Bell Jar*", New Left Review, 28, July-August 2004, pp.65–84.

Kley, R. (1994). *Hayek's Social and Political Thought*, Oxford, Clarendon Press.

Muter, N.B., Çelebi A.K., & Sakınç S. (2012) *Kamu Maliyesi*, 4. Ed., Manisa, Emek Matbaası.

Kongar, E. (2002). *21. Yüzyılda Turkiye: 2000'li yıllarda Türkiye'nin Toplumsal Yapısı*, İstanbul, Remzi Kitabevi.

Kongar E.(2006). *Tarihimizle Yüzleşmek*, İstanbul, Remzi Kitabevi.

Nozick, R. 1974 (1997). *Anarchy, State and Utopia*, Oxford UK and Cambridge, USA: Blackwells.

OECD (2017). *Government at a Glance 2017*, OECD Publishing, Paris http://dx.doi.org/10.1787/gov_glance-2017-en.

Oktayer N. & Susam N. (2008). "*Kamu Harcamaları- Ekonomik Büyüme İlişkisi: 1970–2005 Yılları Türkiye Örneği*". Atatürk Üniversitesi İktisadi ve İdari Bilimler Dergisi, 22 (1), ss.145–164.

Ortaylı, İ. (2018), *Türkiye'nin Yakın Tarihi*, İstanbul, TİMAŞ.

Patterson, R. (2005). "*The Minimal State v the Welfare State: A Critique of the Argument Between Nozick and Rawls*", SCULawRw 7; (2005) 9 Southern Cross University Law Review, pp. 167–182.

Ramazanoglu, H. (1985). *Turkey in the World Capitalist System: A Study of Industrialisation, Power, and Class*, Brookfield, Vt., U.S.A.: Aldershots, Hants, England.

Sandalcı, U. & Sandalcı İ. (2016). "*Kamu Kesimi Ekonomik Büyüklüğü ve Kamu Etkinlik Düzeyi İlişkisi*", Pamukkale Üniversitesi Sosyal Bilimler Enstitüsü Dergisi, 25(1), ss. 413–429.

Simon S. Kean B. MacLeavy J. (2016). *An Introduction to Neoliberalism*, The Handbook of Neoliberalism. NY: Routledge.

Şahin H. (1997) İktisada Giriş, 5. Ed., Bursa, Ezgi Kitabevi.

Tanzi V. & Schuknecht L. (2000). *Public Spending in the 20th Century: A Global Perspective*. United Kingdom: Cambridge University Press.

Tayyar, A., Küçük B. (2013). "*Liberal İktisadi Düşüncede Devlet*", C.Ü. İktisadi ve İdari Bilimler Dergisi, Cilt 14(1), 2013, ss. 107–120.

Teeple, G. (2000). *Globalization and the Decline of Social Reform*, Aurora: Garamond Press.

Teeple, G. (2000). *The Decline of Social Reform*, Toronto, Garamond Press.

Temel A.& Boyar E. & Saygılı Ş. (2002). "Türkiye Ekonomisinde Yapisal Değişim (1946–1999)", http://www.kalkinma.gov.tr/Documents/temela.pdf, (12.02.2018).

Tunçay M. (1997). Siyasal Tarih (1908–1980). Tunçay M. (Ed.). *Türkiye Tarihi 4 Çağdaş Türkiye (1908–1980) içinde*. Cem Yayınevi, ss. 177–184.

Türkiye İstatistik Kurumu Başkanlığı. (2018). Gayri Safi Yurtiçi Hasıla, 1923–2015, http://tuik.gov.tr/PrelstatistikTablo.do?istab_id=2218, (05.02.2018).

Yu B. & Fan S. (2015). "Trends and Composition of Public Expenditures: A Global and Regional Perspective", European Journal of Development Research, 27(3), 353–370.

Zafir, C. Z. (2009). "*NeoLiberalizmin Minimal Devlet Anlayışına Bir Eleştiri*", Yönetim Bilimleri Dergisi 7, ss. 265–282.

Ufuk Selen

The Effects of WTO Agreements on Public Finance

Abstract: The global economic integration of national economies can be achieved through foreign trade policies, which are shaped by the market economy. While foreign trade policies integrate the national economy as a real economy in the global economy, it also influences the approach of other policy areas to market economy conditions. This interaction is also observed in the field of public finance. The (WTO) agreements and mechanisms, which are the main actors in the establishment of the free trade system, have an influence that limits the powers of taxation and expenditure of nation states. From this point of view, in this study, it is aimed to evaluate the reflection of the free trade system on public finance understanding. In today's world trade system, the state, especially for conservation purposes, taxation and expenditure initiatives are significantly limited. The WTO's limitation of the state's power of taxation and expenditure arises at the following points: the Member States in relation to the use of the power of taxation, reduce customs tax rates, fall under tariff commitments and have to comply with the defined procedures for the determination of specific tax subjects and bases.

Keywords: World Trade Organization, Dispute Settlement Mechanism, Power of Taxation, International Trade

JEL Codes: F13, F10, P45, H2

1 Introduction

The global economic integration of national economies is provided by foreign trade policies, which were shaped by the free market economy. While foreign trade policies integrate the national economy in real terms with the global economy, it also influences the approach of other policy areas to free market economy conditions. This interaction is also observed in the field of public finance. WTO Agreements and mechanisms, which are the main actors in the establishment of the free trade system, have a limiting effect on the taxation and spending powers of the nation states (Hoekman and Kostecki, 1995).

From this point of view, the reflections of the free trade system to the understanding of public finance have been studied.

The WTO's limitation of the state's taxation and spending powers arises at the following points:

- rebate in customs tax rates,
- tariff commitments,
- Adhere to defined procedures in the determination of specific tax subjects and bases. Similarly, public spending authority has suppressed from procedural, qualitative and quantitative aspects. At this point, the principles and rules observed in subsidy applications, public commercial operation and public procurement are shaping public spending policies. Under the direction of the minimal state approach, the question arises as to how the opening of authority created by the reduction of the national authority. in the economy will fill. In other words, the problem of global governance has felt. Increasing international interactions in the world economy reveal different areas of conflict.

Increasing international interaction in the world economy reveals different areas of conflict. The most significant example of this is the attempt by developed countries to dominate the international system and to move the national autonomy to the international level (Qureshi, 1996). International autonomy is developing in a confrontational and competitive environment, as the "Realistic State" approach to explaining international relations also implies. At the same time it is dynamic (Bell, 2017). This competitive structure has also observed in the international trade system. The risks associated with conflicting relationships on the system brings with it the need for a global authority (Bell, 2017). For the dominant nation-states are establishing intra-system balances. They cannot directly use the international authority. Therefore, it is necessary to establish a structure of national autonomies and accept autonomy recognised by all states (Potter, 1992).

Today, the free trade system is being tried to be managed by international organisations. International organisations such as the UN, WB, IMF, and WTO, which have been established especially after World War II, have played an essential role in determining and implementing the rules of the free trade system (Kazgan, 1997). These organisations are seeking worldwide acceptance of the standards they have developed in the areas of their activities. These organisations carry out their work with the motive of the conflicts of norms in international law (Yılmaz, 2004). Conflicts of norms, which recognise that international treaty rules are stronger than domestic rules, give these organisations a supranational character.

The WTO regulations, which have become operative under the norm of conflicts of norms, constitute the "constitution" of commercial activities carried out on a wide range of grounds ranging from goods and services trade to intellectual property rights (Will and Winters 1995).

With this feature, the WTO has played an essential role in the operation of the trading system. We summarised the structure and status of the WTO.

2 Structures and Agreements of World Trade Organization

The primary objective of the WTO is to eliminate economic barriers to international trade and ensure tariff reductions are achieved (Nguyen, Perronı and Wıgle, 1993). This objective can be seen in the Agreement Establishing. The objectives of the WTO Agreements include "raising standards of living, ensuring full employment and a large and steadily growing volume of real income and effective demand, and expanding the production of and trade in goods and services"; in other words, developing the world economy under market-economy principles. In order to contribute to these objectives, the WTO Agreements were established to enter into reciprocal and mutually advantageous arrangements designed for the substantial reduction of tariffs and other barriers to trade and the elimination of discriminatory treatment in international trade relations. This means that to introduce market-economy principles into international trade, from the two ideas: (1) reducing trade barriers, and (2) applying non-discriminatory rules. In summary, it expressed that the development of the multilateral trading system aimed at protecting GATT's principles by the market economy. States that the Member States of all agreements are binding on the WTO. Emphasizing that the WTO has established a common institutional structure for the continuation of commercial relations between the Member States[1]. WTO with the Agreement Establishing; implementation of additional agreements, the creation of a forum for continuing the tradition of negotiations, the operation of mechanisms of dispute settlement and trade policy monitoring. Thus, it establishes a platform for the monitoring of international commercial problem settlement and national trade policy applications. Another task of the WTO is to play a role as a tool in regulating trade relations among member countries. In particular, this task comes to the forefront in talks on the development and further liberalisation of the international trade system.

It also emphasised that it has a related aspect as an element in the management of the global economy. In the III / 5th article of the agreement establishing,

---

1 . The typical institutional structure of the WTO and the binding commitment of the Agreement Establishing are related to the additional issues of the WTO beyond the multiple trade agreements, and the issues set out in the legal texts attached to them.

the Member States joined by the expression "the WTO will cooperate with the IMF and the WB and its affiliated institutions to ensure greater consistency in the determination of the global economic policy". With this article, Organization's mission is defined to make it easier for the global economy to fulfil its mission of being an agent.

The Article IV of the Agreement Establishing states that the Member States should fulfil certain obligations in order to fulfil their obligations under the WTO by emphasising the legal personality of the WTO. These obligations are:

I. formation of the legal environment,
ii. Providing the necessary privileges and immunities,
iii. to recognize the necessary privileges and immunities for organizational officials and country representatives to be able to fulfil their WTO related tasks in an independent manner [2],
iv. Guaranteed privileges and immunities.

Another article of the Agreement Establishing, with strengthening the WTO's ability to become a global economic agent, is the IV article. In this article, the General Council is given the authority to make arrangements to improve co-operation with intergovernmental organisations and independent governments related to WTO responsibilities.

Just as the decision-making authority of the WTO does not transfer to the governing body, the administrative or bureaucratic bodies of the institution do not influence the individual policies of the member countries. However, WTO limits its Member States to independent policy-making through sanction mechanisms. Member States supported through sanctions on compliance with WTO rules. However, Member States play a direct role in the implementation of the sanctions, not the WTO. Member countries are working to bring the opposing party and parties that are deviating from the principles of the WTO into line with the principles by operating the Dispute Settlement Mechanism (DSM). If the DSM decisions are not complied with, the complainant is entitled to sanction, and it is defined that the use of sanction by DSM. While this legal infrastructure constitutes the source of power that the WTO has, it also increases expectations from the WTO.

2 It is essential that immunity and privileges ensured by the United Nations General Assembly in accordance with the "Agreement on the Concession and Immunities of the Specialist Institutions" approved on 21 November 1947.

The WTO Agreements, which regulate very different issues related to trade, can be examined in a dual systematic way regarding binding Member States. WTO Agreements are classified in two forms as "Multilateral Agreements" and "Plurilateral Agreements" regarding binding characteristics. Multilateral Trade Agreements are treaties that all Member States and new member countries automatically agree to sign with the WTO Agreement Establishing. Agreements that are not covered by Annex 4 is called "Multilateral Trade Agreements". That is, a state that wants to become a member of the WTO has to recognise and sign all agreements and other regulations attached to them outside Annex 4.

The WTO derives its binding power from the Multilateral Trade Agreements at the point of independent decision-making in member countries' relations with foreign trade. Within the scope of Multilateral Trade Agreements, there is the Agreement Establishing and its three additional agreements.

Annexe 1: The agreements contain agreements and protocols regulating the trade of goods, services and intellectual property rights. Annex 1-A consists of the GATT 1994 agreement and 12 additional agreements aimed at liberalising commodity trading directly. The GATT 1994 includes the GATT Agreement signed in 1947 and the regulations already in place since the establishment of the GATT. Annexe 1B, the General Agreement on Trade in Services, texts on specific services sectors, and individual countries' specific commitments and exemptions; and annexe – 1C, the Agreement on Trade-Related Aspects of Intellectual Property Rights. Collectively, the agreements included in Annex 1 are referred to as the Multilateral Trade Agreements, since they comprise the substantive trade policy obligations which all the members of the WTO have accepted.

The Annex 2 Treaties regulate the structure and functioning of the dispute settlement mechanism that gives the WTO sanction. The Annex 3 Agreement group regulates the structure and functioning of the Trade Policies Tracking Mechanism established to monitor member countries' trade policies.

"Plurilateral Agreements" are agreements that the Member States are arbitrarily parties too. Although Member States have signed the WTO accession treaty, these agreements are not binding on all Member States. In other words, countries that are not parties to the Treaty did not oblige. "Plurilateral Agreements" consist of two agreements[3]: "Civil Aircraft Trade Agreement" and "State Purchase Agreement".

---

3 The "International Dairy Products Agreement" and the "International Cattle Meal Agreement" were also regulated in the context of Plurilateral agreements, but these two agreements abolished in 1997.

In the context of these agreements, the impact of the WTO on public finance has examined in the following section.

3 WTO Agreements Affecting Public Finance

The WTO generally derives its power to influence national economic policies, in particular, public goods, from the Foundation Agreement. It is stated in the Foundation Agreement that the WTO established as a joint institutional structure, which would provide additional cooperation and mechanisms, and that all additional agreements are binding for the member countries. The binding provisions of the enterprise agreement limit the policy-making and enforcement initiatives of Member States.

The impact of the WTO on the use of public finance instruments is as follows: the first observed effect is related to taxation. In this context, Member States must reduce tariff rates, enter tariff commitments, and comply with defined procedures for the determination of specific tax subjects and bases. The second domain is for the use of spending authority. The use of public spending authority is the process, combination and quantity suppression of spending. These effects can see in the context of the "Public Procurement Agreement" and the "Subsidies and Countervailing Measures Agreement" obligations.

3.1 Agreements Affecting Power of Taxation

The impact of the WTO on taxation empowerment arises in the context of economic activities linked to international trade. Under the WTO agreements, the necessary regulations on customs duties can see in the implementation of the "most favoured nations" and "national treatment" rules. As a natural consequence of the "most favoured nations" rule, it has begun to be used as a "tariff concessions list" application tool. Member countries bound by the rates of customs duty on these lists. These lists are lists in which each member is committed to non-discriminatory actions to be applied by the other members. Once a rate of duty is bound, it may not raise without compensating the affected Members. The tariff concessions or "bindings" of each WTO Member are set out in that particular WTO Member's Schedule of concessions on goods. Countries are explaining concession lists linked to these lists themselves. Therefore, Member States cannot abandon their concessions or change the rates of customs unilaterally. However, countries that fall into the balance of payments crisis as an exceptional practice may deviate temporarily from the concession lists, if deemed necessary.

The implementation of the concession lists is binding regarding customs duties received during the customs procedure. That is, the concession lists do not include a commitment regarding internal taxes on imported goods. However, according to Article III of the GATT 1994 agreement, the internal taxation and the laws, regulations and communiqués affecting the sale, sale, purchase and transport of the products in the domestic market shall not apply to domestic, imported products in a way that protects the domestic product. This rule is designed to prevent discrimination in all domestic legislation. According to this arrangement, products imported from a Member State of the WTO shall not be subject to any more unfavourable treatment than those applied to similar products of national origin. This rule, called national treatment, is intended to prevent discriminatory practices.

How to determine the customs tax base is regulated by the two agreements included in the Agreement Establishing. These agreements contain arrangements for the determination of the base of the customs duty and the determination of the rate at which many tariffs apply. The contents of these agreements discussed below.

3.1.1 Customs Valuation Agreement

3.1.1.1 Regulations on the Determination of Customs Validity (Agreement on the Implementation of Article VII of GATT 94)

Magna Carta's day-to-day taxation authority is continually restricted and linked to certain principles. In today's global economic conditions, we see that the taxation authority is limited at the international level as well as nationally. The most concrete example of this can be seen in the WTO agreements. The provisions of the relevant agreements on customs duties limit the areas of action of the Member States at such points as determining the scope and limit of taxation, the use of taxation as a policy instrument, and the determination of tax base and rate regarding tax techniques. For example, countries that declare concession lists may only make the necessary changes within certain rules. The binding declaration of tax rates makes it difficult to use customs taxes as a policy tool. In other words, member countries cannot use customs taxes as they wish in the direction of cyclical fluctuations and other observed economic policy objectives. As a result, determining the customs tax rates for the implementation of the "most favoured country" and "national treatment" rules, and declaring them as concession lists, determines the taxation authority and the tax limit. Regarding the tax technique, the tax rate determines the tax limits as well as the tax base. Regulations for the determination of tax base are attempting to determine the taxation limits of member countries. The aim of these regulations is not to narrow the tax limits of member countries. The primary objective is to provide fair taxation and international economic cooperation. As expressed in the Agreement, Member States have signed an agreement to prevent the use of arbitrary and imaginary customs values, to establish a uniform and impartial customs valuation system, and to accept that customs value should be based on transparent and fair criteria compatible with commercial practice (WTO).

For these purposes, it has been decided that the customs value determination should make by "transaction value". In Article 1 of the related agreement, it states that the customs value of the imported goods is the transaction value, and how the transaction value will apply in the following items explained. The Agreement stipulates that customs valuation shall, except in specified circumstances, be based on the actual price of the goods to be valued, which is generally shown on the invoice. This price, plus adjustments for certain elements listed in Article 8, equals the transaction value, which constitutes the first and most important method of valuation referred to in the Agreement. In order to use "transaction value" in value, it is necessary that there is no restriction which restricts the resale or removal of goods, the condition is not a condition to acquire the asset, or that it is not a matter of acquisition, and that the interest relation between the buyer and the seller does not reflect the commercial relationship.

If one of these three requirements is not met, the "transaction value" cannot be used.

For cases in which there is no transaction value or where the transaction value is not acceptable as the customs, value has distorted as a result of a particular condition. The Agreement lays down five other methods of customs valuation, to be applied in the prescribed hierarchical order[4].

The Agreement, which regulates how these methods are implemented, limits the power of taxation by prohibiting the customs valuation of the Member States concerned. A Member State, by the relevant provisions, may not impose reservations on the provisions of this Agreement without the consent of the other Member States. Regarding the customs valuation, the obligation to obtain the approval of the other member countries of the WTO is necessary for any national savings to be made against the provisions of the agreement. At the

---

4 Other valuation methods in the Agreement: "Transaction value of identical goods", "Transaction value of similar goods", "Deductive method", "Computed method", "Fall-back method".

same time, all WTO members are obliged to make arrangements harmonised with their national legislation and to inform the Customs Valuation Technical Committee about the changes made.

The power of taxation of countries is also affected by the application of tax rate as well as the determination of the value. Primarily, regarding multiple tariff applications, the origin regulations affect the use of the power of taxation.

3.1.1.2 Agreement on Rules of Origin

In the globalisation process, regional economic integrations have become widespread which includes preferential commercial practices. It has made it necessary to use multiple tariffs, which include the rates of discriminatory customs taxes in favour of the parties for the integration. Member countries use different customs duty rates for the same goods at the time of importation from different countries. The use of multiple tariffs has brought about the problem of detecting origin. "Agreement on Rules of Origin" has been signed in the WTO to provide international uniformity in the detection of origin.

In Article 1 of the Agreement, the rules of origin are accepted as administrative savings for the law, regulation and general practice applied by the members to determine the country of origin of the goods. These rules are broad enough to encompass many aspects, such as the operation of the most favoured nation rules, the application of anti-dumping and compensatory taxes, safeguard measures and quantitative restrictions and particular tariff applications. They will also include rules of origin for government procurement and trade statistics.

Due to the globalisation of trade and production relations, the importance of the rules of origin is increasing. Today, the production process of a product can be realised in more than one country. In such a case, it is difficult to determine the origin of the goods. In order to determine the origin correctly, it considered where the production process of the goods completed. If the goods are produced in a single country, they will gain the origin of that country. If the production process of the goods has occurred in more than one country, the product gained the origin of the country where the substantial transformation takes place. Substantial transformation is tied to specific criteria, and these criteria are defined as the rules of origin in the Agreement on Rules of Origin.

The linking of the product to the rules of origin has made it impossible for member countries to apply arbitrary preferential tariffs. Which rules of origin can use are specified in the origin protocols included in the preferential trade agreements. Therefore, Member States have to comply with these protocols in determining the origin of goods. For example, if the importing country does not wish to benefit from the preferential description of a less developed exporting country, it cannot apply a different origin rule than the substantial transformation criteria adopted in the protocol. Where production by the criteria defined in the Agreement on Rules of Origin has performed in the country of origin, the origin of the goods shall be deemed to be that country. Any country cannot object to this provision of the agreement. Thus, in the selection of rates of customs duty, countries are bound by rules of origin.

3.1.2 The Impact of the Agreements on Unfair Competition Elements on Public Finance

The "binding of schedules" and "the most favoured nation" are crucial for the stability of commodity merchandise movements at the international level. WTO agreements support these principles. However, exceptions may occur in certain circumstances. Three points are relevant here. These are: activities against dumping, anti-commercial activities related to state aid, and temporary import restrictions.

The first two of the exceptions are directly related to the use of the power of taxation.

The import which dumped or subsidies may be subject to tax. If the imported goods are dumped and subsidised, there may be an additional tax other than the current customs duty on the import phase. Therefore, this practice contradicts GATT's "national treatment" and "most favoured nation" principles.

These regulations on unfair competition allow Member States to use the "escape clause". It is important to note that the WTO does not allow imports to be carried out at the same time. A description of this topic is given below.

3.1.2.1 The Impact of Anti-dumping Agreement on Public Finance (Agreement on the Implementation of Article VI of GATT 94)

Moving from different micro motivations, selling goods at prices below cost causes market failures. Sales made at a price below cost are defined as dumping and regarded as an element of unfair competition. In order to reduce the trade diversion effect, fight against dumping has been systematised with the "Anti-Dumping Agreement". With this agreement, dumping has been regarded as an unfair competition element at WTO level and regulations have been introduced to prevent it.

The Anti-Dumping Agreement deals only with government policies aimed at preventing dumping, as the dumping claim transferred to DSM in order to implement countermeasures against dumping and the WTO is a body created by the institutions and governments of member countries. In this framework, the WTO is concerned with issues such as whether dumping investigation procedures have adhered to national legislation and whether they have operated correctly. At national level, member countries are obliged to provide the necessary information flow with the relevant institutions and bodies dumping in the WTO. In this context, Member States have the authority to initiate and enforce anti-dumping duties on behalf of the sector and sector claiming anti-dumping.

At the national level, the authority to impose anti-dumping duty is recognised. However, Member States have limited use of this power. First of all, it is necessary to investigate and prove the claim that imports are harmful to domestic producers. If it is proved that the import dampened, a decision must be made by the WTO that antidumping tax can be applied. In this case, the Member State may apply antidumping duty at a limited rate and amount to the margin of dumping. It can say that the application of anti-dumping tax can be used by the Member States in the power of taxation provided they remain bonded to WTO principles and receive WTO approval.

3.1.2.2 Agreement on Subsidies and Countervailing Measures

Subsidy implementations and the government's undertaking of private sector costs cause the price structure to deteriorate. Subsidies cause the price to be determined independently of the cost. Use of subsidies leads to deterioration of price-linked competition and market failure (Alan, 2003). "Agreement on Subsidies and Countervailing Measures" has been signed within the WTO to prevent unfair competition caused by subsidy applications.

The agreement is of two-sided nature and is influential on public finance both regarding taxation and expenditure. Under the terms of the agreement, the definition of the subsidy and the terms of subsidy enable the WTO to influence public expenditure. It benefited from taxation in order to prevent subsidy implementations that cause unfair competition.

In order to protect the national industry from the subsidised imports, the compensatory tax can apply during the import process (Alan, 2003). Compensatory tax is compensated by subsidy application to the competitive advantage provided to the exporter. Thus, local producers are protected by ensuring entry into the country at a price close to the actual cost of imported goods.

Member States cannot act independently in compensatory tax practice. They can use the power of taxation under certain conditions. Compensatory taxes can be used under certain conditions to prevent the use of trade volume in a restrictive manner.

Just as it is the anti-dumping duty, there must be proof of the existence of a causal link between import and damage. This requirement ensures that the taxable event is determined following the procedure defined in the Agreement. The second constraint on the use of taxation authority concerns the determination of the tax rate and amount. The initiative to determine the amount of tax to be collected belongs to the importing country. However, this initiative is tied to an upper limit. The amount of tax to be applied has to be such as to eliminate the amount of subsidy. It is not possible to apply tax over the amount of subsidy determined in the subsidy investigation. However, under the subsidy amount, it may be decided to collect as much tax as required.

Both anti-dumping and countervailing duties offer a legitimate defence to Member States. The use of this right, however, is not intended to shape fiscal policy. Because these taxes are both cyclical insensitive and the base is very narrow. Therefore, while the WTO has limited the state's taxation authority, this restrictive effect is not strong enough to affect fiscal policy.

3.2 Agreements Affecting Power of Expenditure

The assignment of the state to the needs of the economic life makes public entrepreneurship inevitable. However, depending on developments in state understanding, public entrepreneurship has changed over time. The belief is that the state should intervene minimally in economic life in global economic conditions. Based on this belief, the post-1970 full economic policy proposal focused on the necessity of privatisation in order for public enterprises to turn into private sector businesses. Similarly, international elements shaping global economic conditions also draw on policy proposals and regulations on the concept of minimal state. The Treaty of WTO also includes arrangements for the state to remain at a minimal level as an economic unit using resources.

The WTO has included the government's regulations on resource use in the "Understanding on the Interpretation of Article XVII of GATT 1994" and "Agreement on Government Procurement". Both agreements govern the state to carry out non-discriminatory transactions between the private and the public sector in economic life.

3.2.1 Agreement on Subsidies and Countervailing Measures

In Article 1 of the Agreement, the subsidy is defined as any financial contribution that any member of the government has benefited from the government or public bodies. In the same article, financial contributions are explained as follows:

- Direct or indirect transfer of public funds by governments,
- Abandonment of receivables from the public (financial aid such as tax amnesty),
- Government purchasing goods or services other than general services.

In the Agreement subsidies, which resulted in the state undertaking the costs of the private sector, were considered unfair competition elements (Zampetti, 1995). For this reason, as stated above, the prevention and, at the very least, the restriction of its use has been adopted. It is imperative that the subsidy be used with socio-economic necessities. Therefore, limited use of subsidies has adopted since it is impossible to ban subsidies entirely. The necessary measure of the limit is that the subsidy is not given for a specific purpose.

According to the agreement, the incentive must be specific in order to be able to apply countermeasures (Alan, 2003). Specific subsidies are targeted to specific firms, sectors or regions. Subsidies that are expressly limited to "certain enterprises" are specific, that term left undefined. By contrast, when the program does not "favour certain enterprises over others," but is available by "objective criteria or conditions" to enterprises at large, it is not specific – an example given of such a criterion would be the number of employees in an enterprise. Subsidies that appear on their face to be non-specific, however, can become specific as applied.

Further, subsidies that are limited to a particular geographic region within the jurisdiction of the administering authority are defined to be specific. The objective of linking the countermeasure to the specificity criterion is to distinguish the subsidies for economic stimulation in general from subsidies targeting specific firms, sectors or regions (Zampetti, 1995.)

According to the specificity criteria, the subsidies are divided into three groups. These intermediaries are grouped into three groups: "Prohibited Subsidies", "Actionable Subsidies" and "Non-Actionable Subsidies". The assessment of subsidies regarding the specificity in three classes affects public spending authority. Governments are not able to plan expenditures in line with policy priorities, but they also influence the differentiation of expenditure components. Member States have the authority to apply subsidies as they wish. The WTO does not place a direct limitation on countries' spending powers. However, a product that benefits from the subsidy in production can be directed to ask for DSM when it is the subject of foreign trade.

3.2.2 The Agreement on Government Procurement

The Agreement on Government Procurement, which included in multiple agreements, regulates the use of resources by the state and does not want the state to treat nationally in the expenditures it receives in purchasing goods and services from the budget. Government agencies often need to purchase goods and services with public resources and for public purposes to fulfil their functions. Such purchases are generally referred to as government/public procurement (Mutta, 1996).

The agreement specifies how the state can use its budgetary facilities to protect the value of money. Achieving 'value for money' is a primary aim of most procurement regimes. However, how? Open, transparent and non-discriminatory procurement is generally considered to be the best tool to achieve this goal as it optimises competition among suppliers. At the same time, there are competing policy goals: many governments also make use of government procurement to achieve other domestic policy goals, such as the promotion of specific local industry sectors or social groups (Mutta, 1996).

Providing preferential treatment for domestic goods, services and suppliers discriminates against foreign suppliers and therefore acts as a trade barrier in this sector. The multilateral rules of the WTO do not address these barriers as government procurement is explicitly exempted from the primary disciplines of both the General Agreement on Tariffs and Trade (GATT – see Article III: 8a) and the General Agreement on Trade in Services (GATS – see Article XIII:1).

At the first time that we have been able to find a solution to this problem. The multilateral rules of the WTO do not address these barriers as it is exempted from the primary disciplines of the General Agreement on Tariffs and Trade (GATT – see Article III: 8a) and the General Agreement on Trade in Services – see Article XIII: 1).

The liberalisation of the government procurement market has the potential to generate benefits both regarding procurement efficiency and commercial interests. Therefore, the WTO members have worked on this issue on three fronts, namely:

(i) the plurilateral Agreement on Government Procurement (GPA)
(ii) The Doha Development Agenda (DDA) Working Group on Transparency in Government Procurement (which is currently inactive)
(iii) GATS negotiations on government procurement.

Turkey, because it is not a party to this agreement, is exempt from treaty obligations. However, in the process of full membership with the EU, public procurement from the EU has made necessary arrangements in its fiscal legislation to harmonise with the acquis.

3.2.3 Understanding on the Interpretation of Article XVII of GATT 1994

"Understanding on the Interpretation of Article XVII of the GATT 1994" is concerned with the public enterprise and emphasises the meaning of the public enterprise and the state should remain neutral in the context of enterprise activities. In the text of the agreement, the only commercial public enterprise is considered. Commercial public enterprises are defined as governmental and non-governmental companies, including marketing agencies, with exclusive rights and privileges, including statutory and constitutional powers that enable them to influence the level and direction of imports and exports during their purchases and sales.

Each Member State is obliged to inform the Commodity Trade Council regularly about public commercial enterprises and business policies and to ensure transparency that will allow public commercial enterprises activities and the effects of these activities on international trade to be precisely assessed. The agreement does not allow the government to use commercial enterprises as a tool in the direction of national economic policy objectives.

How is this reconciliation text affecting the government's ability to determine and implement policy reflected in policy implementation towards public finance? This question is a question that should answer in the central axis of the study.

The public finance impact of this memorandum is not direct. Here there is an indirect interaction in the context of public expenditure. That is, the text prohibits the use of discriminatory and monopolistic power in the imports and exports of public commercial enterprises. In other words, the concerned enterprises have to act sensitively to the market signals in resource use. Therefore, the state has to act by market conditions in expenditures to be made through these institutions. Note that there is no limit to public expenditure in the treaty. What is desired is only that the government is acting by market signals.

4 Conclusion

In the case of market disruptions linked to international trade, the state benefits from financial instruments. The state can benefit from the power of taxation in fiscal measures. However, the use of the power of taxation takes place not because of the state, but because of the delegated authority of the WTO, which is granted by provisional application. In this respect, it can say that the effect of sanctions and monitoring mechanisms on the public finance is to narrow the initiative of the state to use force.

All this shows that WTO regimes serve to reduce the state in both regulatory and functional sense. The free trade system, which is shaped by the orientation of the hegemon powers with a neoliberal point of view, is being discussed in the process of redefining international distributional relations. These controversies are embodied in practices such as the US putting additional customs duty on the import of iron and steel products contrary to WTO rules. The attitude of the United States in not recognising WTO rules suggests the following question: "Is the border of freedom, the point where the interests of the hegemonic powers are damaged?"

References

Alan O. Sykes. (2003). "The Economics of WTO Rules on Subsidies and Countervailing Measures". John M. Olin Program in Law and Economics Working Paper No. 186.

Bell D. (2017). "Political Realism and International Relations. *Philosophy Compass*", 12: e12403. https://doi.org/10.1111/phc3.12403. (date of access: 15.06.2018).

Hoekman, B. M. (1997). Competition Policy and the Global Trading System: A Developing-Country Perspective", *Policy Research Working Paper 1735*, The World Bank.

Hoekman, B. M. & Kostecki, M. M. (1995). The Political Economy of the World Trading System From GATT to WTO. New York, Oxford University Press.

Kazgan, G. (1997). *Küreselleşme ve Yeni Ekonomik Düzen*, İstanbul: Altın Kitaplar.

Mutta, A. (1996). "The Government Procurement Agreement: Implications of Economic Theory", *Staff Working Paper*, TISD 96-03, World Trade Organisation: Trade in Services.

Nguyen, T., Perronı, C. and Wıgle, R. (1993). "An Evaluating of Draft Final Act of Uruguay Round", *The Economic Journal*, Vol. 103, No. 421.

Potter, D. (1992). "Autonomy of Third World State within The Global Economy", *Global Politics: Globalization and The Nation State*, (Ed: A. Giddens; P. Mc Grew; G. Levis), Cambridge: Polity Press.

Qureshi, A. H. (1996). *World Trade Organization: Implementing International Trade Norms*, Manchester, UK, Manchester University Press.

Weiss, L. (2000). "Globalization and State Power", *Development and Society*, Vol. 29, No. 1.

Will, M. and Winters L. A. (1995). "The Uruguay Round: Widening and Deepening the World Trading System", *World Bank Policy Research Bulletin*, Vol. 6, No. 5, http://documents.worldbank.org/curated/en/387221468764366090/The-Uruguay-Round-widening-and-deepening-the-world-trading-system (Date of access: 07.03.2018).

WTO, Technical Information on Customs Valuation, https://www.wto.org/english/ tratop_e/cusval_e/cusval_info_e.htm. (Date of access: 01.08.2018).

WTO, https://www.wto.org/english/tratop_e/tariffs_c/tariff_data_e.htm.

WTO, Tariffs: Comprehensive tariff data on the WTO website. https:// www.wto.org /English/tratop_e/tariffs_e/tariff_data_e.htm (Date of access: 28.07.2018).

WTO, Government procurement gateway. https://www.wto.org/english/tratop_e/gproc_e/gproc_e.htm. (Date of access: 13.05.2018).

Yılmaz, Müslüm (2004). Dünya Ticaret Örgütü Kuralları Açısından Sübvansiyonlar ve Telafi Edici Tedbir Soruşturması, Doktora Tezi, T.C. Ankara Üniversitesi Sosyal Bilimler Enstitüsü Özel Hukuk (Ticaret Hukuku) Anabilim Dalı file:///C:/Users/kat4/Downloads/2155.pdf (Date of access: 27.06.2018).

Zampetti, Americo B. (1995). "The Uruguay Round Agreement on Subsidies", *Journal of World Competition*, Vol. 19, No. 2.

Orhan Şener

The Irrationality of Consumer Behaviours

Abstract: Neoclassical theory is generally based on the principles of rational consumer behaviours. However, too many business cycles and economic crises showed that consumers are not that rational as Adam Smith stated. As in many Western countries, the overwhelming majority of Turkish consumers act irrationally in making their economic decisions. Irrational consumer behaviour is the outcome of too many social, psychological and economic factors resulting in massive distortions from the equilibrium conditions in both market and public economy. Firstly, it distorts the efficiency of resource allocation, and secondly, it causes unfair income distribution.On the other hand, inefficiency and equity problems result in divergence from macroeconomic stabilisation. Thus, unless irrational consumer behaviours are corrected, it is impossible to secure sustainable economic growth, price level stability, full employment and balance in international trade. This paper includes the approaches developed by Behavioural Economists and Heterodox Economists against mainstream neoclassical economists. Thus, in the first section of the paper, some psychological analyses conducted by Kahneman, Tversky, Akerlof and other economists are mentioned in explaining the irrationality problem. The second section of the paper comprises arguments raised by heterodox economists such as Pareto and Minsky. Since behaviours of Turkish consumers whose economic choices are dominated by conspicuous consumption motivation are entirely different from that of the Western consumers, it results in massive waste both in the market and public economy. For this reason, we prepared a list of the irrational behaviours of Turkish consumers to be corrected by the public authorities through proper education.

Keywords: Behavioural Economics, Heterodox Economics, Conspicuous Consumption, Veblen Effect, Bandwagon Effect

JEL Codes: B5, E2, E7

1 Introduction

As in many capitalist countries, consumers in Turkey behave irrationally due to cultural, religious, social and noneconomic factors, opposing to the mainstream economics thoughts. Adam Smith's Unseen Hand Doctrine dominates the Classical Economics thoughts, which has been used to justify the rational consumer behaviour. However, in real life, this understanding does not hold true as claimed by the behavioural economists and heterodox economists that I refer to. Indeed, if the consumers were rational as mainstream economists claimed, there were no economic crises and market failures. However, there are too many market imperfections due to non-economic factors most of which are based on value judgments, social traditions and religious culture. Irrational behaviours of consumers distort the primary goals of public economy, such as efficiency in resource allocation and fairness in income distribution, and sub-goals of macroeconomic equilibrium affected by growth rate, employment, price level stability and balance in international trade. This paper aims to explain the irrational behaviours that reduce the efficiency of fiscal policies. In explaining the non-economic irrational consumer behaviours concerning Turkish consumers, I give some examples that also affect the behaviours of politicians and bureaucrats. Since the term of consumer also comprises both politicians and bureaucrats, I suggest a comprehensive solution to irrationality problem, regarding general wealth tax and some administrative measures.

2 Theoretical Background

Heterodox economists claim that consumers are not rational as Adam Smith suggested. They also argue that consumer's behaviours are determined not only by economic reasons, but also too many social value judgments, social values, habits and noneconomic factors that shape their economic choices. These behaviours take different forms of showing offs such as important consumption motivations, Veblen Effects, Bandwagon Effects and Snob Effects. Thus, behavioural economists are employing too many concepts in explaining the irrationality of human beings. Some of these are Bounded Rationality, The Market for Lemons, 20 to 80 Law (Power Law), Happiness, Crash-Prone and some ethical considerations (Şener, 2015).

Contrary to Adam Smith's Invisible (unseen) Hand Theory, behavioural economists argue that people are not taking rational decisions. These economists claim that people make decisions based on social values, habits and noneconomic psychological factors. For these reasons, they claim that Adam Smiths' formulation of "people behave along with their self-interest, selfishness and rational motivations" doesn't hold true in real life. There are many examples of irrational human behaviours that do not fit this theory as follows.

Although cigarette smoking is harmful, many people are obese smokers.

Trap prices like 99.90 Liras attract people, especially those thinking of it is less than 100 Liras.

Many types of competitions in business do not rest on economic grounds, but they are related to some psychological and social factors.

Especially in developing countries, people are likely to behave in line with the conspicuous consumption or 'keeping up with Jones' motivations.

Behavioural economics examines the irrational economic activities of people as shown by the examples mentioned above. This new economic theory is based on both economic and psychological factors, rather than traditional and mainstream economic principles. These new approaches profoundly affect the theories on savings and economic policies both in the market and public sector. It also provides insights into the explaining very complex economic behaviours of human beings. Tversky and Kahneman were the pioneers in establishing the basic principles of this new branch of economics in the 1970s. They successfully developed and adopted theories based on brain process information. According to them, when the people face uncertainty, they tend to behave randomly related to their mental shortcuts based on experience. They state that people are strongly influenced by a specific proposition called 'framing' while taking decisions (Kahneman and Tversky, 2003). Another branch of behavioural economics known as 'neuroeconomics' is becoming popular in explaining human economic motivations. Accordingly, the brain reacts to high price offers, as it reacts to abhorrent or disgusting smell.

The other branch of behavioural economics is called 'nudge economics' that explains the decisions based on their self-interest or of their preferences that are closely related to their experiences and environmental preconditions. This means that the assumptions explaining the human behaviour rationality do not rest on self-interested motivation as formulated by Adam Smith because people are very complicated.

2.1 Approaches against Rationality

Although production was the concern of classical economists, early neoclassical economists analysed the consumer preferences based on their behaviours. Especially, institutional economists studied the subject matter and its relevance to physiology and sociology. Although the mainstream economists assume that human beings are rational in making decisions, this does not hold true in their real life. Because a rational human being logically reasons or employs the principles of reasoning consciously based on their daily life. The following cases such as important consumption motivation and Veblen's Effects are the examples of irrational behaviours of consumers.

2.2 Conspicuous Consumption

If someone buys goods that fit his/her exact preferences, as economists assumed, his/her behaviour is considered rational. However, many types of consumer behaviours cannot be accepted as rational. For instance, if you buy a Mercedes car because your neighbour has one, but your purchasing power is not high enough to support. Then, your welfare will decrease since you are paying interest on bank credits, maintenance costs such as insurance, depreciation, gas, etc. On the other hand, your conspicuous consumption behaviour not only reduces your welfare but it also wastes the limited sources of the society. Veblen used this term to explain the behaviour of the wealthy people. He argued that rich people are likely to display their economic and social power by buying very expensive consumption goods called statue goods (Bagwell & Bernheim, 1996). Some people buy these goods to show off that they are "the part of the society" as termed by Bandwagon Effect. There are also some people, exhibiting their consumption behaviour to distinguish themselves from the society known as Snob Effect. Some women enforce their husbands to buy a luxury car or villa because they follow the example Johns Effect, like their neighbours in the USA and Turkey. Sometimes a consumer's demand for a good is closely related to other people's perception. This situation occurs when a consumer wants to show off his high status. This means that he can only own a status good, but others should not have it. Suppose that, somebody else buys this good, he should buy another good that no one could own it. For instance, In Istanbul some rich people urge the restaurant owners, to increase the prices as much as possible so that nobody could access the service quickly. All these types of consumer behaviours violate traditional price setting theory based on supply and demand laws. All these cases show that demand curve becomes upward sloping, rather than downward sloping as economic theory assumed. The upward sloping demand curve displaces the Veblen Effect. According to this effect, higher prices mean better quality and thus higher demand for goods and services opposing to the demanding law. This is why low-income families even demand the expensive goods like mobile phones. Some economists opposed the principle of utility maximisation based on the rational behaviour of consumers. They prefer to use satisfying characteristics of a good rather than their marginal utility. This means that a satisfying quantity is a useful criterion to be used instead of utility maximisation theory.

Another group of economists argue that consumer behaviour is shaped by social forms, value judgments and advises of some friends etc. For instance, during the fasting month demand for the food increases in Muslim countries. On the other hand, some economists prefer to use the term of bounded rationality instead of reasonable consumer assumption, calling for marginal utility theory applies to some extent. Keynes also used this notion of propensity to consume not in the sense of rational consumer behaviour, but in the psychological mean.

3 Heterodox Economics

History of economics has been dominated by orthodox economists who supported the neoclassical economic theory. However, in 1970s economics thoughts were divided into two branches: orthodox and heterodox economics. Heterodox economists strongly opposed to the principles of raised by mainstream economists, who assumed that market mechanism is the best way to optimise consumer utility and profit maximisation goal of the firms. Mainstream neoclassical economics thoughts are based on the following assumptions, which are rejected by the heterodox economists.

Markets are perfectly competitive,

Supply and demand drives the prices to equilibrium,

People behave rationally,

Free markets optimise utility and profit maximisation

Since Orthodox economists became very influential at the universities and financial institutions, they neglected socio-economic and social justice issues. Thus, starting in the 1970s, a number of a heterodox branch of economics thoughts have been developed outside the mainstream economics. They developed many branches of heterodox issues such as behavioural economics, asymmetric information, Power Law, happy economics, financial instability and complex systems of uncertainties. The Bounded Rationality is one of the essential concepts in the Heterodox Economics literature.

3.1 Bounded Rationality

By using the psychological principles Daniel Kahneman and Amos Tversky tested the rational behaviour assumption introduced by neoclassical economists. They found that most of the consumers don't behave rationally and they referred to this attitude known as "bounded rationality". They also stated that consumers have an asymmetric attitude towards loss and gain. So, they often miss out on excellent opportunities. Moreover, Tversky says that consumers also dislike change, which explains why investors often find it hard to let go of underperforming shares (Kahneman and Tversky, 2003). Thus, people just couldn't let go of the rationality.

3.2 The Markets for Lemon

Neoclassical economists assumed that perfect competition conditions exist in markets. They argued that a large number of firms compete to sell the identical products. However, George Akerlof argued that many people might not access the same information about the markets. He investigated what happens when the people are unable to reach the same information. Based on his studies he developed a theory known as the "Markets for the Lemons". He considered a market where the good and bad used cars (or lemons) are sold. If the buyer has less information than the seller has, then the buyer would guess that car is of average quality. So, he is likely to pay the price of an average used car price. If the seller has good quality used car, he will not get high enough price, due to the buyer's lack of information (Akerlof 1970). The result will be as Gresham stated for money: "The bads will drive out goods from the market".

3.3 20 to 80 Laws

Neoclassical economists did not make a necessary investigation on the income inequality, which leads to growing disparities of wealth between rich and poor. The neoclassical economists rest on the Adam Smith's wealth distribution, while the heterodox economists argue that it does not hold true in industrial economies. Smith argued that an unseen (invisible) hand of the markets would divide the wealth between the rich and poor. Opposing to Smith's ideas about wealth distribution, Vilfredo Pareto formulated a law known as "20 to 80 Law" or Power Law. Accordingly, 20% of the population holds 80% of the total wealth. Although Pareto formulated this law in the 19th century, it holds true even in the 21st century. For instance, after the 1970s too high salaries were paid to CEOs in rich countries. At Davos Rounds held in 2018, it was argued that a CEO's four days salary is earned by a worker all his life in Bangladesh. The median salaries stagnated and people around the world struggled to feed. Amartya Sen believed that starvation is the characteristics of some people not having enough food to eat.

3.4 Happy Economics

After 1950s economists argued that there wouldn't be strong relations between happiness and GNP level. Thus, classical economists' interpretation of happiness shows that, once a society reaches a certain level of average income, say 15 000 to 25000 dollars per year, then happiness increases. Economists argue that, based on decreasing utility of income, happiness decreases above this income level. Then, any further increase in income has no significant effect on happiness levels. Veblen argued that use of advertisement and marketing techniques makes people unhappy by buying new products. Conspicuous consumption behaviour of people also makes them unhappy, because they buy goods that they do not need. Studies on life satisfaction revealed that Americans were much happier during the 1950s and 1960s, even though GNP level was less than in later decades. Based on this type of studies, material well-being of society does not necessarily mean that society is happy. Happiness statistics related to material well-being is criticised by heterodox economists (Luigino 2008).

3.5 Feminist Economics

A politician, Marilyn Warings, argues in her book "Counting for Nothing" and stating that many services performed by women and housewives are not included in GNP (gross national product) because they are not paid. Examples of these include bearing children, looking after sick, aged and disabled family members, etc. However, most of these services of women are paid or tax exempted in Scandinavian and some social democratic countries in Europe. Feminist economists highly criticised neoclassical economic theory because it favours for rational economic man. Thus, they criticise male values such as competitiveness and individualism. Contrary to neoclassical economists they argue that women's contribution to social capital needs to be taken into account.

3.6 Crash-Prone

In 1990s economists claimed that the economy is not fundamentally stable as assumed by neoclassical economists. Hyman Minsky argued that the economy is prone to crashes and bubbles. He stated that "During to prosperous times, debt accumulates in the economy as success breeds increasing confidence as Keynes's "animal spirit". According to him this process, known as the Minsky Moment, continues until it finally reaches a crisis point. When the debts get called in, the economy crashes. Minsky's claim that the economy is crash-prone has been evidenced through many bubbles. Mortgage bubble in the USA, Dutch Tulip Mania in the 17th Century and the British South Sea bubble are the historical evidence that is supporting the Minsky's claim (Minsky 1986). Benoit Mantelbrot strongly criticised efficient Market Hypothesis assumed by neoclassical economists. He argued that since 1960 economic data on price changes did not follow the Bell Curve analysis as predicted by that hypothesis (Mantelbrot 1999). This means that the Efficient Market Hypothesis does not hold correct the hypothesis has foreseen. He believed that 20–80 Law distribution is a better tool to predict the crashes. He also argued that, although the price changes are small, if all prices of goods are considered, then income distribution will be adversely affected. Because the Power Law effect becomes significant in developing crashes.

3.7 Ethics

The neoclassical understanding of the economy as stable, rational and self-regulation turned out to be highly misleading. Some fund managers like Soros and

Jean-Philipe Bouchaud believed that neoclassical economics failed to predict what is going on in the markets. The big shock from the subprime crises proved that it was resulted due to irresponsible behaviours of the prominent traders. Some of the Wall Street traders like Goldman Sachs were accused of misleading the investors in financial markets. Traders and mortgage brokers pushed the investors to sign contracts that the investors did not understand, leading to asymmetric information problems, in 2010 subprime crises. Traders in Turkish financial markets undertook speculations and manipulations and also resulted in collapsing in many years. Thus, some economists believe that these problems are due to lacking in ethical behaviours, not considered during the formation of neoclassical theories. This is because the neoclassical economists removed ethical considerations emphasised by Aristotle and Scholastics economics. For this reason, the invisible hand doctrine is not reliable and not satisfactory as far as ethical behaviours are concerned. Thus, a new kind of economics is being emerged nowadays. The behaviour of real people motivations is replacing because reasonable man assumptions as believed by neoclassical economists. Thus, instead of seeing the economy as competition between disconnected people, sustainability of resources and value judgments of people are becoming essential.

4 Some Irrational Behaviours of Turkish Consumers

There are many examples of irrational behaviours of Turkish consumers that fit the principles of Heterodox Economics.

- Boys start to smoke, thinking they could be easily recognised as a grown-up man by the society.
- Trap prices attract many consumers as in Western societies.
- According to a survey conducted in the 2000s, Turkish consumers ranked number 1, all over the European countries in buying Nokia mobile phones.
- A number of the luxury cars produced by foreign countries is the highest in Turkey as compared to European countries.
- Although too many projects such as Third Airport and Third Bosporus Bridge are wasteful and unproductive, however many voters are very proud of even though they do not get any direct benefit.
- Consumers buy houses with one extra room which is used for only a few days by the guests, but they are kept empty all year long.
- Members of low-income families buy very expensive mobile phones even though their income is not sufficient enough to have it.
- Turkey has a very large area to be used in grape production, however, due to religious beliefs, the quantity produced by the wine is the lowest among the

Mediterranean countries. The same applies to the farm products which are mainly imported.

- A number of the summer houses owned by the middle class in coastal areas exceeds 2 million, even though most of them are used only a few weeks in a year, thus kept empty all year long.
- A number of the Mercedes cars in Turkey exceeds the total number of the same brand cars in European countries.
- Wealthy families generally send their kids to universities abroad, without considering the quality of the education.
- Wives urge their husbands to buy luxury cars, villas, and yachts to keep up with their neighbours.
- Businessmen never report their counterparts who evade taxes and conducting unofficial and illegal economic activities.
- Framing and false advertisements change the actual preferences of consumers in buying goods that they need.
- Turkey is abundant in the grape product, however wine production is the least in EU.
- Many investors never deposit their savings at banks, but they prefer to receive profit shares from the İslamic banks, which is more or less equal to the market interest rate.
- Workers, governmental employees, low-income families support the right wing political parties. Whereas intellectuals and middle-income people in business support the social democratic party.
- Turkish workers abroad support social democratic and left-wing parties, whereas they support right-wing political parties at home.
- Many people in Turkey buy medicine on the recommendation from the friends, neighbours or pharmacists.
- Some rich people urge luxury restaurants to charge the highest prices so that everyone would not support to eat there.
- Bicycle transportation is not accessible in Turkey, even though the cost of road transportation is prohibitive. The most popular tourism centres like Antalya and Bodrum are not reached by trains. No sea lines are operating between Istanbul, İzmir, İskenderun and Trabzon, even though it is the cheapest transportation mean.
- More than half of the voters vote for their nationalist and religious feelings, rather than their economic needs, resulting in dissatisfaction with public goods and services.
- Most of the consumers as being voters are not sensitive to the corruption and mismanagement in the public sector, resulting in decreasing utility to be received from the social services.

5 Conclusion

During the Adam Smiths' area, there were no monopolistic and oligopolistic market structures. For this reason, he believed in the existence of perfect competitiveness rather than imperfect competition. However, in modern societies, there are too many imperfections not only in markets but also in the political decision-making process, which induces consumers, bureaucrats, politicians, big business and media to act irrationally. For instance, asymmetric information misleads the consumers, because sellers know more about the technical characteristics of goods than that of the buyers. Consumers are not likely to understand the confusing prescriptions of medicines, insurance policies and mobile phones etc. Thus, many economic activities both in the market and the public economy result in waste, due to irrational behaviours of decision makers. Bureaucrats may be induced to take bribes because they behave under the Veblen and Bandwagon Effects, giving rise to important consumption motivation to operate. This is the reason why the bureaucrats' offices are enormous and luxury. They also employ more people most of them from their hometown, thinking of they may be a candidate for the members of parliament. They also visit foreign countries too often, enjoy many fringe benefits such as luxury state cars and high-quality houses. The same also applies to politicians who are likely to behave under the free rider motivation. Thus, wasteful expenditures increase dramatically, as in the case of more than 2 000 luxury service cars are used by the central government and governmental agencies. To cope with all the irrational behaviours of consumers, politicians and bureaucrats, integrity courses through schools and mass media must be provided to all citizens and students. In addition to these measures, a general wealth tax must be imposed on politicians, bureaucrats and people in business in order to get rid of corruption and mismanagement which are considered irrational behaviour.

References

Akerlof. G (1970), "The Market for Lemons: Qualitative Uncertainty and the Market Mechanism". *Quarterly Journal of Economics*. Vol.84. August. pp. 488-500.

Bagwell L.S. and Bernheim D. (1996), "Veblen Effect Theory of Conspicuous Consumption", The American Economic Review, 86(3), pp. 349–373.

Friedman, M. (1962), Capitalism and Freedom, University of Chicago Press.

Kahneman D. and Tversky A. (2003), Choices, Values and Frames, Cambridge University Press.

Luigino, B. (2008), Handbook on the Economics of Happiness, Edward Elgar Publishing.

Libenstein H. (1950). "Bandwagon, Snob, and Veblen Effect in the Theory of Consumer's Demand", Quarterly Journal of Economics, Oxford University Press, 64(2). p 183–207.

Mantelbrot, B., (1999), "Multiracial Walk down Wall Street", Scientific American, 280(2), pp.70-87.

Minsky, H. (1986), Stabilizing an Unstable Economy, Yale University Press, New Haven.

Nash, J.F. (2002), "Ideal Money" Southern Economic Review, 69(1), pp 4–11.

Şener, O., (2015), Ünlü Ekonomistler Ansiklopedisi, Beta, İstanbul.

Tversky A, and Kahneman D, (1986), "Rational Choice and Framing of Decisions", Oct 1986, p. 251

Wilkinson N., and Kleas M. (2012), An Introduction to Behavioral Economics, Palgrave Macmillan.

Abdullah Tirgil[1] and Recep Yorulmaz

Seasonal Effects of Smoking Bans on Cigarette Consumption in Turkey

Abstract: In this study, we compare monthly aggregate cigarette sales (consumption) data before and after the tobacco control policies (including non-price related) went into effect to see the effects of these anti-smoking measures on declining cigarette consumption in Turkey. We utilise cigarette sales as a proxy measure for cigarette consumption. Our results indicate that the enforcement of the early law in 1996 against tobacco was too weak. As a result, cigarette consumption increased until the 2000s. We also present results after the public smoking regulations were implemented in 2008, which shows an immediate decline in cigarette consumption for the adult population in Turkey.

Keywords: Seasonal Effect, Public Smoking Ban, Anti-tobacco Regulations

JEL Codes: I10, I18

1 Introduction

Tobacco use is becoming a worldwide issue as smoking is foreseen to be the most important cause of death than any other disease by 2020[1]. This will be true especially for developing nations. Cigarette is the first factor of lung cancer disease, cardiovascular death, chronic obstructive pulmonary disease mortality, and many other in all developed nations[2]. In the light of these findings, governments take precautions to prevent their citizens from the harmful effects of smoking by executing tobacco control policies such as increasing taxes on tobacco products. By implying raised taxes on cigarettes, governments aim to increase cigarette prices by which they intend to reduce cigarette consumption and increase public revenues through taxes. In addition, policymakers can reduce smoking by implementing non-price regulations such as tobacco advertisement bans, health warnings on cigarette packages, and indoor smoking bans, etc.

Turkey started its journey in applying tobacco control policies in 1996 by passing Law 4207 "Preventing the Hazards of Tobacco Products". This law banned smoking in health and education institutions, and in public transportation.[3] However, enforcing the law back then was too weak. Therefore Turkey missed a chance to become a smoke-free country at that time.

---

1 Corresponding author.

In 2004, Turkey approved the World Health Organization (WHO) Framework Convention on Tobacco Control (FCTC) through which the goal of joining countries was to protect their citizens from the unfavourable health, social, and economic consequences of tobacco consumption[4]. Turkey also initiated its own "National Tobacco Control Program" to fight against tobacco use in 2006[5].

In this study, we will compare monthly aggregate cigarette sales data before and after the tobacco control policies (including non-price related) went into effect in Turkey to see the effects of these anti-smoking measures on declining cigarette consumption. We use cigarette sales as a proxy measure for cigarette consumption.

There is an enormous amount of literature on smoking worldwide especially for developed nations. Some studies show that anti-smoking policies (price or non-price related) have a positive impact on reducing cigarette consumption[6]. Conversely, some other studies report that public intervention does not affect smoking[7]. For Turkey, studies are missing the most crucial change in public policy affecting tobacco consumption across the country[3, 5, 8-11]. We focus on these anti-tobacco regulations implemented across Turkey to see the impacts of non-price measures on smoking behaviour for the adults by focusing on their seasonal effects.

WHO's convention enforces countries to take part in executing different ways of anti-smoking policies such as raising prices through increased tobacco taxes and implementing non-price measures such as "education, training, and public awareness", "offer help to quit tobacco smoke", "enforce bans on tobacco advertising, promotion, and sponsorship", "regulation of the contents of tobacco products", etc[12].

By the WHO MPOWER package[4], Turkey has adopted rigorous tobacco control policies starting in May 2008 by prohibiting smoking in all enclosed public places and workplaces. On July 2009, this policy was extended to comprise the hospitality sector such as hotels, Turkish cafés, restaurants, bars, etc[13]. Turkey also took significant steps in raising excise taxes on tobacco products to reduce the demand for these types of commodities. In the process of creating a smoke-free zone in Turkey, all participants including government, non-profit organisations and citizens did their part and had given their support in the progression of executing tobacco control policies.

2 Data and Methodology

2.1 Data

We utilise monthly sales data from the Tobacco and Alcohol Market Regulatory Authority (TAPDK) to examine the impact of anti-smoking regulations on cigarette consumption. Individually, we take advantage of per pack per adult aggregate monthly cigarette consumption as our coefficient of interest. The dataset contains information from 2005:1 to 2015:7. We calculate average prices for cigarettes from firms' revenue information which is provided by TAPDK. We also obtain information on income (RGDP) from TurkStat. All monetary terms are adjusted for inflation (using 2003 prices).

2.2 Method

Using monthly aggregate cigarette consumption data per pack per adult for Turkey, we investigate the relationship between indoor tobacco bans (non-price regulations) and cigarette consumption in Turkey. Our dependent variable is per pack per adult monthly log of cigarette consumption in Turkey. In each model, we include monthly dummies and time trend variables to control for seasonality and trend over time, respectively. We also include average real cigarette prices and per capita real income to report price and income elasticities of demand for cigarettes in Turkey. In addition, we include some other anti-tobacco controls in the analysis to see their effects on smoking.

We regress log of monthly cigarette consumption on these variables to isolate the impact of each variable on adults' smoking behaviour. We focus on seasonal effects of the smoking bans to show the consumption patterns of smokers during various seasons after the first indoor ban went into effect in May 2008 in Turkey. We also implement a log-log model to estimate the price and income elasticities of demand for cigarette consumption. The regression equation is set as follows:

$$\begin{aligned} Ln\left(Cigarette\ Consumption\right)_i &= \alpha + \beta_1\ Ln\left(Real\,Price\right)_i \\ &+ \sum_{t=2008}^{2009} \beta_t\ Indoor\ Ban_t + \beta_2\ Warning + \beta_3\ Ad\ Ban + \beta_4\ Trend + \beta_5\ Trend^2 \\ &+ \sum_{m=1}^{11} \beta_m\ Month_i + \beta_6\ Ln\left(Real\,GDP\right)_i + \varepsilon_i \end{aligned} \tag{1}$$

In this equation, the dependent variable is the logarithm of the per pack per adult (+15 above) monthly cigarette consumption, $Real\,Price$ is cigarette prices adjusted for inflation (2003 prices), $Indoor\ Ban$ refers to the first and second public smoking bans in Turkey, $Warning$ is for health warnings introduced in May 2010, $Ad\ Ban$ stands for advertisement ban started in July 2012, $Trend$ and $Trend^2$ are linear and squared time trends, $Month$ is for monthly dummies, $Real\,GDP$ is for income adjusted for inflation, ε is the error term, and t i are for years (2008 and 2009) and months, respectively.

In this study, we have three sets of models as can be seen in Tab 1. The first model in Tab 1 refers to our main equation, which is specified above as equation (1). The second model runs the regression of cigarette consumption on the same variables without logs, and the rest is the same as in equation (1). For the third model, we create an interaction term by multiplying seasonal (monthly) dummies and the first smoking ban (2008) and add these interaction terms to the first model. Then, we add these interaction terms, monthly dummies, and the first smoking ban up to see the effect of seasonal changes on smoking behaviour after the first indoor ban went into effect in May 2008 in Turkey (see Fig 4 and Tab 1 Continued for full covariates).

3 Results

We perform a descriptive analysis to see how the tobacco control policies affect the cigarette consumption in Turkey. Fig 1 illustrates that cigarette consumption declines since the early 2000s in Turkey. This reduction can partially be attributed to the 2001 economic crisis in Turkey. By the time indoor bans along with other measures (raised tobacco taxes) had introduced we see a much more significant decline in cigarette sales in Turkey occurring around 2008.

Fig 2 shows monthly log cigarette consumption and monthly log price levels from 2005 to 2015. Demand for cigarettes depends on cigarette prices considerably during the relevant time frame such that as price goes up, cigarette consumption declines significantly.

We want to elaborate on the period right after the indoor smoking bans in 2009 and raised excise taxes in 2010. We observe that there is a substantial reduction in cigarette consumption over these years in Turkey. Based on Fig 3, we could firmly state that anti-tobacco smoking policies which were implemented in 2008 and 2009 affect cigarette consumption in Turkey substantially.

Tab 1 shows the regression results for three various models in this study. The first model indicates that the price elasticity of demand for cigarettes is -0.812 which means that when cigarette prices go up by 10%, cigarette consumption will go down by 8%. First indoor ban significantly (at 5% significance level) reduces the cigarette consumption by about 12%. Other anti-tobacco regulations such as health warnings on cigarette packages, advertisement bans do not show any statistically significant results on declining smoking behaviour. Trend variable shows the positive and significant result of cigarette consumption however when we control for squared time trend this effect fades away and eventually becomes zero. We also control for seasonal dummies in our regressions. First four months (Jan-April) show greater and statistically significant decline in cigarette consumption. After that, we observe an increase in smoking in July and

Tab 1. OLS Results of the Effects of the Indoor Smoking Ban on Cigarette Consumption

	(1) **Log-log**	(2) **Linear**	(3) * **Log-log**
Log (Real Price)	-0.812***		-0.715***
	(0.186)		(0.175)
Real Price		-2.455***	
		(0.381)	
First Indoor Ban	-0.125**	-0.750*	-0.069
	(0.049)	(0.381)	(0.080)
Second Indoor Ban	-0.016	-0.140	-0.029
	(0.043)	(0.333)	(0.042)
Warning	0.029	0.218	0.015
	(0.034)	(0.267)	(0.031)
Ad Ban	0.009	0.286	0.003
	(0.041)	(0.307)	(0.039)
Trend	0.005**	0.030*	0.004*
	(0.002)	(0.016)	(0.002)
Trend Square	-0.00002*	-0.001	-0.00002*
	(0.0001)	(0.0001)	(0.0001)
January	-0.241***	-1.643***	-0.166***
	(0.046)	(0.328)	(0.054)
February	-0.287***	-1.856***	-0.158*
	(0.046)	(0.331)	(0.062)
March	-0.170***	-1.139***	-0.175*
	(0.047)	(0.359)	(0.090)
April	-0.102***	-0.741***	-0.079*
	(0.032)	(0.245)	(0.045)
May	0.015	0.173	0.032
	(0.035)	(0.259)	(0.056)
June	0.053	0.553*	0.073
	(0.035)	(0.291)	(0.062)
July	0.112***	0.880***	0.192***
	(0.042)	(0.330)	(0.054)
August	0.102*	0.746*	0.196***
	(0.047)	(0.372)	(0.050)
September	0.042	0.182	0.001
	(0.046)	(0.361)	(0.091)
October	-0.022	-0.168	-0.068
	(0.045)	(0.365)	(0.104)

(*continued on next page*)

Tab 1. (continued)

	(1) **Log-log**	(2) **Linear**	(3) * **Log-log**
November	-0.044	-0.351	-0.014
	(0.030)	(0.229)	(0.050)
Log (Real GDP)	-0.591**	-3.245*	-0.553*
	(0.229)	(1.760)	(0.249)
Constant	7.482***	39.939***	7.080***
	(1.807)	(13.923)	(1.998)
Number of Observations	127	127	127
R2	0.79	0.78	0.83
			(3) *
JanuaryxFirstIndoorBan			-0.111*
			(0.070)
FebruaryxFirstIndoorBan			-0.195***
			(0.072)
MarchxFirstIndoorBan			0.012
			(0.100)
AprilxFirstIndoorBan			-0.034
			(0.062)
MayxFirstIndoorBan			-0.026
			(0.072)
JunexFirstIndoorBan			-0.029
			(0.078)
JulyxFirstIndoorBan			-0.117*
			(0.069)
AugustxFirstIndoorBan			-0.142**
			(0.070)
SeptemberxFirstIndoorBan			0.052
			(0.101)
OctoberxFirstIndoorBan			0.065
			(0.113)
NovemberxFirstIndoorBan			-0.043
			(0.064)
Constant			7.080***
			(1.998)
Number of Observations			127
R2			0.83

Note: *** indicates that a coefficient is significant at the 1% level, ** significant at the 5% level, and * significant at the 10% level. Robust Standard Errors are reported in parenthesis. The complete set of regression equation (3) * is shown in the appendix.

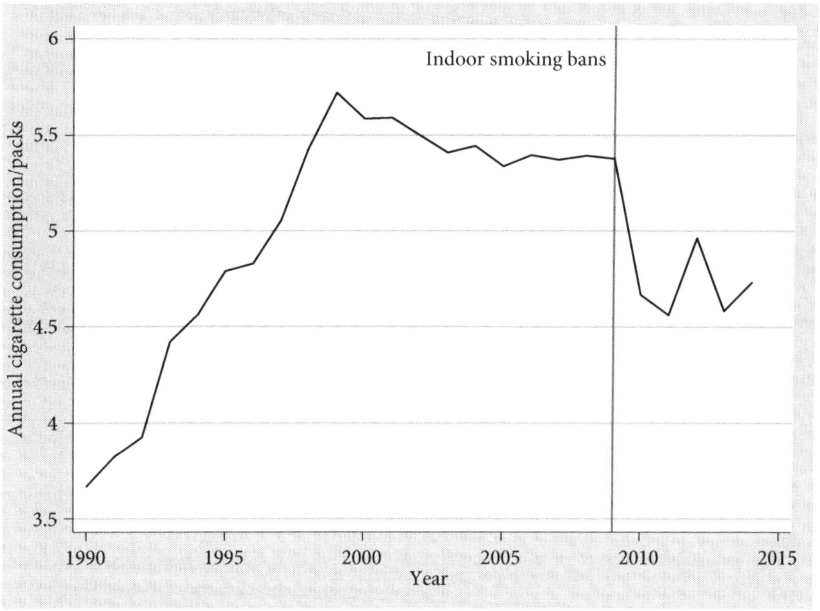

Fig 1. Annual Cigarette Sales

August. Another impressive result that we found is that income elasticity of cigarette demand is negative unlike other studies in Turkey[5, 13].

More importantly, when we look at the impact of the anti-tobacco policies on cigarette consumption altogether, we see a dramatic shift in the trend of cigarette consumption.

Fig 4 illustrates seasonal smoking patterns for adults in Turkey before and after the indoor bans in 2008. People in Turkey smoke more over a year without the indoor bans (blue colour). However, with the implementation of indoor smoking regulations people reduce smoking noticeably (red colour). Especially during the autumn and winter months, smoking goes down much. Then, it starts to increase during the spring and summer months. Overall, executing indoor smoking bans reduce smoking by adults considerably.

4 Conclusion

In this study, we looked at the correlation between anti-tobacco smoking bans and cigarette consumption in Turkey. Specifically, we focus on the seasonal effects of tobacco regulations on smoking behaviour.

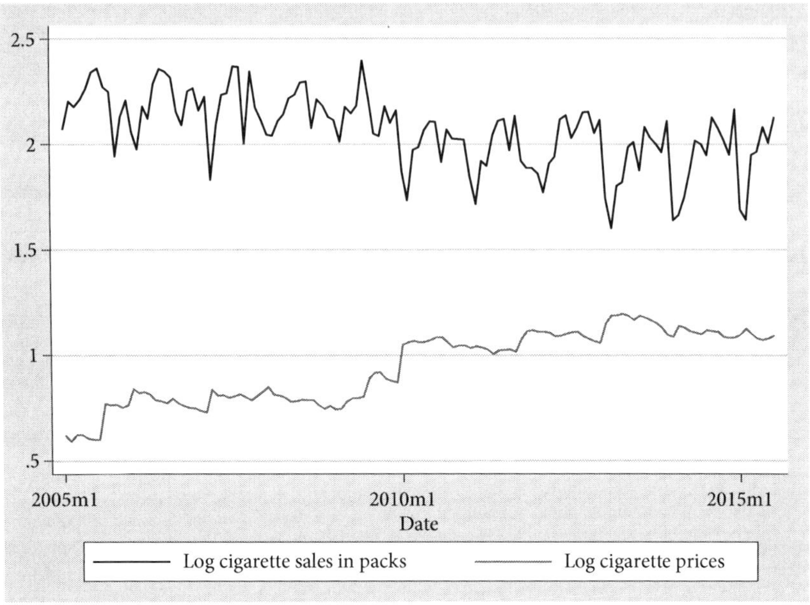

Fig 2. Cigarette Sales vs. Real Cigarette Prices

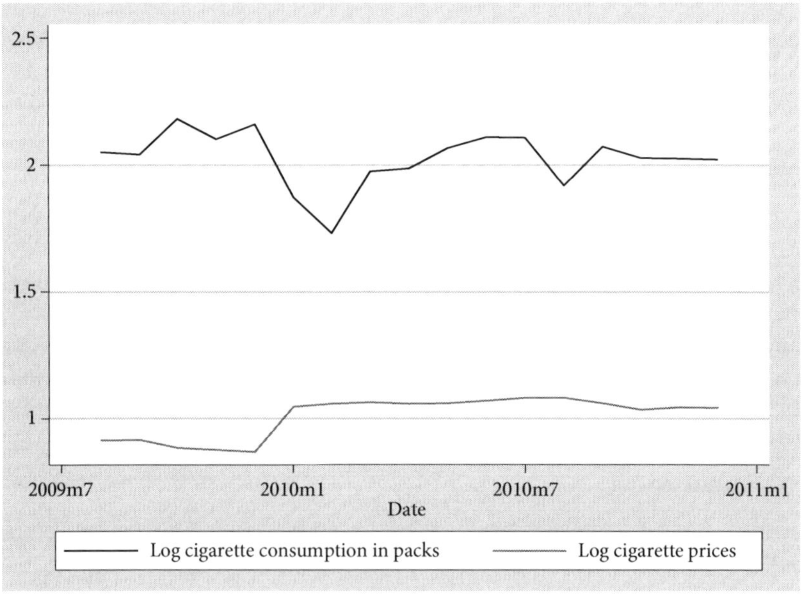

Fig 3. Cigarette Sales vs. Real Cigarette Prices After the First Ban

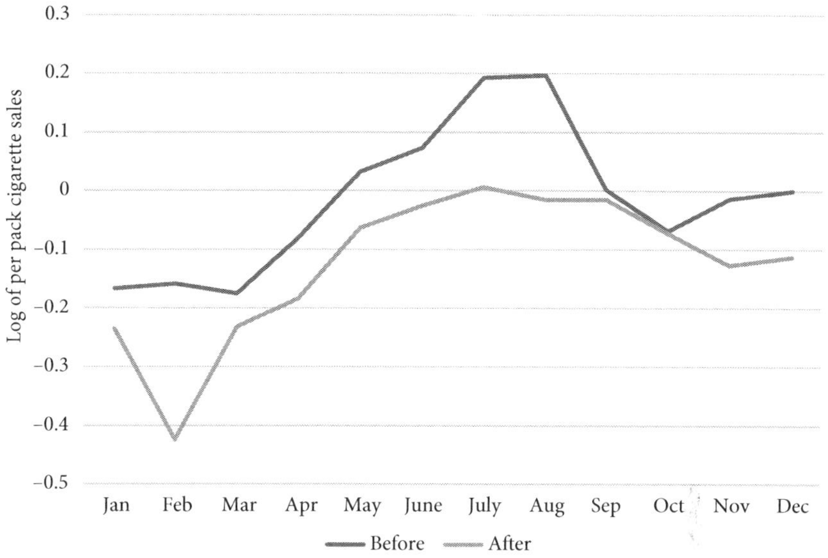

Fig 4. Seasonal Changes in Smoking Behaviour in Turkey

Although there are mixed results on the effects of anti-tobacco policies on cigarette consumption across the world, we find that anti-tobacco regulations in Turkey with strong enforcement could reduce cigarette consumption considerably. In this manner, it is also essential to get support from the society and non-profit organisations to execute smoking laws, which we profoundly experience in Turkey.

More importantly, our findings indicate anti-tobacco regulations have more substantial seasonal impacts on declining cigarette consumption by adults. Another impressive result that we found in this study is that cigarettes are inferior goods unlike other studies in Turkey. Our findings also indicate inelastic demand for cigarettes like other studies in Turkey but more significant. Considering all these, we could firmly state that when implemented with price-related measures anti-tobacco regulations will help reduce smoking.

References

Cetin, T. (2017), "The effect of taxation and regulation on cigarette smoking: Fresh evidence from Turkey", *Health Policy*, 121(12): 1288–95.

Chaloupka, F. J., & Warner, K. E. (1999), *The Economics of Smoking*, Cambridge, Mass: National Bureau of Economic Research.

Jones, A. M., Laporte, A., Rice, N., & Zucchelli, E. (2015), "Do public smoking bans have an impact on active smoking? Evidence from the UK", *Health Economics*, 24(2): 175–92.Top of Form.

Murray, C. J. L., Lopez, A. D., Harvard School of Public Health, WHO., & WB. (1996), *The global burden of disease: A comprehensive assessment of mortality and disability from diseases, injuries, and risk factors in 1990 and projected to 2020*. Cambridge, Mass: Published by the Harvard School of Public Health on behalf of the World Health Organization and the World Bank, distributed by Harvard Univ. Press.

Onder, Z. (2002), *THE ECONOMICS OF TOBACCO IN TURKEY: New evidence and demand estimates*, (Tobacco Control) eScholarship, University of California. Bottom of Form.

Tansel, A. (1993), "Cigarette demand, health scares and education in Turkey", *Applied Economics*, 25(4): 521–9.

Türel, O. (1975), "An analysis of demand for tobacco products and alcoholic beverages in Turkey". *State Planning Organization, DPT* 1975; 1454.

Warren, C. W., Erguder, T., Lee, J., Lea, V., Sauer, A. G., Jones, N. R., & Bilir, N. (2012), "Effect of policy changes on cigarette sales: the case of Turkey", *European Journal of Public Health*, *22*, 5, 712–6.

Wasserman, J., Manning, W. G., Newhouse, J. P., & Winkler, J. D. (1991), "The effects of excise taxes and regulations on cigarette smoking", *Journal of health economics*, 10(1): 43–64.

World Health Organization (2003), Framework Convention on Tobacco Control. Geneva, 2003. http://www.who.int/fctc/text_download/en/ (accessed 1/4/2018).

World Health Organization, & Research for International Tobacco Control. (2008), *WHO report on the global tobacco epidemic, 2008: The MPOWER package*. Geneva: World Health Organization.

Yürekli, A., Önder, Z., Elibol, M., et al. (2015), "The economics of tobacco and tobacco taxation in Turkey", International Union Against Tuberculosis and Lung Disease, 2015; 5, Paris.

Ayşe Yiğit Şakar

The Financial Incentives in Financing of Energy Efficiency in Buildings: A Comparison between Turkey and European Union

Abstract: The energy efficiency achieved in sectors such as building, transportation, service, industry, technology and agriculture contributes to achieving sustainable development, energy independence, protection of the environment and success in combating climate change. Energy efficiency in buildings refers to the reduction of energy consumption without lowering living standards, health conditions and service quality of the residents in the buildings. The aim of this study is to comparatively address financial incentives used to finance energy efficiency in buildings in terms of Turkey and European Union and to make inferences for Turkey. In the study, firstly, financing methods of energy efficiency in buildings and the legal regulations regarding energy efficiency targets of the European Union have been addressed.

Moreover, financial incentives in financing energy efficiency and at the supranational level, the applications of European Union, and at the national level, applications of countries such as United Kingdom, France, Germany, Poland and Italy and the applications of Turkey have been discussed. As a result of the study, it is determined that the same financing methods have been adopted both in Turkey and European Union; however, Turkey, compared to European Union, has newly begun to implement the tax incentives. European Union supports financial incentives at the supranational level. While supports in EU countries are provided as low-interest loans and grants rather than tax incentives, in some countries tax credits and tax reductions are also applied. In Turkey, the expenses made for the thermal insulation of buildings as well as low-interest loans can be deducted from income tax, and Stamp Tax and Fee exceptions are applied. Providing Value Added Tax reduction, title deed fee reduction, property tax reduction, Banking and Insurance Transaction Tax exception in energy efficient buildings in the construction sector will create positive results.

Keywords: Energy Efficiency, Energy Efficiency in Buildings, Financial Incentive, Grant, Tax Deduction, Subvention

JEL Codes: H21, H26, K34.

1 Introduction

Having first emerged in 1973, the concept of energy efficiency, whose significance was recognised as a result of the Energy Crisis, is not regarded as a very new concept now as it has been developing for over forty years (Yang ve Yu, 2015: 11).

Additionally, it continues to draw attention as a critical resource for economic and social development in all world economies, and it is getting more important to appreciate its real value (Yiğit Şakar, 2017:208). The vital importance of energy efficiency for Turkey has been recognised for the last ten years, and policies towards increasing the energy efficiency has begun to be developed.

Energy efficiency is a vital source of energy in the context of national and international efforts to achieve sustainability goals. This reflects a shift in paradigm that has begun to rely on both supply and demand-side actions in pursuit of achieving economic growth while promoting energy security, competitiveness and environmental sustainability (OECD/IEA, 2014: 18). Energy efficiency is called "hidden fuel" which promotes energy savings and energy security, reduces carbon emissions and promotes sustainable economic growth. The International Energy Agency (IEA) emphasised that energy efficiency should be considered as "first fuel" instead of "hidden fuel". It has also suggested that the global energy efficiency investments and the impact on energy supply are equal to the net contribution of other energy sources (OECD/IEA, 2013: 3). The IEA considers that two-thirds of economically profitable investments will not be used to increase energy efficiency in most of the building sector by 2035 (Deloitte, 2016:7).

Energy efficiency is a concept which complements national strategical objectives such as ensuring energy supply security, reducing the risks from external dependency, making energy costs sustainable, increasing the effectiveness of climate change and fighting and protecting the environment. Energy efficiency refers to the reduction of energy consumption without causing the quality of life and quality of service in the buildings and the quality and quantity of production in industrial enterprises (Enerji Verimliliği Kanunu, m. 3-j).

Energy efficiency represents all the measures taken to reduce energy losses in energy efficiency, fuel use, gas, steam, heat, air and electricity, to use the wastes by recycling, to reduce energy demand by using advanced technology without decreasing production, to implement advanced industrial processes and to increase energy efficiency (Tuğrul, 2017:11).

Regarding energy efficiency in buildings, in 1970 the Council of Europe adopted that "*the improvement of thermal insulation in buildings leads to a significant reduction in fuel consumption*" (Sudhakara Reddy et al. 2009:186).

The Organisation for Economic Co-operation and Development (OECD) added to the Environmental Guidelines in 1974 that "*the establishment of regulations and high standards for better thermal insulation in new buildings is a useful way to increase productivity*" (Sudhakara Reddy et al. 2009:186).

Increasing the energy efficiency of the buildings is creating an environment for the residents of the buildings to live in a more comfortable and healthy way. It is possible to improve community health by reducing illnesses and deaths caused by poor climatic conditions and lousy heating systems in buildings, thanks to buildings with high energy performance. In this context, energy efficiency can provide many economic, social and environmental benefits.

Turkey's energy supply is dependent on imports with the rate of 75.9%. There is 4.4% annual increase on average in energy demand in the building sector in Turkey. The share of the building sector in final energy consumption has passed the industrial sector at the rate of 32.8%. As of 2017, approximately 87% of the 9.1 million buildings in Turkey constitutes a qualified residential building (Ulusal Enerji Verimliliği Eylem Planı, 2018:8). The rate of energy consumption in buildings is similar to the European Union countries, and energy efficiency is implemented as government policy both in Turkey and in the European Union countries.

The construction sector accounts for about 9% of Europe's GDP. Construction activities involving renewal work and energy increases and construction of new buildings almost double the value of the economy and SMEs contribute to added value in EU's building sector more than 70% (https://ec.europa.eu/energy/en/topics/energy-efficiency/buildings).

Policies to be implemented for energy efficiency can be divided into three groups. These are (OECD/ IEA, 2014: 75):

- Establishing regulatory standards that require the improvement of energy performance on a sectoral basis,
- Providing financial incentives,
- Conducting educational and informative activities by creating awareness in the field of energy efficiency.

Energy efficiency that serves sustainable development is a broad topic that covers sectors such as building, transport, agriculture, industry, technology and service. The aim of this study is to consider financial incentives used in financing energy efficiency in the building sector comparatively in terms of Turkey, European Union and selected EU countries and to make inferences for Turkey.

2 Financing Methods of Energy Efficiency in Buildings

While energy efficiency is considered as an essential element of economic and environmental policy, there is no consensus on energy efficiency targets and the strategies to be pursued to achieve these targets (Sudhakara Reddy vd., 2009:76).

Energy efficiency policies consist of energy market intervention instruments which intend to remove obstacles against energy efficiency investments. Although these instruments have standard policy measures such as taxation, subventions, legislation, regulations, information or service provision, different applications are seen for each sector (Sudhakara Reddy et al. 2009:100).

The following methods are used in the financing of energy efficiency in the buildings: (http://beva.csb.gov.tr/Sayfa.aspx?id=29):

> *"Financial instruments can be classified as free loans, public financing, credit lines for SMEs and households, subventions (internal financing) and grants (external financing), loan guarantee programs for private banks, energy tariff reforms during non-repayable periods.*
> *Taxes include carbon, energy and environmental taxes.*
> *Financial incentives include tax credit, tax reductions, VAT reductions, investment incentives.*
> *Distribution Mechanisms can be counted as Technical Assistance for project identification and preparation in loan and public procurement, Energy Service Company (ESCO) market, performance contracts and third-party financing, legal obligations for utilities, energy efficiency funds and voluntary agreements."*

International Energy Efficiency Financing Protocol-IEEFP provides guidelines for local financial institutions around the world to evaluate and finance energy efficiency and savings-based renewable projects. The protocol is intended to be developed and updated on a country basis (Efficiency Valuation Organization, 2012: x). The first edition of the International Performance Measurement and Verification Protocol (IPMVP), entitled "North American Energy Measurement and Verification Protocol", was published in March 1996. It was renamed as "International Performance Measurement and Verification Protocol" in December 1997. The protocol was updated in 2001 and 2002. In 2002, IPMVP Inc. was established as an independent non-profit corporation to involve the international community and alleviate its responsibilities as the organiser of Ministry of Energy of USA. In 2004, IPMVP Inc. was named EVO (Productivity Evaluation Organization). EVO updated its protocol in the years of 2007, 2009 and 2010 (Efficiency Valuation Organization, 2012: x). The regularly updated Protocol has been translated into 11 languages and is used in more than 40 countries. (https://www.metering.com/regional-news/north-america/international-energy efficiency-financing-protocol-ieefp-available/).

2.1 Financial İncentives in the Financing of Energy Efficiency in Buildings: EU Application

2.1.1 Energy Efficiency Targets of EU

The main policy strategies affecting the building sector and energy efficiency practices in the EU can be classified as:

- Energy-focused initiatives,
- Regulations targeting buildings,
- Climate change and product-focused work.

(CEPMC, 2012: 43).

"*Action Plan for Energy Efficiency: Achieving Potential (EEAP)*" adopted on 19 October 2006 is essential for the European Union energy policy (COM/2006/0545 final). In late March of 2007, the Council of Europe identified energy efficiency as an essential part of the comprehensive strategy on climate change and energy. It also underlined the need to achieve 20% reduction in the EU energy consumption by 2020 (Buildings Performance Institute Europe -BPIE, 2010:9).

Sustainability, supply security and competitiveness constitute the three pillars of the European Union's energy policy. In the Energy Action Plan, energy efficiency has been combined with the measurable "20/20/20" targets that define the European energy policy (Yüksekkkaya, 2016: 7). It is not surprising that energy efficiency is tightly linked to the three pillars of the European Union energy policy: security (supply security, import independency, safe production), sustainability (reducing greenhouse gas emissions) and competitiveness (for cost-efficient energy users) (Deloitte, 2016:7). According to data from the year 2014, 30% of the amount of greenhouse gas emissions in the European Union comes from the buildings. This is equal to about 40% of the total energy consumption of the European Union, and 75% of the buildings are energy inefficient (European Commission,2016: 2). Houses built between 1945–1980 consume much energy, and due to the recent economic crisis, these facilities are inadequate for renewal funds (European Commission, 2017:10). Increasing building energy efficiency will ensure that the European Union complies with the United Nations Framework Convention on Climate Change (UNFCCC) and the Kyoto Protocol (Buildings Performance Institute Europe- BPIE, 2010: 9).

The European Union has set targets for greenhouse gas emissions, renewable energy sources and energy efficiency for the years of 2020, 2030 and 2050. In 2010, the European Commission issued a statement entitled "*Energy 2020 – A Strategy for Competitive, Sustainable and Secure Energy*" (European Commission, 2010). The 2020 Energy Strategy covers the priorities of the EU, known as the "20-20-20 targets" between 2010 and 2020. These are (https://www.avrupa.info.tr/tr/enerji-abnin-hedefleri-58):

- At least 20% reduction of greenhouse gases,
- Increasing the share of renewable energy in energy consumption by at least 20%,
- Increasing energy efficiency by at least 20%.

The European Commission regards the building as a significant potential to achieve 20% energy efficiency by 2020 and anticipates the development of financial programs aiming the projects in this area. (CEPMC, 2012: 44).

The European Union's "2030 Framework for Climate and Energy Policies" was officially adopted in 2014 (European Commission, 2014b). EU member states have also agreed on the following objectives for 2030 (https://ec.europa.eu/energy/en/topics/energy-strategy-and-energy-union/2030-energy-strategy):

- Reducing greenhouse gas emissions by 40% compared to 1990 levels,
- Providing 27% of the energy consumed from renewable energy sources
- Increasing energy efficiency by at least 25%.

The European Commission aims a reduction in greenhouse gas emissions at the rate of 80% to 95% by 2050 compared to 1990 in the direction of the "*Roadmap for a Competitive Low Carbon Economy in 2050*" (European Union, 2012: 10). One of the actions that it has set out to achieve this goal is to encourage and support renovation investments (CEPMC, 2012: 44). In 2050 Energy Road Map, it is stated that energy efficiency should remain as the primary focus, higher energy efficiency should be aimed in new and existing buildings; the use of products and devices should become a rule in the buildings with almost zero energy that meets the highest energy efficiency standard; recycling and lean production should be used and the life of products should be extended; tax incentives, grants, specialist counselling support, are needed to ensure the use of energy efficient vehicles and to change people's consumption habits, and thus, a significant increase in productivity can be achieved (European Union, 2012: 10).

2.1.2 Amendments Regarding the Financing of Energy Efficiency in Buildings

2002/91/EC Energy Performance of Buildings Directive – EPBD is an important part of the European Union Legislation. It was arranged with the inspiration of Kyoto Protocol which aimed the reduction of 5.2% of the levels in 1990, and in which the EU committed to reduce greenhouse gas emissions below 8% of 1990 levels until 2010. The EPBD anticipates the development of all the EU countries' construction regulations by using energy certification schemes for buildings, and by ensuring that boilers and air conditioning in use are controlled (Yüksekkaya, 2016:9).

Directive 2010/31/EU of the European Parliament and of the Council of 19 May 2010 on Energy Performance of Buildings Directive and Directive 2002/91/EC of the Energy Performance Directive were amended. As emphasised in the

7th, 9th and 10th articles of the new Directive 2010/31/EU, more importance is given to the buildings which underwent the major renovation. Article 10 of the Directive regulates financial incentives and market barriers (Official Journal of the European Union L 153, 18.6.2010, p. 22):

"Article 10:
Financial incentives and market barriers

1. *In view of the importance of providing appropriate financing and other instruments to catalyse the energy performance of buildings and the transition to nearly zero energy buildings, Member States shall take appropriate steps to consider the most relevant such instruments in the light of national circumstances.*
2. *The Member States shall draw up, by 30 June 2011, a list of existing and, if appropriate, proposed measures and instruments including those of a financial nature, other than those required by this Directive, which promotes the objectives of this Directive. The Member States shall update this list every three years. The Member States shall communicate these lists to the Commission, which they may do by including them in the Energy Efficiency Action Plans referred to in Article 14(2) of Directive 2006/32/EC.*
3. *The Commission shall examine the effectiveness of the listed existing and proposed measures referred to in paragraph 2 as well as of relevant Union instruments, in supporting the implementation of this Directive. On the basis of that examination, and taking due account of the principle of subsidiarity, the Commission may provide advice or recommendations as regards specific national schemes and coordination with Union and international financial institutions. The Commission may include its examination and possible advice or recommendations in its report on the National Energy Efficiency Plans referred to in Article 14(5) of Directive 2006/32/EC.*
4. *The Commission shall, where appropriate, assist upon request Member States in setting up national or regional financial support programmes with the aim of increasing energy efficiency in buildings, especially of existing buildings, by supporting the exchange of best practice between the responsible national or regional authorities or bodies.*
5. *In order to improve financing in support of the implementation of this Directive and taking due account of the principle of subsidiarity, the Commission shall, preferably by 2011, present an analysis on, in particular: (a) the effectiveness, the appropriateness of the level, and the actual amount used, of structural funds and framework programmes that were used for increasing energy efficiency in buildings, especially in housing; (b) the effectiveness of the use of funds from the EIB and other public finance institutions; (c) the coordination of Union and national funding and other forms of support that can act as a leverage for stimulating investments in energy efficiency and the adequacy of such funds for achieving Union objectives. On the basis of that analysis, and in accordance with the multiannual financial framework, the Commission may subsequently submit, if it considers this appropriate, proposals with respect to Union instruments to the European Parliament and the Council.*
6. *The Member States shall take account of the cost-optimal levels of energy performance when providing incentives for the construction or major renovation of buildings.*

7. *The provisions of this Directive shall not prevent the Member States from providing incentives for new buildings, renovations or building elements which go beyond the cost-optimal levels."*

According to the new Directive 2010/31/EU, the Union financial instruments and other measures shall be introduced or adapted in order to promote energy efficiency measures. The Union financial instruments are (Official Journal of the European Union L 153, 18.6.2010, p. 15):

- European Regional Development Fund,
- Public-private partnership on "European Energy Efficient Buildings" initiative to encourage green technologies and develop energy efficient systems and materials in new and renovated buildings,
- The European Investment Bank-EIB initiative aims to encourage investments in energy efficiency,
- Investments of energy efficiency and "Marguerite Fund" under the leadership of the European Investment Bank: 2020 European Energy, Climate Change and Infrastructure Fund,
- Council Directive 2009/47/EC of 5 May 2009 amending Council Directive 2006/112/EC on VAT rates and the application of VAT at a reduced rate of not less than 5% in the repair and renovation of private homes,
- JEREMIE Structural Funds (Joint European Resources for micro to medium enterprises),
- Energy Efficiency Finance Facility,
- The Competitiveness and Innovation Framework Programme including the Intelligent Energy Europe II Programme aims to eliminate energy efficiency and energy-related market barriers from renewable sources, primarily through technical assistance organisation ELENA (European Local Energy Assistance),
- The Covenant of Mayors,
- Entrepreneurship and Innovation Program,
- Information and communication technology (ICT) Policy Support Program 2010 and the Seventh Research Framework Program,
- The European Bank for Reconstruction and Development is also financing to promote energy efficiency measures.

The European International Financial Institutions (IFIS), national programs and private sector financing instruments are also used in financing energy efficiency (European Commission, 2013:7–8).

The Energy Efficiency Directive 2012/27/EU, which entered into force on 04 December 2012 has been implemented by the Member States since 5 June

2014. The Energy Efficiency Directive contains restrictive measures to help the EU achieve its 20% energy efficiency target by 2020. This Directive introduces additional energy-saving requirements on EU countries' buildings. Examples of these requirements are that central government buildings should be built more energy efficient and EU countries should prepare national plans for the renovation of all building stock.

The Energy Efficiency Directive No. 2012/27/EU covers the renovation of public buildings, increasing energy efficiency in public services, mandatory energy audits for all major companies and the other similar energy efficiency provisions. With the new Directive, the following applications have been introduced.

- **Renovation of at least 3% of the public buildings each year:** Regulation requires that 3% of the surface area of public buildings with utility areas of 500 m2 and above, which are heated and/or cooled, not meeting the minimum energy performance criteria in the EU BEPD, are requested to be renovated annually. This limit, which was 500 m^2 by July 2015, has become 250 m^2 after July 2015.
- **Annual energy saving measures:** Member countries are obliged to undertake new energy efficiency regimes between 2014 and 2020 to provide at least 1.5% less energy use annually.
- **Public procurements:** The governments of the Member States are obliged to make energy-efficient decisions that are exemplary for public administrations when purchasing certain types of products or services and purchasing or leasing buildings.
- **The use of smart meters:** Member countries shall provide the use of individual smart meters, defined in EU BEPD, reflecting energy used for electricity, natural gas, central heating and cooling to the users correctly, having competitive prices, notifying end-user about energy consumption and usage in real time.
- **The use of individual consumption meters in multi-apartment buildings:** Individual smart meters shall be used for each unit in central heating/cooling systems used in multi-apartment or multi-purpose buildings, in separate heating system units and in heating/cooling systems serving more than one building in order to measure the consumption of heat and water until the date of 01 January 2017.
- **Billing and consumer information:** By 1 January 2015, Member States are obliged to ensure that the billing information is based on correct and actual consumption and the end user determines their own energy consumption. Billing information will be provided at least twice a year or quarterly, or upon actual consumption on request.

According to Article 12 of the Energy Efficiency Directive 2012/27/EU, The Member States shall take appropriate measures to encourage and facilitate the efficient use of energy by small energy customers, including domestic customers. These measures, which may be part of national strategies, can be a range of instruments and policies to encourage behavioural change in consumers, such as financial incentives, access to finance, grants or subventions, provision of information, sample projects and workplace activities.

Directive No. 2006/32/EC on energy end-use efficiency and energy services, emphasises the need to improve energy end-use efficiency and energy services, mainly by creating stronger incentives for the demanding side. Within the scope of the Directive, each EU Member State has prepared the National Energy Efficiency Action Plan which describes the energy efficiency improvement measures planned at the national level to achieve the energy saving target of the Directive (Buildings Performance Institute Europe -BPIE, 2010: 11).

On November 30, 2016, the European Commission proposed an update to the Buildings' Energy Performance Directive to encourage the use of smart technology in buildings, to streamline existing rules and to accelerate the renovation of buildings. This updated proposal was approved by the EU Council of Ministers on 14 May 2018 (https://ec.europa.eu/info/news/commission-welcomes-council-adoption-new-energy-performance-buildings-directive-2018-may-14_en).

The European Commission also published the EU Building Stock Observatory, a new building database so as to monitor the energy performance of buildings across Europe. The Commission has initiated a Smart Financing initiative for Smart Buildings to guide the investment in renewing of building stock. This has the potential to open additional public and private funds of 10 billion euros for energy efficiency and renewable energy consumption in the buildings (https://ec.europa.eu/energy/en/topics/energy-efficiency/buildings).

2.1.3 Obstacles against Energy Efficiency Investments in Buildings

There are many obstacles against energy efficiency investments in buildings. Those can be summarised as such (Buildings Performance Institute Europe-BPIE, 2010:13–14; CEPMC, 2012:60):

- **High transaction costs:** The time and effort required to make a decision and to receive sufficient information, the application of a loan and the arrangement of the work can be perceived as not worth returning in terms of energy saving.
- **Institutional handicaps:** Current acts or practices hinder the developments in energy efficiency.

- **Lack of information:** The lack of consumer awareness about the benefits of energy efficiency, both financially and environmentally, contributes to the difficulty of consumer behaviour and habits which are hard to change.
- **Energy prices:** Another obstacle involved in lack of information is known as price inflation. The unnecessary subvention of energy prices may disrupt the markets and hinder correct price formation which reflects the real marginal cost of energy use of the customers.
- **Lack of trained personnel or technical or administrative expertise**: The majority of actors in the building chain do not have enough training and knowledge of energy efficiency. Suppliers, producers, investors and financiers alike do not have the necessary skills to promote energy efficiency products to their customers properly.
- **Uncertainty about energy saving**: The inability to pinpoint the level of energy savings that both investors and customers will obtain, prevents these investments from being made.
- **Split incentives:** These incentives emerge when there are not many direct benefits for the person, which means that the person cannot benefit from the investments made for energy savings and it counts for both residential and commercial buildings. Although energy saving investments are to be made by the building owner, the one who benefits from these investments is the tenant or the occupier by paying lower energy bills. As a result, there is no direct incentive for landlords to invest in energy savings. On the other hand, if energy bills are meant to be paid by the landlord, the tenant will not do anything special in order to save energy. In either way, it is not natural to invest in energy efficiency measures for the actors in question.
- **Externalities:** The environment, energy security, social policy and employment can create a barrier to the investment in energy efficiency. Like environmental damages, how to internalise the costs of externalities is still an important issue.

2.1.4 Financial İncentives: EU Application

European Union legislation promotes Member States to provide tax incentives to encourage energy efficiency investments (European Commission, 2014a).

"Member States are at the centre of the realisation of energy efficiency policy and EU intervention should be well targeted and supportive to their actions. The EU's role is in:

(a) *establishing a common framework which creates the basis for coherent and mutually reinforcing mechanisms while leaving in being the responsibility of Member States to set the means to achieve the agreed objectives;*

(b) *creating a platform for exchanging best practice and stimulating capacity building;*
(c) *setting minimum requirements in areas where there is a risk of internal market distortions if the Member States take individual measures;*
(d) *using EU instruments to promote energy efficiency, e.g. through financing.*"

The resources required to finance energy efficiency in the European Union are planned centrally with the decisions of the EU Commission. The control and use of these resources are carried out by the European Bank for Reconstruction and Development (EBRD) and the Council of Europe Development Bank (CEB). These institutions provide long-term low-interest loan sources to the governments of member states, local governments, public banks and commercial banks to use in Efficiency Improvement Project (EIP) at all premises, primarily for housing and public banks. In addition to these, the Horizon 2020 programme, which EU Member States have established to support R&D projects, is also supporting innovative activities to increase energy efficiency in the buildings (Tarım, 2017: 20).

Member States re-plan and disseminate the financial resources they receive from the funds provided by the central government, by taking into account the population, income distribution and economic conditions in their respective countries. Whereas some of these resources are awarded as grants to small incomes, some are used to promote EIP applications. In addition, member states distribute the resources through public banks that they allocate from the state budget according to the size of the energy potential in the buildings which they specify through energy surveys (Tarım, 2017:20).

"National governments also use their own budgets to support energy efficiency in buildings. Many of the existing measures have been reported to the Commission through the National Energy Efficiency Action Plans (NEEAPs) and under the EPBD. These reports show that building-related measures represent a very high share of the reported energy savings (e.g. 58% for Italy, 63% for Ireland, 71% for Slovenia and 77% for Austria). Over three-quarters of the reported measures are grants and 'soft' loan schemes, followed by tax incentives. Instruments such as energy performance contracting, the use of assigned amount units under the Kyoto Protocol and energy suppliers' obligations are also used" (European Commission, 2013: 7).

Financial instruments used in energy efficiency in the EU member states are (Tarım, 2017:6):

- Grants and direct subventions,
- Interest rate subvention,
- Tax exemption, tax deductions and tax refunds,

- Reduced VAT rates,
- Risk Assurance,
- Performance Guarantees,
- Energy performance contracts,
- Energy efficiency programs of energy companies.

2.1.4.1 Grants and Direct Subventions

In order to encourage the use of effective construction methods and/or equipment, member states provide direct subventions to individuals or groups at a level of 10% -30% of the cost of energy savings, in cash-paid grants (Tarım, 2017:6).

2.1.4.2 Interest Rate Subventions

With this incentive, governments aim to accelerate the application of the Efficiency Improvement Project (EIP) in housing and to reduce the loan interest burden on the homeowners. In EIP applications the banks which give loans are paid from the state budget to cover all or some of the accrued interest of the loans. Sometimes, subvention support can also be given by the International Finance Agency or by in forms of long-term low-interest rate loans (Tarım, 2017:6–7).

2.1.4.3 Risk Assurance

"Risk assurances are issued by governments or International Finance Organizations to reduce the risk of borrowing in markets where political or economic risk is high and traditional banks are reluctant to give loans and thus to make getting loans more accessible" (Tarım, 2017:7). These loans play a role as a kind of incentive because of their reduced interest rates, due to the fact that the governments or International Financial Institutions are to pay the lender's financial damage when borrowers cannot pay their loans back (Tarım, 2017:7).

Risk assurances encourage sustainable commercial financing as it reduces risk concerns for commercial banks and makes them more willing to invest in energy efficiency projects. Most importantly, it can be extended to include customers who are not considered eligible for a loan (Tarım, 2017:7).

2.1.4.4 Energy Performance Contracts – EPC

"The EPC is a turnkey service that offers a variety of energy services to its customers, including the application of energy efficiency measures. In its simplest form, the EPC is the means by which expected savings on energy bills can be used to pay for the renovation of buildings. The building owner and the

Energy Services Company (ESCO) sign a performance contract that requires a certain level of energy savings. If the savings are below the guaranteed value, ESCO pays the difference as a penalty (Tarım, 2017:8)".

EPC contracts are mostly preferred for non-residential buildings, public buildings and commercial buildings. These contracts are appealing to building owners as they allow the up-front payment to be taken as a refund and the amount of money saved as a result of renewal. It is an appealing for the ESCO as it will generate revenue because of its share of energy savings to be provided as a result of the efficient design of the project (Tarım, 2017:8).

The Energy Performance Contract is different from other incentives in terms of promoting commercial financing or financing from the private sector. However, there are some ESCOs operating partly or wholly of state-owned enterprises as well (Tarım, 2017:9).

2.1.4.5 Energy efficiency programs of energy companies

"The Energy Efficiency Directive No. 2006/32/EC brought certain obligations for EIP applications to energy companies, industries and buildings (mainly residences, public buildings and commercial buildings). EU Member States benefit from various options when applying these obligations. In most countries, they are focused on making suppliers inform customers about their energy consumption and provide information about their energy saving options. However, some Member States have expanded this area of responsibility and have introduced energy-saving targets (legally enforceable obligations) for gas and heating companies. These energy-saving obligations have become a condition in the Energy Efficiency Directive No. 2012/27/EU, and have become a commitment in the Energy Community, and there are now ten EU energy saving obligations (Tarım, 2017:9)."

2.1.4.6 Tax Exemption, Tax Deductions, Tax Refunds and VAT Reduction

In the European Union countries some tax incentives, such as property tax exceptions, income tax reduction, income tax refund and reduced VAT rates, are provided to generate energy efficiency in buildings (Tarım, 2017:7).

Property Tax Exception: Some governments apply a partial or full exception to the property tax, limited to a specified period, to a building built with high energy efficiency performance.

Income Tax Deductions: It is the method that some member states apply. Deductions, within the amount to defray some of the portions of project expenses, are made from the income tax that will be paid by the homeowners who apply VAP to save energy in their residences.

Income Tax Refund: Some member states prefer to make refund from the income tax they have collected before.

Tax deduction and tax refund methods are the most common type of tax incentive preferred by the EU Member States to encourage increased energy performance in existing buildings.

Reduced VAT rates: Reduced VAT rates can be used in specific categories of products to encourage the consumption of energy efficient technology products and devices with high purchasing costs.

2.2 Financial Incentives in Financing of Energy Efficiency in Buildings: Applications in European Countries

2.2.1 United Kingdom

Government support is provided for projects to build renewable energy systems in order to reduce external dependency on natural gas consumption in heating of houses in the United Kingdom (Tarım, 2017:25).

The Domestic Renewable Heat Incentive (RHI): This incentive is a long-term financial support programme initiated by the government for homeowners to set up renewable heating systems in their residences located in the UK (England, Scotland and Wales). It is an incentive that anyone can apply for; however, it is most likely that those who live on by gas grids can benefit from this incentive more. If the rules of the programme are followed and implemented, payments are received every three months for seven years. The size of the payment relies on the size of the property and the kind of the heating system to be set up. https://assets.publishing.service.gov.uk/government/uploads/system/uploads/attachment_data/file/318080/domestic_rhi.pdf).

The Enhanced Capital Allowances: The Enhanced Capital Allowances (ECA) program can reduce 100% of investment spending on energy saving technologies listed in the Energy Technology Criteria List against the taxable profits of the period they invested. ECAs are requested in the same way as other capital allowances on the Corporation Tax Refund for companies, and Income Tax Refund for Individuals and Partnerships. One of the qualified technologies is high quality "Combined Heat and Power- CHP". In order to qualify for ECAs, it is a must for CHP plant to have Energy Efficiency Certificate. (https://www.gov.uk/guidance/combined-heat-and-power-incentives#climate-change-levy-exemption).

Climate Change Levy Exemption: The Climate Change Levy was initiated by the UK Government in 2001 and is collected from non-domestic energy sources used as fuel for lighting, heating and power. It is designed to promote energy efficiency and investment in energy-saving equipment, and thus to reduce greenhouse gas emissions. In order to benefit from this exemption, it is necessary to obtain an exemption certificate. This exemption will be used if 20% energy efficiency is met in the fuel used. Otherwise, this exemption will be taken back (https://www.gov.uk/guidance/combined-heat-and-power-incentives#climate-change-levy-exemption).

VAT Reduction: A VAT rate of 5% is implemented for specific energy-saving materials if used on premises or in village halls in the UK. In addition, all installations are covered in this reduced rate (including conventional systems) if this reduced rate is employed in a single or principal dwelling of whom are over 60 years old. These facilities are central heating systems and heating appliances, grant-funded installations of hot water tanks built in the factory, combined internal heat and power units and heating systems using renewable energy (Cansino et al., 2011: 3809).

Stamp Tax Exception: No stamp tax is paid for all new residences that meet the zero carbon standards and have a value of 500,000 British Pounds (605,080 Euros)(Cansino et al., 2011: 3809).

2.2.2 France

In France, there are government incentives called "*tax credits*" to support projects to increase energy efficiency in residential buildings (Tarım, 2017: 28). VAT Reduction of 5.5% is provided for energy efficiency of buildings over two years old (Directorate- General for Energy and Climate, 2017:27). In addition, 10-year interest-free loans are provided for buildings built before 1 January 1990 (Tarım, 2017:31).

The Housing Energy Renovation Plan (PREH), announced on March 21, 2013, has committed to renovating 500,000 houses annually by 2017. The plan includes multiple measures covering all aspects of renovation (Directorate-General for Energy and Climate, 2014: 21):

- Decision making (single points of contact, thermal renovation messengers);
- Financing (sustainable development tax credit, interest-free eco-loans and social housing eco-loans, energy saving certificates, private bonuses, application of third-party financing);
- Structuring the sector and developing a network that can respond correctly to questions and requests (training and competence of professionals).

The aim of the financial support package is to support the income of every household. Zero-interest eco-loan (eco-PTZ) and sustainable development tax credit are applied for private housing. To encourage a more profound renovation, the tax credit runs at two rates (Buildings Performance Institute Europe – BPIE, 2014: 38):

- 25% for work packages with at least two measures;
- 15% for low-income households of those who take a single action.

Interest-free eco-loan (eco-PTZ): Interest-free eco-credit (eco-PTZ), which has been applied since 1 April 2009, is being implemented to finance significant renovations of those who rent their homes or those who live in their own homes (Directorate- General for Energy and Climate, 2017:27).

This loan finances up to 30,000 euros to undertake the necessary work to improve the energy performance of a home for over a period of 10 years. The time period of the loan can be extended to 15 years by the bank. In this case, it is not possible to benefit from the tax credit for the interest accrued between the tenth and fifteenth years (Directorate- General for Energy and Climate, 2014:25).

Energy transition tax credit (crédit d'impôt transition énergétique – CITE): Individuals have been taking advantage of the tax credit for the purchase and installation of the equipment that will be used in existing buildings to provide energy saving since 2005. With the aim to encourage the use of energy efficient equipment and technologies, equipment list and necessary performance criteria for the tax credit have been revised regularly since it was created. The tax programme (CITE) was improved on 1 September 2014 by enforcing the rule of a single rate of 30% without any income requirements so as to accelerate the rate of energy renovations (Directorate- General for Energy and Climate, 2017:26).

Property Tax Deduction: In 2006, Finance Act was amended and an exception at a rate of 50%–100% was granted for five years from the property tax on real estates developed by local governments. Since 1 January 2009, this exception has been made available to all buildings completed before 31 December 2008 and to new houses (on the condition that they have LEB (low-energy building) label) completed (Directorate-General for Energy and Climate, 2017:28–29).

VAT Reduction: As of 1 January 2014, VAT rates on energy modifications of buildings that are older than two years and eligible for the tax credit requirements, has been reduced to 5.5% with the Article 9 of the Finance Act (Buildings Performance Institute Europe –BPIE, 2014:39; Directorate-General for Energy and Climate, 2014:26, Directorate-General for Energy and Climate, 2017:2).

2.2.3 Germany

Germany initiated the National Action Plan on Energy Efficiency (NAPE), the central building stone of the energy efficiency strategy, by the end of 2014. In this context, for example, a series of urgent actions have been launched, including the introduction of new competitive bidding processes for energy efficiency, the development of promotional activities for building renovation and the market incentive programme for the use of renewable energies (Federal Ministry for Economic Affairs and Energy-BMWi, 2015:5).

On 18 November 2015, the German Federal Government adopted the Energy Efficiency Strategy for Buildings. By effectively combining renewable energy with measures to improve energy efficiency, it provides a vision of how to reach an almost carbon-neutral building structure by 2050 (https://www.bmwi.de/Redaktion/EN/Textsammlungen/Energy/napeverbraucher.html?cms_artId=255692).

On 1 January 2016, the Federal Ministry of Economics and Energy initiated the new Energy Efficiency Incentive Program (APEE), which will be financed for the modernisation of home heating and ventilation systems. The aim of the program is to create an incentive that will include tax reductions for innovation and investment in efficient and renewable based heating systems. The program will improve and strengthen existing financing programs (https://www.bmwi.de/Redaktion/EN/Textsammlungen/Energy/napeverbraucher.html?cms_artId=255692).

The Energy Efficiency Incentive Program is government supported for three years. The cost of the project is financed in the form of low-interest loans and grants. Once the investment is completed, 600 Euros and 35% of the project fee are paid back (Tarım, 2017: 26).

German Development Bank – KfW is the primary funding institution for energy efficiency. Since 1996, KfW has gained significant experience in promoting thermal improvement investments in the housing sector through preferential loans and grants. The bank has two main specially designed programs. Energy efficiency investment in the housing sector: "Energy Efficient Renovation – Energieeffizient Sanieren" and "Energy Efficient Construction – Energieeffizient Bauen" (Neuhoff vd., 2012: 242).

Those who are interested in establishing a fossil-fuel-based heating system can apply for funding under a ventilation and heating package by using the same application procedure as the KfW Energy-Efficient Modernization Programme. Financing can be used either as a grant or as a loan. Within the scope of the heating and ventilating package, grants will be increased from 10% to 15% of the investment costs (https://www.bmwi.de/Redaktion/EN/Textsammlungen/Energy/napeverbraucher.html?cms_artId=255692).

Funding for fuel cell heating systems is offered under the heading Energy-efficient Construction and Retrofitting-Fuel Cell Grant. This program completes existing financing programs for energy efficient construction and strengthening. Residential households have been able to apply for financing under the program since August 2016. In July 2017, it became open to small and medium-sized businesses (SMEs), contractors, charities and local authorities once involving the non-residential buildings in the program (https://www.bmwi.de/Redaktion/EN/Textsammlungen/ Energy/napeverbraucher.html?cms_artId=255692).

Individuals wishing to set up a renewable energy heating system can apply for financing under a ventilation and heating package by using the same application procedure under the Market Incentive Programme (MAP) for renewable energy in the heating market. Those who apply for financing under the heating package can receive a 20% refund of the previously paid funds for the heating system backups and 600 € for the heating system optimisation under the Market Incentive Programme (https://www.bmwi.de/Redaktion/EN/Textsammlungen/Energy/napeverbraucher.html?cms_artId=255692).

All commercial enterprises, self-employers and contractors can benefit from the funds under the CO2 Building Modernization Programme for the construction and modification of energy-efficient buildings. Since 1 October 2015, municipalities and social institutions have been entitled to get support through the KfW for the construction of new, especially energy-efficient buildings (Federal Ministry for Economic Affairs and Energy-BMWi, 2015:69). This programme financed by KfW has been very successful. Since 2006, more than 4.6 million residences have been built or modernised. The duration of the program has been extended until 2018 (https://www.bmwi.de/Redaktion/EN/Textsammlungen/Energy/napeverbraucher.html?cms_artId=255692).

Tax deduction of craftsmen's bills: If other public funds weren't received, landlords and tenants could deduct 20% of the labour costs (1.200 euros maximum) of craftsmen bills from their income tax. The owner can regard the costs of energy efficiency measures as maintenance costs, and thus tax expenses can be reduced (Federal Ministry for Economic Affairs and Energy-BMWi, 2015:70).

2.2.4 Poland

By using market-based mechanisms, Poland has provided substantial energy efficiency gains in all economic sectors. Within the government's strategy to improve energy efficiency, the energy efficiency framework is based on three fundamentals: (Dünya Bankası, 2011: 52)

- Direct regulation (standards),
- Supporting the market with economic and financial incentives,
- Supportive instruments such as information, education, research and development.

The Thermo-Modernization Fund, which has been in service in Poland since 1998 and is managed by the Polish State Development Bank – Gospodarstwa Krajowego (BKG), is an excellent example of one of the major national programs in energy efficiency applications (Tarım, 2017: 33; Dünya Bankası, 2011: 53). It provides financial support as grants to investors that carry out thermo-modernization and renovation projects (apartment management, residential cooperative management, residential sites, detached dwellings, municipalities, local governments, regional heating systems or heat power plants, etc.) to reduce energy consumption (Tarım, 2017: 34). The Fund provides financial support through a premium (refunded by the state through participating financial institutions) that covers up to 20% of the loans used to finance thermal insulation improvements in buildings (Dünya Bankası, 2011: 53).

2.2.5 Italy

Since 2007, Italy has been offering tax incentives for energy efficiency improvements in existing buildings. The program provides tax deductions on strengthening measures such as heat insulation, installation of solar panels, changing of heating and air conditioning systems, or extensive reinforcement work for dwellings and companies. The tax credit can cover 55% of the energy cost, but the measure cannot exceed the maximum monetary value determined according to the type. Tax credits are refunded within ten years, starting with the completion of the job (Neuhoff vd., 2012: 236–237).

2.3 Financial İncentive in Financing of Energy Efficiency in Buildings: Turkey Application

2.3.1 Legal Regulations

The aim of the Energy Efficiency Law No. 5627, enacted in 2007, has been defined as an effective use of energy, prevention of waste, reduction of energy costs on the economy, and improvement of the efficiency of energy resources and energy use to protect the environment.

The National Climate Change Strategy Document covering the years between 2010 and 2023 aims to increase energy efficiency and reduce greenhouse gas emissions in the building, industry, transport and energy sectors.

With the Energy Efficiency Strategy Document covering the years between 2012 and 2023, a policy supported by outcome-oriented targets and actions to achieve the targets have been planned.

In addition, energy efficiency measures to be taken during the planning period have been determined with respect to "Development of Energy Efficiency Program" of the Tenth Development Plan covering the period 2014–2018 (T.C. Kalkınma Bakanlığı, 2014).

The targets for energy efficiency have been defined in the Ministry of Energy and Natural Resources 2015–2019 Strategic Plan.

Within the scope of the Directive 2012/27/EU on energy efficiency, published by the European Parliament and the Council on 25 October 2012, member states have been obliged to prepare national energy efficiency action plans that provide a common structural framework for energy efficiency and methods for application.

The targets of the National Energy Efficiency Action Plan under the National Energy and Mine Policy, prepared by the Ministry of Energy and Natural Resources in 2017, were also included.

The National Energy Efficiency Action Plan (2017–2023) was put into force on 2 January 2018 with the publication of the Official Gazette. According to the National Energy Efficiency Action Plan, macro-economical analyses will be conducted for the rehabilitation of existing buildings within the scope of *Rehabilitation, and Energy Efficiency Improvement of Buildings* and one or more of the methods of incentive, support, taxation or penal sanction shall be applied in the direction of these analyses.

2.3.2 Financial İncentives

Within the scope of the "*Law on the Amendment of Certain Laws for the Improvement of the Investment Environment*" numbered 6728, which was enacted on 15 July 20, in "*Income Tax Act*" *No*. 193 and "*Stamp Tax Act*" No. 488 incentives were provided for the works carried out to provide heat insulation and energy saving in the buildings. With this regulation, due process of the article 40/7 of the Income Tax Act expenses made to save energy and heat insulation can be deducted as expense from the tax base.

As required by Income Tax Act a. 74/6, which entered into force on 7 September 2016, the expenditures for heat insulation and energy saving which are made by the lessor and which increase the economic value of the property can be deducted from the real estate capital. (These expenditures can be treated as a cost if they exceed the amount (1000 TL for 2018) set out in Article 313 of the Tax Procedural Law within a calendar year.)

With the amendment in the Stamp Tax Act No.6728 a.29, tax exception has been provided for all kinds of documents set during the expenditures made for heat insulation and energy saving (Stampt Tax Act, List II, Article IV/47).

With the paragraph added to Article 123 of Act of Fees no. 492, transactions made to provide heat insulation and energy saving are exempted from the fees.

In addition to these incentives, public banks and commercial banks have been provided resources in different amounts for different purposes. Additionally, KOSGEB provides grant support to small and medium-sized enterprises (SME), which operate in health, tourism, education and culture sectors, for EIP applications and energy surveys in their buildings.

3 Conclusion

Energy efficiency is of vital importance for both Turkey's and the European Union's present and future. Turkey has adopted the financing methods within the same respect of the European Union's applications. In the European Union countries, loans are provided in the form of grants with lower interest rates than tax incentives. Energy efficiency in residences and industries in many countries are also improved with the help of low-interest loans and grants (Geller et al., 2006: 566). In some countries tax credits and tax deductions are also provided, while in Turkey expense reduction in Income Tax Act, exceptions in Stamp Tax Act and in Act of Fees have been implemented by 2016 for transactions to provide heat insulation of buildings. VAT reduction, title deed fees reduction, property tax reduction and Banking and Insurance Tax exception are demanded for energy efficient buildings in construction sector (Acuner, 2014:34). The satisfaction of this demand will create positive results in terms of energy efficiency in the buildings.

References

Acuner, E. (2014). *Binalarda Enerji Verimliliği ve Finansmanı Raporu*, İMSAD Yayın No. İMSAD-R/2014-11/376, İstanbul. http://imsad.org/Uploads/Files/imsad_bev_ rap_kasim_2014.pdf (10.03.2018).

Buildings Performance Institute Europe- BPIE. (2010). *Financing Energy Efficiency (EE) in Buildings*, Background Paper, November, Brussels.

Buildings Performance Institute Europe- BPIE. (2014). *Renovation Strategies of Selected EU Countries, A Status Report on Compliance with Article 4 of The Energy Efficiency Directive*, November, Brussels.

Cansino, J.M., Pablo-Romero, M.P, Roma´n, R. and Yn˜iguez R. (2011) "Promoting Renewable Energy Sources for Heating and Cooling in EU-27 Countries", *Energy Policy*, Volume 39, Issue 6, June 2011, Pages 3803–3812.

CEPMC (2012). *Binalarda Enerji Verimliliği Finansmanı, Türkiye'nin Yol Haritasi AB'nin Durum Analizi, AB Mevzuatı Çerçevesinde Binalarda Enerji*

Verimliliğinin Finansmanı ve Hukuki Düzenlemeler ile İlgili Sektörlerarası İşbirliği Projesi Rehber Kitabı, Editör: Özden Özkan Çayırlı, İstanbul, İMSAD Yayın No İMSAD-R/2012-11/373. http://imsad.org/Uploads/Files/rehber_ana.pdf (10.03.2018).

Deloitte (2016). *Energy Efficiency in Europe*. https://www2.deloitte.com/global / en/pages /energy-and-resources/articles/ energy-efficiency-in-europe.html (17.11.2017).

Directorate- General for Energy and Climate (2014). *Energy Efficiency Action Plan for France – 2014*, https://ec.europa.eu/energy/sites/ener/files/documents/2014 _neeap _en_france.pdf (29.04.2018).

Directorate- General for Energy and Climate (2017). *Report of France Pursuant to Articles 24(1) and 24(2) of Directive 2012/27/EU of the European Parliament and of the Council of 25 October 2012 on Energy Efficiency*, 2017 Update. https://ec.europa.eu/energy/sites/ener/files/documents/fr_neeap_2017_en.pdf (22.11.2017).

Dünya Bankası (2011). *Türkiye'de Enerji Tasarrufu Potansiyelini Kullanmak*, Sürdürülebilir Kalkınma Bölümü (ECSSD) Avrupa ve Orta Asya Bölgesi (ECA), Ocak. http://documents.worldbank.org/curated/en/521081468318313907/pdf/522100Energy0S0ential0Energy0Turkey.pdf (22.04.2018).

Enerji Verimliliği Kanunu, (2007, 2 Mayıs). T.C. Resmi Gazete (Sayı: 26510).

Efficiency Valuation Organization- EVO (2012). *International Performance Measurement and Verification Protocol, Concepts and Options for Determining Energy and Water Savings Volume 1*, January, EVO, 10000-1:2012, Canada.http://www.eeperformance.org/uploads/8/6/5/0/8650231/ipmvp_volume_i__2012.pdf (09.03.2018).

European Commission (2010). Communication From The Commission to The European Parliament, The Council, The European Economic And Social Committee, The Committee Of The Regions And The European, *Energy 2020 A Strategy For Competitive, Sustainable And Secure Energy* {SEC(2010) 1346}, Brussels, 10.11.2010, COM(2010) 639 final. https://mgimo.ru/files2/y11_2013/243404/10.3.1_com_2010_0639_energy_2020.pdf (08.03.2018).

European Commission (2013). *Report from The Commission to The European Parliament and The Council, Financial Support for Energy Efficiency in Buildings*, Brussels, 18.4.2013, COM(2013) 225 final. https://ec.europa.eu /energy/sites/ener/files/documents/report_financing_ee_buildings_com_2013_225_en.pdf (23.04.2018).

European Commission (2014a). *Commission Staff Working Document Executive Summary of The Impact Assessment Brussels*, 23.7.2014, SWD (2014) 256 final. https://ec.europa.eu/energy/sites/ener/files/documents /2014_ eec _ executive_summary _ 0.pdf (23.04.2018).

European Commission (2014b), *Communication from The Commission to The European Parliament, The Council, The European Economic And Social Committee and The Committee of The Regions A Policy Framework for Climate and Energy in The Period From 2020 to 2030*, Brussels, 22.1.2014, COM (2014) 15 Final. http://eur-lex.europa.eu/legal-content/EN/TXT/PDF/?uri= CELEX:52014DC0015&from=EN (05.05.2018).

European Commission (2016). *Accelerating Clean Energy in Buildings to the Communication From The Commission to The European Parliament*, The Council, The European Economic And Social Committee, The Committee Of The Regions And The European Investment Bank Clean Energy For All European, Brussels, 30.11.2016, COM(2016) 860 final ANNEX 1 https://ec.europa.eu/energy/sites/ener/files/documents/1_en_annexe_autre_acte_part1_v9.pdf (08.03.2018).

European Commission (2017). *Good Practice in Energy Efficiency For a Sustainable, Safer and More Competitive Europe*, Belgium: European Union.

European Union (2012). *Energy Roadmap 2050'* (COM(2011) 885 final of 15 December 2011), Luxembourg: Publications Office of the European Union, 2012.https://ec.europa.eu/energy/sites/ener/files/documents/2012_energy_roadmap_2050_en_0.pdf (01.05.2018).

Federal Ministry for Economic Affairs and Energy-BMWi (2015). *Energy Efficiency Strategy for Buildings*, Berlin. https://www.bmwi.de/Redaktion /EN/Publikationen/energy-efficiency-strategybuildings.pdf?__blob=publicationFile&v=6 (24.10.2017).

Geller, H., Harrington P., Rosenfeld A.H., Tanishima S. & Unander F. (2006). "Policies For Increasing Energy Efficiency: Thirty Years of Experience in OECD Countries", *Energy Policy* Volume 34, Issue 5, March, Pages 556–573. https://www.sciencedirect.com/science/article/pii/S0301421505003113 (01.12.2017).

Neuhoff, K., Stelmakh, K., Amecke, H., Novikova, A., Deason, J., Hobbs, A. (2012). "Financial Incentives for Energy Efficiency Retrofits in Buildings", ACEEE Summer Study on Energy Efficiency in Buildings. https://aceee.org/files/proceedings/ 2012 data/papers/0193-000422.pdf (05.05.2018).

Official Journal of the European Union L 153, 18.6.2010.

OECD/IEA (2013). *Energy Policies of IEA Countries Germany, 2013 Review,*Paris.http://www.iea.org/publications/freepublications/publication/UK2012_free.pdf (27.10.2017).

OECD/IEA (2014). *Capturing the Multiple Benefits of Energy Efficiency*, OECD/IEA, Paris. http://www.iea.org/publications/ freepublications/publication/Multiple_Benefits_of_Energy_Efficiency.pdf (20.09.2017).

Sudhakara Reddy, B., Assenza, G.B., Assenza D. & Hasselmann, F (2009). *Energy Efficiency and Climate Change Conserving Power for a Sustainable Future*, New Delhi: SAGE Publications India Pvt Lt. http://sk.sagepub.com/books/energy-efficiency-and-climate-change (08.03.2018).

Tarım, M. (2017). *Binalarda Enerji Verimliliğini Arttıracak Projeler İçin AB ve Türkiye'de Bulunan Finans Kaynakları Mali Politikaları ve Araçlar*, Ankara: Binalarda Enerji Verimliliğinin Artırılması İçin Teknik Yardım Projesi.

T.C. Kalkınma Bakanlığı (2014). *Onuncu Kalkınma Planı (2014–2018).* http://kkp.tarim.gov.tr/sp/Onuncu%20Kalk%C4%B1nma%20Plan%C4%B1(2014-2018).pdf (15.01.2018).

Tuğrul, B. (2017). *Sanayide Enerji Yönetimi ve Yönetişimi*, Toprak İşveren Dergisi, Sayı 113, Mart, ss.8–13.

Yang, M. & Yu, X. (2015). *Energy Efficiency Benefits for Environment and Society*, XXVIII. 180p. Springer. http://www.springer.com/gp/book/9781447166658 (20.09.2017).

Yiğit Şakar, A. (2017). *Enerji Verimliliği Alanında Yapılacak Yatırımlara Sağlanan Vergisel Teşvikler: Türkiye Uygulaması*, Eurasian Academy of Sciences Eurasian Business & Economics Journal, 201, Volume: 11: Pages 208–222. Published Online Otober2017 (http://busecon.eurasianacademy.org) http://dx.doi.org/10.17740/eas.econ.2017-V11-12.

Yüksekkaya T. (2016). *Binalarda Enerji Verimliliği AB ve Türk Mevzuatı*, Ankara.

https://assets.publishing.service.gov.uk/government/uploads/system/uploads/attachment_data/file/318080/domestic_rhi.pdf (04.05.2018).

https://www.avrupa.info.tr/tr/enerji-abnin-hedefleri-58 (05.05.2018).

http://beva.csb.gov.tr/Sayfa.aspx?id=29 (18.10.2017).

http://beva.csb.gov.tr/Sayfa.aspx?id=64 (18.10.2017).

https://www.bmwi.de/Redaktion/EN/Textsammlungen/Energy/napeverbraucher.html?cms_artId=255692 (23.04.2018).

https://ec.europa.eu/info/news/commission-welcomes-council-adoption-new-energy-performance-buildings-directive-2018-may-14_en (28.05.2018).

https://ec.europa.eu/energy/en/topics/energy-efficiency/buildings (01.05.2018).

https://ec.europa.eu/energy/en/topics/energy-strategy-and-energy-union/2030-energy-strategy (05.05.2018).

https://www.gov.uk/guidance/combined-heat-and-power-incentives#climate-change-levy-exemption (04.04.2018).

https://www.metering.com/regional-news/north-america/international-energy-efficiency-financing-protocol-ieefp-available/ (05.05.2018).

Mesut Yücesan

Trade Wars and Turkish Search for New Foreign Trade Markets under the Pressure of Foreign Exchange Rate

Abstract: The concept of trade wars is usually considered as a product of the US President Trump; yet, it has a deeper historical background. Trade wars can be associated with the periods when the focus is on protective foreign trade policies, with free foreign trade assumptions taking a backseat. There have been many periods that could be described as trade wars during the development of the global economic system. It is remarkable that countries resort to protective policies to be less affected by the consequences of the negative conjunctures, usually following wars or crisis. In this sense, similarly, after the 2008 Global Financial Crisis, countries relied on protective policies. The US President Trump has enforced protective policies in the foreign trade activities with many countries, especially China, which contributed to the emergence of trade wars. Turkey seeks to make the best of its foreign trade potential, despite the fluctuations in exchange rates amid the negative outlook caused by the current conjuncture. Also, Turkey must increase its share in existing foreign trade markets and enter new foreign trade markets to meet the desired amount of 500 billion dollars, which is the country's target exports for the year 2023. This study analyzes how the groups of target and priority countries, which are assigned by the Ministry of Economy to serve as a roadmap for Turkish exporters and are annually updated, react to the changes in foreign currency rates in the period of Trade Wars. The findings of the study demonstrate that foreign exchange volatility does not have an impact on the exports of the countries included in the analysis. However, there is a statistically significant and negative correlation between the imports of the mentioned countries and foreign exchange volatility. As fluctuations in foreign exchange rates increase, the imports of the countries in the analysis decrease. The size of this negative correlation is small enough to be overlooked.

Keywords: Trade Wars, Foreign Exchange Wars, New Foreign Trade Markets, Protective Foreign Trade

JEL Classification Codes: F01, F10, F31

1 Introduction

The first question to which the Spaniards coming to an unknown shore in the following years after the discovery of America sought for an answer, was whether there was gold or silver hidden in the surroundings. They then considered whether the shore was worth establishing a settlement or the country was worth conquering, based on the answer. Plano Campino, who was a monk sent as an envoy to one of the sons of the famous Genghis Khan by the King of France, reported that the Tatars constantly asked him if there were many sheep and cattle in the Kingdom of France or not. The question asked by the Tatars and the question asked by the Spaniards served the same purpose (Smith, 2002: 5). While a country needed to have silver and gold mines to be worth conquering for the Spaniards in a country with precious metals as the source of wealth, the new lands to be conquered by the Tatars in a country with sheep and cattle as an important indicator of wealth needed to sustain herds of sheep and cattle. No matter how differently they defined the concept of wealth, it is a fact that all nations seek for wealth. The search for wealth, which was previously through wars or colonialism, is now through foreign trade. It is needless to say that this previous search for wealth has evolved into the search for new foreign trade markets where the countries in the global economic system could market their export goods. By benefiting from their foreign trade potential to the greatest extent possible, countries seek to increase their wealth.

Many countries implemented protective policies until the late 1970s. These practices, called import substitution policies, were a limiting factor in the foreign trade volume on the world economy. With the Cold War erupting between the USA and Russia in the years following the World Wards and ending in favor of the USA, these protective policies were gradually replaced by open economy policies. Today, many countries have adopted an export-led growth model as their growth strategy. There were fluctuations in exchange rates with the collapse of the Bretton-Woods System and the question whether these fluctuations negatively affected the foreign trade volumes of countries due to their exports or not has become a significant subject of study. Besides, particularly in recent years, the USA and China adopted an export-led growth strategy after January 24, 1980, economic package. Adopting an export-led growth strategy after 1980, Turkey is a developing country which enhances its degree of integration into the global economic system day by day. The country set the goal to increase its total exports to 500 billion dollars for the year 2023, which will mark the 100th year anniversary of the foundation of the Turkish Republic. It stands to reason that with its total exports of 142,6 billion dollars in 2016, Turkey must increase its share in existing foreign trade markets and accelerate its search for new foreign trade markets in within a short period of seven years to meet the desired amount of 500 billion dollars. Further, to that end, Turkey needs to minimize the challenges brought about by the currency and trade wars as much as possible.

2 Trade Wars

All the countries of the world were affected, albeit to different degrees, by the global economic crisis, which originated in the real estate markets of the United States and broke out with the bankruptcy of Lehman Brothers in the second half of 2007. This negative conjuncture, called the 2008 Global Financial Crisis, impacted developed countries as well as many developing countries and thus turned into a worldwide crisis. The crisis that started in the USA first led to the foreign debt crisis in the Greek economy and then caused problems in many European countries. It has even raised doubts over the European Union and its institutions. Being felt worldwide, the crisis narrowed the volume of global foreign trade. Many countries focused on protective foreign trade policies to avoid the problems caused by the global crisis.

Following the recent global financial crisis, the protective foreign trade policies implemented by the countries to achieve their political and economic objectives, have become more evident. It is particularly striking that the G20 countries have increasingly adopted protectionism. Due to the deterioration of the economic indicators in the post-crisis period and the effects of such deterioration, which was greatly felt by the actors, it has become widely believed that the protective measures, which undermine the basic rationale of international agreements and free-market economics, serve as a way out for many countries in the long term (Ünay & Dilek, 2018: 13).

In a broad sense, protectionism is defined as arrangements that aim to limit the entry of the goods of foreign origin into the domestic market or to ensure that the domestic goods are preferred over the goods of foreign origin in the domestic market. Accordingly, various measures such as restrictions on imports, quantity restrictions, customs duties, restrictions on foreign exchange allocation are applied. In other words, protectionism is considered a foreign trade policy based on the perception that a country must protect its domestic manufacturers against all kinds of destructive foreign competition (Ertürk, 2017: 91).

In economics, the basis of protectionism goes back to the Mercantilist period. The reason is that during this period, the countries generally followed certain policies that promoted exports and considered imports as a threat to themselves. That is to say, the most common policy in the Mercantilist period was to prevent the import of precious metals, regarded as the source of wealth. It was believed that any foreign trade activity between countries would result in a winner and a loser in an absolute manner. The pro-free trade views of the liberal economic approach that emerged in later periods led to the destruction of the protective policies of the Mercantilists. In the light of the classical theories of foreign trade, liberalism became prevalent all over the world. Besides this radical transformation, the following chronological list demonstrates the periods when protectionism was promoted in foreign trade as well:

- Years between 1875–1914 (golden age and trade liberalization)
- Years between 1914-1929-1944 (war period, stagnation, protectionism, depression)
- Years between 1944–1970 (the period of institutional capitalism, commercial liberalization)
- Years between 1970–1980 (Opec crisis, stagflation, new protectionism period)
- Years between 1980–2000 (neoliberal policies, multinational corporations, trade liberalization, competition, non-tariff instruments)
- Years between 2000–2008 (financial globalization)
- Year 2008-.... New protectionism period until today (Mangır & Acet, 2014: 95).

It is certain that the 1930s were the years when the protective reflexes were most intense. The US Administration and Congress, panicking after the 1929 crisis, increased the average of customs duties to 60% in 1930, which inflicted a fatal blow on the trade with Europe and the economy of the continent; such a blow was regarded as one of the key factors leading to fascism and the World War II by many writers (Kuneralp, 2018: 1). Since 2009, the World Trade Organization (WTO) has been monitoring the Member States regarding protectionism in international trade and regularly reporting their findings to the public. In this framework, according to the report released on July 10, 2017, the member countries implemented a total of 251 trade barriers between October 2016 and May 2017. Such figure corresponds to 36 commercial trade barriers per month. These barriers can be analyzed under two main categories. The barriers in the first category, which can be called restrictive trade barriers, consist of traditional trade barriers, including new customs tariffs to import and export or upgrading of existing customs tariffs, import prohibitions or quantity restrictions (quotas), mandatory use of domestic content, mixed and lengthy customs procedures as well as temporary or permanent taxation on imports and exports. The barriers in the second category, which can be called administrative measures and mostly consist of anti-dumping taxes, are restrictions on preventing unfair competition in international trade, rather than promoting protectionism as a principle (Türkiye Cumhuriyet Merkez Bankası, 2018).

Although protective policies have become prevalent on a global scale, it can be stated that the US President Trump and his explanations caused what is today called the Trade Wars. During his presidential campaign, President Donald

Tab 1: US Foreign Trade in China (Million Dollars)

YEAR	EXPORT	IMPORT	FOREIGN TRADE DEFICIT
2000	16,185.2	100,018.2	83,833
2008	69,732.8	337,772.6	268,039.8
2009	69,496.7	296,373.9	226,877.2
2010	91,911.1	364,952.6	273,041.6
2011	104,121.5	399,371.2	295,249.7
2012	110,516.6	425,619.1	315,102.5
2013	121,746.2	440,430	318,683.8
2014	123,657.2	468,474.9	344,817.7
2015	115,873.4	483,201.7	367,328.3
2016	115,545.5	462,542.0	346,996.5
2017	129,893.6	505,470.0	375,576.4

Source: https://www.bloomberght.com/haberler/haber/2132677-abd-nin-cin-ile-imtihani-astronomik-ticaret-aciklari (Date of access: 22.08.2018).

Trump promised to implement protective policies on the assumption that the orderly trade system promoted and led by the USA since its establishment in the World War does not serve US interests anymore, and now, President Trump started to implement these policies.

The first move that possibly led to a trade war between China and the United States was taken by President Trump on March 8 (Aran, B. 2018: 2). Following the moves by the USA, China declared to make similar moves, and after that, many statements were made regarding the advent of a potentially global-scale trade war. This tension, which started between the USA and China being the first two countries in the global trade volume, is still escalating.

The USA and China have a long history of trade partnership. The following table clearly shows the figures regarding the foreign trade of the USA with China and the resulting foreign trade deficit. It is evident that the commercial relations between the two countries have been rapidly strengthened since 1985. The USA had a negligible foreign trade deficit of only six million dollars in 1985.

As seen in the table above, there were improvements in the foreign trade between the USA and China in favor of China every year, particularly after 2008. In its foreign trade with the USA, which is the leader of the global trade, China had a large foreign trade deficit of 375 billion dollars. It can be stated that the USA rationally took protective measures for the closure of such a large foreign trade deficit.

3 Foreign Exchange Wars

The concept of "Foreign Exchange Wars" is not a new concept. In the 1930s, to explain a similar situation, the economist Joan Robinson used the concept of beggar-thy-neighbor that defines the policies implemented at that time. It is reported that Robinson inspired from a British card game and coined the term "beggar-thy-neighbor." Today, this kind of games, where a player eliminates the other, and his or her gain equal to the other's loss, are called the zero-sum game. In economics, a beggar-thy-neighbor policy means that a country has its policy applied against its trading countries and implements import restrictions and foreign exchange policies damaging the trading country to overcome certain problems in its economy such as inflation, the balance of payments and unemployment (Pınar & Uzunoğlu, 2013: 5).

The periods considered as trade wars in the historical process can be grouped under three sub-headings, which are respectively: the period where gold standards were used until the Bretton Woods meeting (1907–1945), the period from Bretton Woods to Oil Crises (1971–1992) and today, where there is an international system in the multipolar world. In the first part of the foreign exchange wars, the monetary system based on gold standards collapsed and the United States, as a rising force, was on the world stage. Coal was considered as the most important natural resource in this period. In the second part of the foreign exchange wars, the Bretton Woods system changed in the international monetary system. The rising force of this period was Japan, and the most important natural resources were oil and nuclear energy. In the third period, the monetary system became completely based on the dollar currency. The rising force was China, and the most important natural resources were oil and natural gas (Arana, V, G. 2014: 76).

Lastly, the Minister of Finance of Brazil Guido Mantega claimed that the countries weakening their monetary values to increase their competitiveness started an "international foreign exchange war," which put the foreign exchange wars on the world agenda once again. Following this statement, the topic of the foreign exchange wars has become one of the most controversial topics on a global scale. Another current topic is the impacts of the fluctuations in foreign exchange rates on the foreign trade of countries. These topics are relevant for Turkey as well. Setting the goal to increase its total exports to 500 billion dollars for the year 2023, Turkey must continue its foreign exchange activities without slowing down in this period called the foreign exchange wars.

4 Econometric Method and Method Application

With the current foreign trade activities, it seems very difficult for Turkey to meet the 2023 export goals. The global topics such as the foreign exchange wars and trade wars have particularly narrowed the global trade volume. It is a necessity for Turkey to search for new foreign trade markets regardless of global negatives. The main reasons for such a necessity were the inability to meet domestic demand for energy, the dominance of the European Union countries in the foreign trade volume and the current account deficit problem evolving into a structural problem. Due to such reasons, it has become a prerequisite for Turkey to be in search of new foreign trade markets. To that end, the 2023 Turkey Export Strategy and Action Plan were prepared by the Ministry of Economy of the Republic of Turkey. In concordance with this action plan, the Ministry of Economy classified the countries in the world as target and priority countries to serve as a road map for the exporters in Turkey. The classification aims to increase the level of exports in existing foreign trade markets and also to boost export figures by opening to new foreign trade markets.

This present study performed a time series analysis to show how the countries specified by the ministry were affected by the changes in foreign exchange rates. Further, the study individually analyzed the export and import equations for these countries.

4.1 Country Selection and Limitations

The Ministry of Economy utilized a two-step method in determining the target and priority countries among the countries in the global economy. The first step involved the classification of the world countries based on certain criteria related to foreign trade and the size of national income and decided on 127 countries. The second step involved the selection of 17 Target Countries and 27 Priority Countries among these 127 countries.

During the process of selection, the data obtained from the IMF database were used, and the countries were selected according to the following two criteria:

Criterion 1: With a GDP higher than 10 billion dollars
Criterion 2: With total imports exceeding 5 billion dollars

Based on the above criteria, the countries with no relevant data and those which do not play an important role in global trade were excluded from the study; and, a total of 127 countries were selected, representing 99% of the world's GDP and 98.4% of the world's imports.

The countries selected in the first step were reviewed based on the following four methods in the second step:

Method 1: Views of Relevant Headquarters and Country Desks (95 Countries)
Method 2: Macroeconomic Indicators Analysis

Tab 2: The Countries with the Highest Potential for Turkey's Exports

China	Brazil	Indonesia	Kazakhistan
Russia	Iran	Saudi Arabia	Japan
India	Nigeria	Iraq	
USA	Egypt	South Africa	
Poland	Libya	Ukraine	

Source: Ministry of Economy, Targets, and Priority Countrieshttp://www.ekonomi.gov.tr/portal/faces/ home/ihracat/pazaraGiris/hedef-ve-oncelikli-ulkeler?

Tab 3: The Countries That Will Be Favored in Market Entry Activities to Promote Turkey's Exports

Turkmenistan	Vietnamese	Romania	Sweden
Azerbaijan	Kenya	Ethiopia	Norway
Mexico	Algeria	Singapore	Angola
Peru	Ghana	Kuwait	Canada
Chile	Tanzania	Argentina	Jordan
S. Korea	UAE	Colombia	Qatar
Malaysia	Germany	Slovakia	

Source: Ministry of Economy, Targets, and Priority Countries http://www.ekonomi.gov.tr/portal/faces/ home/ihracat/pazaraGiris/hedef-ve-oncelikli-ulkeler?

Method 3: Growth-Share (BCG) Matrix Analysis
Method 4: Other Factors (Socioeconomic and Demographic Indicators, Other Expert Opinions).

Following the steps outlined above, the Ministry of Economy of the Republic of Turkey established two groups of countries as target and priority countries. As per the description of the Ministry, the group of target countries is the countries with the most important potential for Turkey's exports, whereas the group of priority countries is the countries that will be the focus for Turkey while performing its market entry activities. Tab 2 and 3 below show the group of countries assigned by the Ministry.

The countries in Tab 2 above are the countries with the highest potential for Turkey's exports. Among them, there are some countries with a leading role in the global foreign trade, like the USA, Russia, and China.

The countries in Tab 3 demonstrate the countries that will be favored in market entry activities to promote Turkey's exports. The countries in this group,

Tab 4: The Countries That Were Included in the Analysis

Countries included			**Countries excluded**
Angola	Kazakhstan	Romania	USA
Argentina	Kenya	Singapore	Germany
Brazil	Colombia	Slovakia	Russia
Algeria	Kuwait	Saudi Arabia	Japan
China	Libya	Chile	Canada
Indonesia	Malaysia	Tanzania	Jordan
Ghana	Mexico	Ukraine	Qatar
South Africa	Egypt	Vietnam	Ethiopia
South Korea	Nigeria		UAE
India	Norway		Azerbaijan
Iran	Peru		Turkmenistan
Sweden	Poland		Iraq

except for Germany, are those with a relatively lower share in the global foreign trade volume, compared to the group of target countries.

As seen in the tables above, a total of 44 countries, including 17 target countries and 27 priority countries, are recommended to Turkish exporters by the Ministry of Economy. The study did not present the analysis of all these 44 countries. The reason for this is the variable of foreign income and the lack of access to the data related to the foreign trade and foreign exchange rates of some countries via the World Bank database. Tab 4 presented the countries included in and excluded from the model.

As evident in the table above, a total of 32 countries were included in the analysis while 12 countries were excluded. Since the variable (F), which was used as the income of the external world in the study, is composed of the national income of the G8 countries, the USA, Russia, Germany, Japan and Canada were excluded from the analysis. Furthermore, some countries were excluded due to the problems experienced while accessing to their data, resulting from insufficient data on their exchange rates or the changes in their foreign exchange systems during the period of the study.

4.2 Econometric Model

In the economics literature on the impacts of the changes in foreign exchange rates on foreign trade, there are two different models as foreign trade export and import equations in the study by Benson U. Omojimite and Godwin

Akpokdje (2010), and the study by Celal Kızıldere, Burhan Kabadayı and Ömer Selçuk Emsen (2013), which underlie this present study. These models are as follows:

Model 1: $X_{i,t} = \alpha_i + \beta_1 VOLREER_{i,t} + \beta_2 M_{i,t} + \beta_3 GDPX_{i,t} + \beta_4 F_{i,t} + u_{i,t}$

Model 2: $M_{i,t} = \theta_i + \delta_1 VOLREER_{i,t} + \delta_2 GDP_{i,t} + v_{i,t}$

The study probes into the effects of foreign exchange rate volatility on foreign trade, as mentioned above. The first model considers the variables of import, export-free gross domestic product and external income as the control variables while discussing exchange rate volatility; on the other hand, the second model considers only the variable of the gross domestic product as the control variable while discussing exchange rate volatility.

4.2.1 Findings from Export Equation

Before the establishment of the panel data model, the study examines the stability of the series. Stability analysis has two types of root tests according to the presence of cross-sectional dependence in the series: the first-generation unit root test and the second-generation unit root test. For that reason, the study first analyzed the presence of cross-sectional dependence to determine the appropriate test for stability analysis. As T, the time dimension of the series in this study is 12 years and N, the unit number of the series is 33, the study used Pesaran (2004) test, which is applicable for N>T (Pesaran, H, M., 2004: 84). Table 5 presents the test results of the Model 1.

As seen in Tab 5, the results of Pesaran's (2004) test regarding the model is 3.97, and the p-probability value regarding this test statistic is 0.0001. Therefore, the null hypothesis of cross-sectional dependence is rejected at a 99% confidence

Tab 5: Cross-sectional Dependence regarding the Export Equation (Model 1)

VOLREER	0.0001 (0.2830)*	**Constant**	10.7135 (0.0000)*
M	1.0994 (0.0000)*	**R2**	0.9808
GDPX	-0.0070 (0.2860)*	**F-Test**	3637.2300 (0.0000)*
F	-0.0001 (0.7110)*	**Pesaran (2004) Test**	3.9700 (0.0001)*

*The values inside parentheses indicate p probability values.

level. In conclusion, the test revealed that the second-generation unit root test was appropriate for stability analysis.

4.2.1.1 Findings from Unit Root Test

Pesaran (2007) test is one of the second-generation tests, which are frequently used in the literature (Pesran, H, M. 2007: 269). The test includes the following components:

- Only constant
- Constant and trend.

Tab 6 shows that the p-probability value regarding the test statistics, which were calculated regarding the variable X in the model with only constant and the model with constant and trend, is calculated as 1. For that reason, the null hypothesis of the presence of a unit root is not rejected for the variable X. Thus, the first order difference (DX) for this variable was included to perform the test once again, and the null hypothesis of the presence of unit root in the model with constant is rejected at 90% confidence level.

On the other hand, as for the variables of VOLREER, M, GDPX, and F, their p-probability values regarding the test statistics, which were calculated in the model with only constant, are lower than 0.1. Therefore, the null hypothesis of the presence of a unit root is rejected for these variables. In conclusion, the

Tab 6: Results of Unit Root Test regarding Model 1

	Number of lags	**Constant**	**Constant and trend**
		t statistics	**t statistics**
X	0	-0.950 (1.000)*	-1.268 (1.000)*
DX	0	-1.984 (0.082)*	-2.103 (0.791)*
VOLREER	1	-2.552 (0.000)*	-2.617 (0.032)*
M	1	-2.437 (0.000)*	1.700 (1.000)*
GDPX	1	-2.107 (0.021)*	-1.465 (1.000)*
F	2	-2.997 (0.000)*	-3.340 (0.000)*

*The values inside parentheses indicate p probability values.

first order difference of the variable X and the other variables in the level were included in the model.

4.2.1.2 Findings from Hausman Test

Panel data models can be grouped into two types of models: fixed effects or random effect models. Hausman developed a test for the difference between the parameter estimators for the fixed effects model and those for the random effects model. To that end, he compared the generalized least squares estimator and the intra-group estimator. The resulting test statistics have an asymptotic distribution. The null and alternative hypotheses regarding the test are developed as follows:

H_0: Individual effects are random.

H_1: Individual effects are fixed.

Thus, the resulting test statistic is calculated as 42.28 with the p-probability value being close to 0. Therefore, the null hypothesis that individual effects are random is rejected, and the fixed effects model is valid (See Tab. 7).

When the cross-section data in a study are collected from a large population by random methods, it would be more reasonable to analyze the individual effects randomly using cross-sectional observations, since the sample is not large enough to cover the entire population (Karabulut, 2009: 126). Econometrically, the random effect refers to the lack of correlation between the observed explanatory variables and the unobserved effect. In this sense, the expression of fixed effect does not always mean that c_i is not random. Fixed effects allow the correlation between the unobserved effect and the observed explanatory variables

Tab 7: Results of the Hausman Test for Export Equation (Model 1)

	Coefficients			
	b	**B**	**b-B**	**Sgrt (diag(V_b-V_B**
	Fixed Effect	**Random Effect**	**Difference**	**S.E**
VOLREER	-0,0000349	-0,0000188	-0,0000161	0,0000751
M	0.3190929	0,1479813	0.1711116	0,0491038
GDPX	-0,0738671	-0,0099145	-0,639526	0,0121023
F	0,00002261	0,00002211	0,0000491	0,0003584
χ^2	42,28			
Prob	0,00000			

(Şentürk, 2016: 214). As the units in this study were fixed units, the study utilized fixed effects panel data models.

4.2.1.3 *Outputs for Export Model*

Tab 8 presents the calculations regarding the model, which shows the effect of foreign exchange volatility on the exports of the countries included in the study as the fixed effects model.

The estimations regarding the model I are demonstrated in Table 3.10. The standard model primarily shows that the variable VOLREER does not have a statistically significant effect on the variable DX. Here, the coefficient of the variable VOLREER has been estimated as a value close to 0, and the p-probability value for this estimator is 0.716. Therefore, the null hypothesis that the coefficient of the variable VOLREER is equal to 0 is rejected.

On the other hand, the coefficient of the variable M is 0.3191, statistically significant; the coefficient of the variable GDPX is -0.0739, statistically significant and the coefficient of the variable F is 0.0023, statistically significant.

Tab 8: Findings from Export Equation (Model 1)

	Standard Model	**Prais Winsten Standard Error**	**Driscoll Kraay Standard Error**
VOLREER	0.0000 (0.7160)*	0.0000 (0.7660)*	0.0000 (0.4010)*
M	0.3191 (0.0000)*	0.1521 (0.0000)*	0.3191 (0.2400)*
GDPX	-0.0739 (0.0000)*	-0.0102 (0.2410)*	-0.0739 (0.2180)*
F	0.0023 (0.0030)*	0.0026 (0.0000)*	0.0023 (0.0350)*
sabit	68.4119 (0.0030)*	84.8650 (0.0000)*	68.4119 (0.0030)*
R^2	0.2248	0.4238	0.1049
F Test	9.5500 (0.0000)*		
Wald Test	54954 (0.0000)*		
Wooldridge Test	12.8740 (0.0011)*		
Pesaran CD Test	43.5380 (0.0000)*		

*The values inside parentheses indicate p probability values.

The presence of cross-section dependence, autocorrelation, and heteroscedasticity in the established model was examined, respectively, using Pesaran CD test, Wooldridge test, and Wald test.

- The result of the Pesaran CD test is calculated as 43.538, with the p-probability value being close to 0, which indicates a cross-sectional dependence problem.
- According to the results of the Wooldridge test, the test statistic is 12.874, with the p-probability value being 0.0011, which indicates an autocorrelation problem.
- According to the results of the Wald test, the test statistic is 54954 with the p-probability value being close to 0, which indicates a heteroscedasticity problem.
- While the model of the Prais Winsten standard errors may be used to overcome the heteroscedasticity problem and the autocorrelation problem, the model of the Driscoll Kraay standard errors may be used to overcome all these three problems.

The model of the Driscoll Kraay standard errors demonstrates that the variable VOLREER, which is not considered significant in the standard model, is still non-significant. On the other hand, the p-probability values of the variables M and GDPX, which are considered statistically significant in the standard model, have increased to 0.24 and 0.218, respectively. It can be thus stated that upon overcoming their cross-section dependence, autocorrelation and heteroscedasticity problems, these variables have become non-significant. The coefficient of the variable F is estimated as 0.0023 in the model of the Driscoll Kraay standard errors, with the p-probability value being 0.035. More precisely, an increase of 1 billion US dollars in foreign income causes an increase of 0.0023 billion US dollars in exports. The coefficient of determination for the established model is estimated as 0.1049. Therefore, it can be stated that 10.49% of the changes in the dependent variable results from the changes in the explanatory variables.

4.2.2 Findings from Import Equation

As in the export equation, the findings from the import equation present the findings from cross-sectional dependency, unit root, and Hausmant tests. Tab 9 shows the results from the cross-sectional dependence regarding the import equation, in other words, the model 2.

As seen in Tab 9 the results of Pesaran's (2004) test for cross-sectional dependence indicate the presence of a cross-sectional problem. The test statistic is

Tab 9: Cross-sectional Dependence regarding the Import Equation (Model 2)

VOLREER	-0.0001 (0.5790)*
GDP	0.2082 (0.2012)*
Constant	44.8152 (0.0000)*
R^2	0.8876
F-Test	47.5700 (0.0000)*
Paseran (2004) Test	1691.1600 (0.0000)*

*The values inside parentheses indicate p probability values.

calculated as 1691.16 with the p-probability value being close to 0. Therefore, the null hypothesis of cross-sectional dependence is rejected in the model 2 too. Table 3.11 presents the results of Pesaran's (2004) test for the variable GDP, which is used in the model 2, in addition to the variables used in the model 1.

4.2.2.1 Findings from Unit Root Test

The variables of import, foreign exchange volatility, and national income are used in the model 2. The unit root tests for the data of import and foreign exchange volatility are available in the section for the model I. Since the variable of national income (GDP), rather than the variable of export-excluded national income (GDP-X), is used in the model 2, Tab 10 also presents the results of the unit root test for the variable of GDP.

According to the results of the variable GDP in the model with constant and the model with constant and trend, the null hypothesis of the presence of unit root is rejected. Here, the test statistic in the model with constant is calculated as -2.305 with the p-probability value being 0.001.

4.2.2.2 Findings from Hausman Test

The study performed a Hausman test to determine the method in the import equation, like in the export equation. The hypotheses regarding the Hausman test are as follows:

H_0: Individual effects are random.

H_1: Individual effects are fixed.

Tab 10: Results of Unit Root Test regarding Import Equation (Model 2)

	Number of lags	Constant	Constant and Trend
		t statistics	t statistics
VOLREER	1	-2.552 (0.000)*	-2.617 (0.032)*
M	1	-2.437 (0.000)*	1.700 (1.000)*
GDP	2	-2.305 (0,001)*	1.700 (1.000)*

*The values inside parentheses indicate p probability values.

Tab 11: Results of Hausman Test for Import Equation (Model 2)

	Coefficients			
	b	B	b-B	Sgrt (diag(V_b-V_B
	Fixed Effect	Random Effect	Difference	S.E
VOLREER	-0,0005	-0,0000576	7,59e -06	0,0000154
GDPX	0,2082127	0,2091425	-0,0009298	0,0008535
χ^2	1,34			
Prob	0,5115			

The results of the Hausman test for the model 2 show that the test statistic is calculated as 0.5115 with the p-probability value being 1.34. As the p-probability value is higher than 0.1, the null hypothesis that individual effects are random is not rejected. As stated above, since the units in this study were fixed units, the study utilized fixed effects panel data models in the model 2 (Tab. 11).

4.2.2.3 Outputs for Import Model

The table below indicates the direction and size of the effect of foreign exchange volatility on the exports of the countries included in the study, according to the import equation based on the groups of target and priority countries assigned by the Ministry of Economy. The outputs for the established import model is presented in Tab 12.

Tab 12 shows the calculations regarding the model 2. The Standard model demonstrates that the variable VOLREER does not have a statistically significant

Tab 12: Findings from Import Equation (Model 2)

	Standard Model	Prais Winsten Standard Error	Driscoll Kraay Standard Error
VOLREER	-0.0001 (0.5790)	-0.0001 (0.0380)	-0.0001 (0.0130)
GDP	0.2082 (0.0000)	0.2205 (0.0000)	0.2082 (0.0000)
Constant	44.8152 (0.0000)	37.5314 (0.0000)	44.8152 (0.0000)
R^2	0.8876	0.9666	0.9036
F-Test	1691.1600 (0.0000)		
Wald Test	6100000 (0.0000)		
Wooldridge Test	97.8550 (0.0000)		
Pesaran CD Test	27.3200 (0.0000)		

*The values inside parentheses indicate p probability values.

impact on the variable M. Here, the coefficient of the variable VOLREER is calculated as -0.0001 with the p-probability value being 0.579. Hence, the null hypothesis that the coefficient of the variable VOLREER is equal to 0 is not rejected.

On the other hand, the coefficient of the variable GDP is 0.2082, statistically significant.

The presence of cross-section dependence, autocorrelation, and heteroscedasticity in the established model was examined, respectively, using Pesaran CD test, Wooldridge test, and Wald test.

- The result of the Pesaran CD test is calculated as 27.32, with the p-probability value being close to 0, which indicates a cross-sectional dependence problem.
- According to the results of the Wooldridge test, the test statistic is 97.855, with the p-probability value being close to 0, which indicates an autocorrelation problem.
- According to the results of the Wald test, the test statistic is 610000 with the p-probability value being close to 0, which indicates a heteroscedasticity problem.

In the model of Driscoll Kraay standard errors, the variable VOLREER, which is not considered significant in the standard model, is significant. The coefficient of the variable is estimated as -0. 0001, with the p-probability value being 0.013. Therefore, the null hypothesis that the coefficient of the variable VOLREER is equal to 0 is rejected at 95% confidence level. In conclusion, it can be stated that there is a reverse correlation between the variable VOLREER and the variable M, and a unit increase in the variable VOLREER results in a reduction of 0.0001 units in the variable M.

On the other hand, the variable GDP, which is considered statistically significant in the standard model, is significant in the models of the Driscoll Kraay standard errors. More precisely, an increase of 1 billion US dollars in GDP causes an increase of 0.2082 billion US dollars in imports. The coefficient of determination for the established model is estimated as 0.9036. Therefore, it can be stated that 90.26% of the changes in the dependent variable results from the changes in the explanatory variables.

5 Conclusion

Because of the recent negative effects of the 2008 Global Financial Crisis, excessive fluctuations in foreign exchange rates, sudden changes in the price of an important commodity like oil and political transformations such as the Arab Spring, the global economy itself has too many risks. In addition to these risks, the trade wars that broke out due to the statements made by the US President Trump have narrowed the global foreign trade volume. The USA and Chinese economies are now the two largest economies in the world. The foreign trade activities between the USA and China have been developing in favor of China, particularly in recent years. In its foreign trade with the USA, China had a large foreign trade deficit of 375 billion dollars in 2017. Ongoing foreign trade relations between the two countries mean that China will take over the title of the world's largest economy from the USA. It is remarkable that the USA forced China to change its foreign exchange policy, but China did not decide in favor of changing its policy, during the period called the foreign exchange wars, before the advent of the concept of trade wars. Unable to achieve the desired outcome about foreign exchange, the USA implemented protective policies to directly restrict trade in goods. In other words, the competition between the USA and China, which originally broke out as foreign exchange wars, has evolved into trade wars, where trade barriers are imposed. Trade wars is a global issue today, given that the USA continues to impose similar trade barriers for foreign trade on other countries.

Global trade has been shrinking day by day due to the adverse conditions mentioned above. All countries around the world seek to avoid the negative effects of the current conjuncture as much as possible. Many countries have turned to protective policies, and the trade wars have gradually developed into a global threat. Despite the negativities caused by the current conjuncture, countries make a great effort to benefit from their foreign trade potential as far as possible. In this regard, Turkey is targeting exports of 500 billion dollars in the 100th year anniversary of the foundation of the Turkish Republic. To that end, the 2023 Turkey Export Strategy and Action Plan were prepared by the Ministry of Economy of the Republic of Turkey. In concordance with this action plan, the Ministry of Economy classified the countries in the world as target and priority countries to serve as a road map for the exporters in Turkey. The classification aims to increase the level of exports in existing foreign trade markets and also to boost export figures by opening to new foreign trade markets.

Focusing on the countries specified by the Ministry of Economy, this study concluded that the most important determinant of the exports of the countries included in the analysis is the imports of these countries. The coefficient of export (M) is estimated at 0,31, which is statistically significant, in the import equation, calculated through the fixed effects method. That is to say, to increase one unit of their exports, these countries need to increase 0,31 units of their imports. This finding indicates that the countries included in the analysis, like Turkey, import the intermediate goods used in the production of their export goods from other countries. Thus, it would be reasonable that Turkish exporters give priority to the exports of intermediate goods that are demanded by these countries. There is a statistically significant and negative correlation between the imports of the countries in the study and foreign exchange volatility; yet, the correlation is weak enough to be overlooked. According to the results of the import equation, a change of one unit in exchange rates decreases imports by 0.0001 units, and due to the small size of the negative impact, there is no important correlation between foreign exchange volatility and imports, like in the export equation.

References

Aran, B. (2018). "A.B.D, Çin, Ticaret Savaşları Ve Türkiye", Türkiye Ekonomi Politikaları Araştırma Vakfı, Değerlendirme Notu, pp. 1–7.

Arana, V. G. (2014). "Currency Wars: The Lack of a Global Monetary System", Working Paper, Zürich, pp. 75–76.

Ekonomi Bakanlığı, Hedef ve Öncelikli Ülkeler, http:// www.ekonomi.gov.tr/portal/faces/home/ihracat/pazaraGiris/hedef-ve- oncelikli-ulkeler (15.03.2017).

Eroğlu, E. (2010). "Türkiye'de Yoksulluk ve Yoksullukla Mücadelede Uygulanan Kamusal Politikaların Değerlendirilmesi", Uludağ Üniversitesi Sosyal Bilimler Enstitüsü, (Yayımlanmamış Yüksek Lisans Tezi), Bursa.

Ertürk, N. (2017). "Ticaret Savaşları ve Dünya Ekonomisine Etkileri", *Fiscaoeconomia*, Vol: 1, No: 2, pp. 88–112.

Karabulut, R. (2009). "Hisse Senedi Getirilerinin Panel Veri Analizi ile Tahmini: İstanbul Menkul Kıymetler Borsasında Bir İnceleme", İnönü Üniversitesi Sosyal Bilimler Enstitüsü, Yayımlanmamış Doktora Tezi, Malatya.

Kızıldere, C., Kabadayı, B & Ö,S, Emsen. (2013). "Dış Ticaretin Döviz Kuru Değişimlerine Duyarlılığı: Seçilmiş Gelişmekte Olan Ülkeler Üzerine Bir İnceleme", *Atatürk Üniversitesi İktisadi ve İdari Bilimler Dergisi*, Vol: 27, No: 3, pp. 41–54.

Kuneralp, S. (2018). "Korumacılık Savaşları Mı Başlıyor?", Ekonomi ve Dış Politika Araştırma Merkezi, Ekonomi ve Küreselleşme 2018/1, pp. 1–5.

Mangır, F. & Acet, H. (2014). "Serbest Ticaret ve Korumacılık, Avrupa Birliği'nde Malların Serbest Dolaşımı ve Türkiye'nin Uyumu", *Selcuk University Journal of Institute of Social Sciences Dr. Mehmet YILDIZ Special Edition*, pp. 93–108.

Omojimite, U, B. & Godwin, A. (2010). "A Comparative Analysis of the Effect of Exchange Rate Volatility on Exports in the CFA and Non-CFA Countries of Africa", *Journal of Social Sciences*, Vol: 24, No: 1, pp, 23–31.

Pesaran, H, M. (2004). "General Diagnostic Tests for Cross Section Dependence in Panels", Discussion Paper No. 1240.

Pesaran, H, M. (2007). "A Simple Panel Unit Root Test in the Presence of Cross-Section Dependence". *Journal of Applied Econometrics*, Vol: 22, No: 2, pp. 265–312.

Şentürk, H. (2016). "Çevresel Kuznet Eğrisi: Doğrusal Olmayan Regresyon Analizi", Gazi Üniversitesi Sosyal Bilimler Enstitüsü, (Yayınlanmamış Doktora Tezi), Ankara.

Smith, A. (2002). *Ulusların Zenginliği*, (Çev.) Tanju M. Akad, İstanbul, Alan Yayıncılık.

Türkiye Cumhuriyet Merkez Bankası. (2018), Uluslararası Ekonomik İlişkiler, Kutu 2.1. http://www.tcmb.gov.tr/wps/wcm/connect,(28.08.2018).

Ünay, S. & Dilek, Ş. (2018). "Yeni Korumacılık ve Ticaret Savaşları", Siyaset, Ekonomi Ve Toplum Araştırmaları Vakfı, Vol: 228, pp. 13–14.

FSC
www.fsc.org
MIX
Papier aus verantwortungsvollen Quellen
Paper from responsible sources
FSC® C141904

Druck:
Canon Deutschland Business Services GmbH
im Auftrag der KNV-Gruppe
Ferdinand-Jühlke-Str. 7
99095 Erfurt